Future of Business and Finance

The Future of Business and Finance book series features professional works aimed at defining, describing and charting the future trends in these fields. The focus is mainly on strategic directions, technological advances, challenges and solutions which may affect the way we do business tomorrow, including the future of sustainability and governance practices. Mainly written by practitioners, consultants and academic thinkers, the books are intended to spark and inform further discussions and developments.

More information about this series at http://www.springer.com/series/16360

Stefan Güldenberg · Ekkehard Ernst ·
Klaus North

Editors

Managing Work in the Digital Economy

Challenges, Strategies and Practices
for the Next Decade

 Springer

Editors
Stefan Güldenberg
University of Liechtenstein
Vaduz, Liechtenstein

Ekkehard Ernst
Research Department
International Labor Organization
Geneva, Switzerland

Klaus North
Wiesbaden Business School
RheinMain University of Applied Sciences
Wiesbaden, Hessen, Germany

ISSN 2662-2467   ISSN 2662-2475   (electronic)
Future of Business and Finance
ISBN 978-3-030-65172-5   ISBN 978-3-030-65173-2   (eBook)
https://doi.org/10.1007/978-3-030-65173-2

This Springer imprint is published by the registered company Springer Nature Switzerland AG.
The registered company address is: Gewerbestrasse 11, 6330 Cham, Switzerland

"There seems a general rule that, the more obviously one's work benefits other people, the less one is likely to be paid for it."
In memory of David Graeber (12.2.1961, New York City – 2.9.2020, Venice)

Prologue

It is the year 2030; digital technologies are pervasive in complementing and augmenting human capabilities. However, despite earlier fears, humans have not been replaced with robots. For most people, work remains the key source to make a living. Not everybody has benefited from these changes to the same extent, though. Social and economic divisions run deep between "digital losers" and "digitally enabled value creators" and between those who have stable jobs and those who "clickwork" on a short-term contract basis (the "gig economy"). People with the right skills and competences can look for meaningful and fulfilling jobs. Self-employment has grown considerably along with changed contractual relations and new forms of learning.

In 2030, we live in a world that has changed: for some radically and for others so far barely noticeable. Changes coexist with old organizational and leadership practices. The COVID-19 crisis at the start of the 2020s accelerated several trends like increased digitalization, automation, e-commerce, and remote work. Most importantly, it triggered policy and sentiment shifts in the EU and elsewhere that had many societies questioning their work cultures. It also demonstrated which jobs are "systemically relevant" and which are not, starting a societal dialogue about how we value these jobs and how much we are willing to pay for them.

This social dialogue had already started much earlier in the aftermath of the global financial crisis of 2008. Despite a seeming acceleration in technological change, much heralded with the introduction of the smartphone, working conditions, livelihoods, and productivity did not improve much. What little productivity gains were observed were eaten up by "bullshit jobs", employment so completely pointless, unnecessary, or pernicious that even the employee cannot justify its existence.[1] Instead of enjoying our lives, benefiting from reduced working time through a 15-hour workweek or a 4-hour workday already called for by John Maynard Keynes in the 1930s, we continue to struggle in jobs that the more relevant to society they are, the less they pay. Instead, the superfluous nature of many of our jobs creates

---

[1]See Graeber, D. (2018) Bullshit Jobs: A Theory, Simon & Schuster, as well as the German documentary film *The Cleaners* released in 2018, which shows the character of these bullshit jobs specifically in the digital economy relentlessly open and very vivid.

psychological discontent and stress. Employees, as part of their conditions of employment, feel obliged to give sense and meaning to their occupation. The rise of these jobs is intimately linked to the specific nature of current technological change, which is focused on increasing interconnectivity and the need to manage and oversee ever more complex networks of people and transactions. Or to give a concrete example from the care industry: Rather than seeing more doctors and nurses, we observe a rapid increase in compliance officers, adding little value to patients' health.

In the process, we have lost the meaning of work: Work is not working any more for us. To claim back the future of work, therefore, we do not only need to address the economic and technological challenges that the digital transformation brings. We also have to consider the point that David Graeber and other Occupy Wall Street activists have made and face its cultural and societal challenges. When we think about the future of work, we should think about our lives and societies as work and life are much closely linked together than we might think. The average person will spend 90,000 hours of their life working. For some of us, it is even well over 100,000 hours, as the line between professional and private life and work has blurred.

Because work is so central to our lives, the future of work lies at the heart of a peaceful coexistence and a sustainable society. The way in which we shape the world of work rather than leaving it to itself makes a decisive contribution to our economic prosperity and social peace. Therefore, we should not only be observers of the digital transformation and technological development but actively intervene where we see undesirable consequences and where the world of work is too far removed from basic human needs. Work is such a profoundly basic human need, not only because it still secures the economic basis for our survival, but also because it contributes decisively to creating meaning for our lives. Our work is not only part of our life, but it is our life. So let's make work again: for us as human beings and our world as a whole.

How, then, can we confront the changes yet to come to our working lives? Will the digital transformation replace some of our jobs? Will we simply move on and create new ones, or will we take this opportunity and reinvent the meaning of our lives? If so, can we afford to do so? Even though we cannot possibly answer these questions yet, one thing is certain: Because work is so important for us and our lives, discussions about the future of work will intensify on all levels, political, organizational, and individual. By 2030, new solutions for managing work must have been found and tested in daily business, including answers for the following questions:

- What are the most pressing challenges of the digital transformation of work for employees, leadership, and organizations? Which new ways of value creation are emerging? And how do human beings interact with machines in 2030?
- What impact will these changes have on individual lives by 2030? In particular, how will the meaning of life and work change in 2030? And how do we learn in 2030?

- How does leadership change in 2030? What does human resource management look like in 2030? How have labour relations evolved? How have social partners and trade unions' actions evolved in 2030?
- Which recommendations and guidance can be given for managing one's work and the work of others in a digitalized, globalized, and turbulent world?

The purpose of our book is to answer these questions. Written as though we are in 2030, it offers different perspectives on what the world could look like a decade from today. It asks: How did we end up here? What could we have done differently? How could we have shaped things to accelerate change to improve outcomes for more people? This book offers a unique chance to understand and analyse the path that brought us to this juncture. It allows us to think ahead and work to reshape those trends that we do not want to define in the decade between 2020 and 2030. How could we have avoided certain challenges and dead ends? And how could we have sped up certain transformative processes to reap and share the benefits of change more broadly? Most importantly, how can we create a virtuous circle of shared prosperity that will leave us much better off by 2030?

Looking forward to the year 2030, this book collects insights from different scholars in the field on the world of work and provides well-founded insights and guidance to (self-)manage work in a globalized and digitalized economy. International researchers and practitioners who have contributed to this volume draw a picture of the type of jobs and work, their dynamics, and location that we are likely to experience in 10 years' time. Adopting the "persona" approach, the book also illustrates how these changes will impact on people. Many cases and examples make this work a compendium for learning and implementing new leadership and management practices.

This book assists entrepreneurs, managers, knowledge workers, human resource professionals, consultants, trainers, and coaches in business, public administration, and non-profit organizations to shape the future of work.

This book would not have been possible without the engagement of renowned international contributors who furthered our insights into the topic. We extend our thanks to Prashanth Mahagaonkar, Senior Editor at Springer, for actively supporting the book project. We would also like to thank, in particular, Michael Muscat for language editing and proofreading and the Springer production team.

We wish you inspiring reading and look forward to your feedback.

Vaduz, Liechtenstein   Stefan Güldenberg
Geneva, Switzerland   Ekkehard Ernst
Wiesbaden, Germany   Klaus North
Spring 2021

Contents

About the Editors

Stefan Güldenberg is a pioneer and leading expert on the future of work, digital strategies, sustainable leadership, and knowledge management. He is a university professor, platform founder, strategy consultant, executive coach, and knowledge entrepreneur. He studied Business Mathematics, Philosophy, and English at the University of Ulm and then received his doctorate and habilitation at the Vienna University of Economics and Business. Stefan has 25 years of experience in research, knowledge transfer, and practice. He conducts research on and supports the development of strategy and transformation processes. Stays abroad led him, among others, to Harvard University, the Massachusetts Institute of Technology (MIT), and the National University of Singapore. He is the current Vice President Practice of the European Academy of Management (EURAM) and President of the New Club of Paris, a think tank and agenda setter for the knowledge economy.

Ekkehard Ernst is an internationally recognized expert on the future of work at the International Labour Organization. His work focuses on the impact of technological change, demographic shifts, globalization, global warming, and political vagaries on productivity, employment, wages, and inequality. In particular, he has studied the implications of artificial intelligence, robots, and blockchain applications on job growth, inequality, and the transition to a sustainable society. In 2017, Ekkehard co-founded Geneva Macro Labs, a Swiss Do-Tank, to offer a platform to identify, develop, and implement solutions to address global challenges and existential risks to promote and advance the United Nations Sustainable Development Agenda. Previously, he worked at the Organisation for Economic Co-operation and Development (OECD) and the European Central Bank. Ekkehard Ernst has studied in Mannheim, Saarbrucken, and Paris and holds a PhD from the École des Hautes Études en Sciences Sociales. He regularly advises external partners on labour market issues, including the Conference Board, the UK Productivity Insights Network, McKinsey, Roland Berger, and Foresight Alliances.

Klaus North is a Professor of International Management at Wiesbaden Business School, Germany, and was previously a senior researcher at the International Labour Office (ILO). He has widely published on knowledge and innovation management as well as digital transformation. His textbook *Knowledge Management—Value Creation Through Organizational Learning* (Springer Texts in Business and Economics) has been translated into multiple languages and has become a reference work on the subject. He frequently consults with major companies and public institutions worldwide and teaches in business programmes internationally.

Part I

Life in 2030

The World in 2030: Looking Back Ten Years from Now

Sabina Dewan, Ekkehard Ernst, and Eric Gravel

1 From the News: "Global Leaders to Reach Agreement on a New Stakeholder Model"

After 10 years of intensive debate, the recently established Group of 40 adopted the Agenda 2040 in its meeting yesterday to promote a new, sustainable way of doing business. Bringing together governments from the richest 40 countries in the world, the G40 sets up several principles initially put forward by the 2019 Business Roundtable of the CEOs of major American companies who led the call for a shift to a stakeholder capitalism model.

A fundamental guiding principle behind Agenda 2040 is the use of legal innovations around blockchain technology that has become a business standard over the last 10 years in many areas. Whether in supply chain management, e-identity, or international payment systems, blockchain has become the industry norm. With Agenda 2040, governments hope to lay the ground for cross-system standards that help regulate existing contractual relationships while at the same time ensure that international legal norms, such as labour rights, are properly protected. The stakeholder business model enshrined in these guidelines adds several important elements that will strengthen business leaders' incentives to take a more holistic view of their companies and to integrate different interests into their strategic outlook.

Advanced economies among the G40 group hope that with these new principles, a more equitable sharing of gains from technological dividends, especially in the digital economy, can be achieved. Rewarding consumers for their data is expected to be strengthened by the Agenda 2040. Emerging countries, on the other hand, place their hope in stronger

S. Dewan
JustJobs Network, New Delhi, India
e-mail: sabinadewan@justjobsnetwork.org

E. Ernst (✉)
Research Department, International Labour Organization, Geneva, Switzerland
e-mail: ernste@ilo.org

E. Gravel
International Labour Standards Department, International Labour Organization, Geneva, Switzerland
e-mail: gravel@ilo.org

© Springer Nature Switzerland AG 2021
S. Güldenberg et al. (eds.), *Managing Work in the Digital Economy*, Future of Business and Finance, https://doi.org/10.1007/978-3-030-65173-2_1

recognition of the wealth of natural capital they have to offer as well as more substantial incentives to improve working conditions, both of which are highly valued by the guiding principles that make up the Agenda 2040.

Governments in their final statement at the last G40 summit expressed hopes that this new Agenda 2040 will finally produce the shared prosperity for their countries that current technologies have promised for so long.

(From the Global Legal Chronicle, Cancun, 15 May 2030).

2   The Pendulum of Global Wealth Has Swung Back

A decade ago, the global balance of economic power seemed to shift away from advanced economies to emerging ones. Now in 2030, a decade after the COVID-19 pandemic swept the globe, advanced countries, spearheaded by the United States, have once again consolidated their position in the global economy. The health crisis wiped out the development gains that emerging and developing nations had slowly accumulated following a period of economic liberalization and globalization that had started in the late 1990s. Large emerging economies such as India, in particular, saw a significant set-back in their quest to improved living standards. Global income distribution had been dubbed the "global elephant" as a large middle class emerged in less well-off countries in the 2010s. With the changes that occured over the last ten years, however, income distribution started to resemble the traditional (inverted) income distribution pyramid again, underscoring the idea that the richer you are, the faster you grow (Milanovic 2020).

Yet, it was not so much that economic growth accelerated in the small number of OECD countries. Instead, emerging and developing countries saw their growth rates slow during the crisis, and they were unable to find their way back to precrisis levels. The pandemic erected barriers to growth that stymied a global convergence in living standards. Growth rates did not recover much in advanced economies either, and the impression of accelerating technological progress remained confined to sectors that benefited from investment in information and communication technologies.

From the vantage point of 2030, new technologies neither delivered on their promise to boost aggregate productivity significantly nor did they act as an equalizer. Over the last decade, technology continued to become an integral part of people's lives, but it did not lead to the massive restructuring that many had expected. Virtual meetings over smartphones or computers have become a standard way of communicating without replacing more traditional meetings and conferences. Tracing apps, from goods to people, have become routine, whether to know where your shipment is or whom you might have been in contact with. Indeed, the pandemic helped establish new standards and protocols that struck a balance between public policy and privacy concerns. Earlier fears of massive rates of unemployment due to technological advances did not materialize but neither did the wave of technological innovation bring substantial productivity gains. Instead, we have found new ways of keeping our workforce relevant, providing it with the necessary skills to use the latest tools and apps. This has helped to keep them in the labour market but did not deliver massive gains in income or living standards.

Some promising trends are emerging but have not yet developed their full potential. For instance, cryptocurrencies and their underlying technology, blockchain, have disrupted supply chain management over the past 10 years. The pandemic in 2020 also helped to promote this trend. Nevertheless, the potential of cryptocurrencies and blockchain to produce a better, more efficient allocation of scarce resources, thanks to digitally defined property rights, remains unrealized. The hype over the potential of artificial intelligence made way for disillusionment as gaps in regulatory governance and legal challenges prevented a more comprehensive adoption of potentially path-breaking technologies. The world in 2030 has turned out to have more gadgets with few gains.

This first chapter sets the stage against which these technological changes have been taking place and discusses some of the other concurrent megatrends. Many of these trends were already visible in 2020. Demographic shifts, accelerating climate change, and a (partial) retreat from globalization were already in the making when we entered the last decade. New challenges emerged as the decade unfolded, but most of them were grounded in these deep-running trends. Disenchantment after the hype over the potential of artificial intelligence arose quickly as new technologies faced significant technical shortcomings and regulatory barriers. And after two global crises, most states lacked the capacity to instigate new, innovative changes. Instead, in many countries, civil society organizations emerged, but their combined ability to act has not increased sufficiently by 2030 to substitute for what state institutions were not able to deliver. Let us explore the path that we have taken over the last 10 years and discuss what obstacles we have faced and how we overcame them. Let us also look at the challenges that we still need to confront. Let us look back at our journey to 2030.

3 Global Growth Has Slowed, Not Least due to Demographic Challenges

Global growth has slowed as major economies drew back from globalization and struggled with their ageing populations. As a result of these developments, the decade between 2020 and 2030 only saw a lacklustre expansion of production and incomes despite an initially rapid recovery from the pandemic-induced recession.

Investment remained flat, mostly owing to high uncertainty and depressed demand in the first half of the decade. Reduced consumption, especially in services, led to a decline in production, which induced further job losses. Firms that survived the COVID-19 crisis took the opportunity to automate their processes, making the recovery job-poor and doing little to stem the unemployment rates in developed countries and informal employment in developing ones.

From the United States to China, from Germany to Japan, most advanced economies, and some emerging ones, started to struggle with ageing populations (see Fig. 1). Most developed countries saw a rise in their silver economy as the rising number of older people expanded their demand for care services. On the other hand, the pandemic had brought significant disruption to other services, wiping out a large

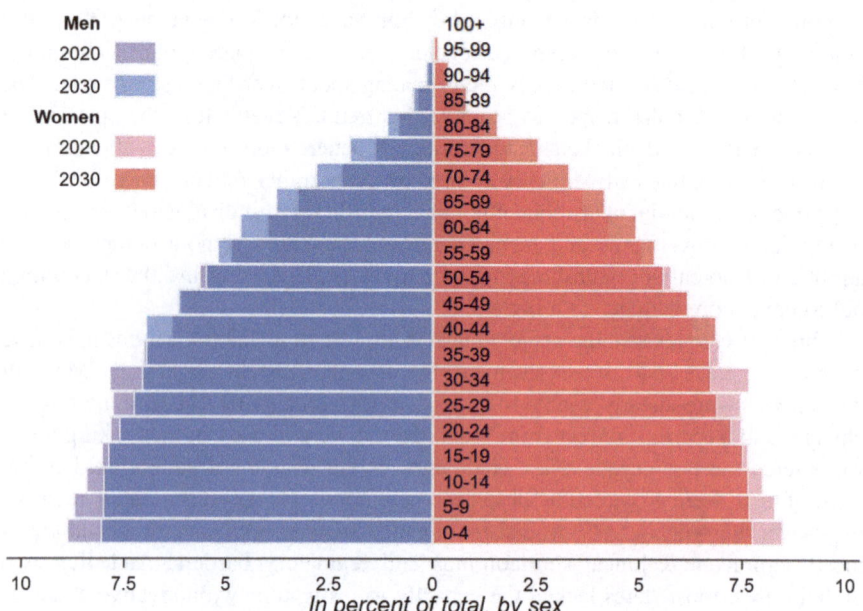

Fig. 1 Population pyramid—2020 vs 2030. Note: the chart compares the relative size of different age groups for men and women between 2020 and 2030. Age group shares are measured with respect to the total population size for men and women separately. Source: https://www. populationpyramid.net/world/

part of job-intensive activities. Moreover, rising dependency ratios continued to strain welfare systems and fiscal budgets as more pensioners demanded health care at the same time as fewer earners paid into the system, further depressing economic growth.

The faltering demographics in these countries did not only affect the growth and composition of consumption. It also had a direct impact on the provision of essential services. As more of the workforce retired, shortages of labour reappeared over the past decade. This shortage is more pronounced in sectors like health care that are seeing growing demand. As the labour force participation rate declined, the burden of performing existing work fell to fewer people intensifying questions about a work-life balance and quality of life. As a consequence, women's labour force participation rates started to decline again over the past decade as the burden of taking care of elderly relatives fell disproportionally on them.

These labour market shortages were not compensated by a fast-growing youth population in developing economies over the 2020s. The rising population in countries such as Nigeria and India has been straining infrastructure and public services—from utilities to health care and the provision of quality education and skills training—preventing these countries from reaping the full benefit of their demographic dividend. In addition, the pandemic caused significant collateral damage to international migration, preventing labour supply from evolving more in sync across countries and continents. Overall, even though demographic development in low- and low middle-income countries has been more dynamic than that of advanced economies, it has not provided sufficient stimulus for global growth, having had little impact on the world economy.

The reallocation of jobs across industries and occupations, accelerated by the pandemic, constituted a further drag on economic growth. High value-added services in tourism and transportation have since been replaced by more local, domestic consumption. Protectionism, already a concern before the outbreak of the pandemic, has become more fervent. Global supply chains have become more fragmented and complex as firms attempted to limit their exposure to a single supplier. This trend has, however, reduced efficiency gains from international trade and specialization. Activities that were hitherto offshored to emerging and developing countries in an attempt to save on labour costs have now been brought back, thanks to flexible automation, to protect against disruption in supply chains. Such reshoring, although limited in size, has prevented emerging countries from further technological and capital transfer, which is much needed for their continued development. Even though most economies have since returned to a more stable growth path, productivity gains remained meagre, and global living standards in 2030 barely exceed those of a decade ago.

One important consequence of the continued low growth over the last decade was a further increase in inequality. The labour income share, measuring the sum of all wages and earnings distributed in an economy as a share of national production, continued its downward trend in most major economies as labour markets struggled to recover from the severe hit they took in 2020. Personal income distribution also became increasingly skewed, with a few billionaires reaping large gains from their investment in selected, fast-growing industries, especially around digital technologies.

4   Job Market Challenges Prevail. . . Amidst Some Green Sprouts

The pandemic undid most of the meagre gains in jobs and earnings that had been hard-won prior to 2020. Since then, several forces that accelerated the destruction and reallocation of jobs continue to weigh on a full labour market recovery, not least the fallout from the pandemic, automation, and climate change. A key barrier to a successful transition is the lack of sufficient public resources to address and accompany these shifts.

With slow growth and strained fiscal budgets, governments across the world have struggled to provide their populations with sufficient public services necessary to assist them in their labour market transitions, a trend already visible before the crisis (Alvaredo et al. 2018). Workers who lost their jobs due to accelerating automation in the aftermath of the pandemic could not rely on sufficient support to transit to new occupations through education and reskilling programmes. The transition to clean energy sources or simply anaemic growth further limited their success in finding alternative job opportunities. Certain occupations were particularly hard hit, as were people who lacked the right competencies to shift out of their previous job profiles. In particular, many medium-skilled occupations proved to be dead-ends, out of which a career switch proved exceedingly difficult (Del Rio-Chanona et al. 2020).

Skills gaps widened further as young people struggled to enter or complete education, partly as a consequence of school closures during the pandemic. Even after the immediate health crisis had been overcome, governments struggled to provide education and skills to the growing number of job seekers. Private sector initiatives that promised to fill the gap mostly targeted the lucrative high-skilled workers transiting between jobs. This exacerbated the mismatch between the requirements of existing jobs and the labour supply, even as the economy struggles to generate enough employment for the growing cohort of labour market drop-outs. In developed nations, a shortage of labour resulting from an ageing population was compounded by insufficient reskilling and upskilling of prime-age workers despite increasing attempts to find innovative solutions for lifelong learning. In developing countries and despite their growing populations, insufficient investment in education and training continued to exacerbate a lack of skilled personnel to supply talent for higher value-added sectors. In addition, these countries faced severe brain drains as "qualified migrant programmes" invited skilled and credentialed workers from developing countries into developed ones, thereby causing the most skilled workers to leave. The compensatory income flows through remittances is an essential source of income for many families in these countries but provide little to support long-term economic prosperity as they are mostly spent on consumption rather than on building assets (Chami et al. 2018).

Climate change caused additional strain on labour markets, especially in many developing countries, where a large percentage of the population still relies on agriculture for employment. Rising surface temperatures meant worsening working conditions, especially for all those who are working outdoors, such as construction, mining, or agricultural workers. The resulting heat stress was particularly severe for workers in countries that could provide little infrastructure to protect against the rise in temperatures (Kjellestorm et al. 2019). Possibilities for workers to move to milder climates were often prevented due to tightening migration laws despite obvious mutual benefits.

The costs of insufficient job creation, however, were shared unequally across different labour market groups. Besides young people, women faced a particularly challenging jobs decade. Partly as a result of the shock brought about by the pandemic, barriers to entry for women to the labour market went up again. The restructuring of global supply chains meant less demand for (female) employment in apparel and footwear in many developing and emerging economies. Moreover, even though the awareness for women's rights continued to grow over the 2020s, gender norms and biases continue to relegate women into low-level jobs in many parts of the world. As working conditions deteriorated further during the crisis at the beginning of the decade, for many women, the trade-off of working in inferior conditions was no longer worth it, and they decided to drop out of the workforce instead. In addition, those developing countries that saw an increase in their per capita incomes experienced a particularly sharp decline in the rates of female participation in the labour force. Rising incomes allowed second-income earners (mainly women) to leave the labour market and allowed young women, in particular, to stay longer in education. Other culprits include migration and the nuclearization of families where there are fewer women in the household to contribute to domestic work.

Green sprouts started to appear at the end of the decade. Despite the skills gaps and mismatch, education levels did continue to rise across the board; however, this was simply not fast enough. This increase in education levels has benefited mainly (young) women. In advanced economies, the share of highly educated women has caught up to or even exceeded that of men, and gender pay gaps gradually declined but have not yet disappeared. Educational gaps between men and women continue to be larger in emerging and developing countries but are closing there as well, especially among those countries with ambitions to catch up to advanced economies. Even in countries and regions where traditional role models continue to be prevalent, the rising educational achievement of women has strengthened their role in the labour market. This is exemplified by Saudi Arabia that managed to implement major milestones of its Saudi Vision 2030 enacted back in 2016.

5   The Nation-State Returned to the Commanding Heights. . . Exhausted

The previous decade had started with a novel experience: Concerns about the state of the economy were demoted in favour of public health considerations. More importantly, policymakers had been swift in recognizing the extraordinary challenge the situation represented to maintain existing lifestyles and provide substantial lifelines. This included not only major state guarantees to businesses and monetary and fiscal support measures but also considerations to bring back large parts of the economy under the protection of the (national) state, essentially reverting three decades of neoliberal state disengagement of the economy. In other words, we were observing a return of the state to the commanding heights of the economy, last experienced in the aftermath of the war economy of the 1950s.[1]

But this return of the state came at a price. Two major socioeconomic crises in less than 15 years left many advanced economies exhausted. Economic resources that were meant to improve infrastructure, education, and health care were diverted to keep the economy afloat. The funds were used to provide minimum income security to those most in need and to pay back the large amounts of debt that had to be piled up to address the previous crises. The situation looked even worse in emerging economies where lack of capacity to respond led to a much deeper crisis, with little room to recover quickly. Ten years after the crisis, most of the countries in the Global South have still not made up for the loss in livelihood and jobs that they

---

[1]https://www.pbs.org/wgbh/commandingheights/hi/story/index.html

had lost during the global pandemic. And many only survived, thanks to the support from the international community through debt restructuring and donor aid.

Piling up debt to respond to the crisis was not a free lunch. Indeed, much debate during the previous decade focused on the merit of paying back this debt or trying to grow out of it. As growth did not pick up and inflation did not accelerate, it became increasingly clear that only a conservative management of public finance and hence a continuous reduction in public debt through fiscal savings would allow countries to have sufficient ammunition to address another economic slowdown in the future. Resilience, thus understood, became the mantra of the decade and created a further drag on economic growth. More importantly, choices made on how to repay the debt caused significant spending constraints. Only infrastructure, education, and non-essential health care or innovation spending could be easily cut back but with adverse consequences for growth and productivity potential that would usually have been boosted by such public investment.

The pandemic also accelerated the debate on the right institutional model and on institutional innovation that opened new avenues, albeit often in diverging directions. The return of the state had offered openings for a neo-authoritarian approach. Initial experiences in China, South Korea, and Israel had seemed to suggest that a strict, centralized approach to disease management, together with the detailed tracking of large proportions of the population, offered an efficient way of limiting the outbreak and further spread of the virus. As the crisis unfolded, however, decentralized and democratic approaches demonstrated their strength in finding tailor-made, country-, region-, or even city-specific answers to both the health and the socioeconomic crisis. Both models showing merit in different phases of the crisis, the world came up even more polarized regarding their institutional set-up: Democracy vs command control is no longer only a philosophical question but shapes geopolitics and our multilateral system and depended largely on the conditions found prior to the pandemic.

Another institutional innovation that was born out of the crisis and that has started to develop into a new, powerful instrument of the state is sovereign wealth funds that were set up out of necessity to deal with the crisis. Indeed, one of the key challenges at the beginning of the crisis was to ensure that economic supply would not collapse. Many small- and medium-sized enterprises but also big companies in transportation or tourism would not have survived without the helping hand of the state. To avoid overburdening these companies with debt, many countries resolved to setting up funds similar to the German Stabilization Fund that took equity stakes in companies in exchange for support. As these funds matured and economies recovered, their managing boards decided to enlarge the portfolio of companies in which they invested, mostly to direct their investments towards digital companies, benefiting from the extraordinary capital gains and returns these companies offered. As we enter the fourth decade of the century, these sovereign wealth funds have become an essential tool both for macroeconomic stabilization management and for regulating the microeconomy, notably in digital services.

6   Major Challenges Have Remained Without an Answer

Despite the return of the strong state, whether in its authoritarian or democratic form, major global challenges have remained largely unaddressed. Climate change, ramping urbanization, and the adverse consequences from ever-increasing digitalization have yet to be resolved. Working poverty, informal work, and poor working conditions continue to be widespread and have even increased in many parts of the world. To a large extent, the challenges to the multilateral system that the global polarization over the last 10 years has created prevented political energy being directed towards these challenges.

Take climate change, for example.

The greater incidence of natural disasters, changing weather patterns, and fluctuations in temperature are not one-off events, but unmistakably the effects of intensifying climate change. Restrictions following the pandemic that struck the world in 2020 led to a sharp decline in economic activity, trade, air, and other forms of travel. This made a significant dent in carbon emissions, but as the crisis subsided, these activities resumed. The pandemic reinforced the belief that coordinated action across countries, to counter global challenges such as pandemics and climate change, is both possible and necessary.

Nevertheless, attention to climate change remains fickle at best and varies across countries depending heavily on the nation's respective level of development. In developed economies, public awareness has fuelled a decline in consumption-based emissions, but the outsourcing of emission-intensive production to developing and emerging economies offsets these gains (Jiborn et al. 2020). Production and growing populations in developing countries demand more energy. In many of these countries, renewables such as solar and biofuel expanded, but dirty coal continues to be a key source of energy. Managing the transition from carbon-based fuels to clean fuels, particularly in terms of the associated employment shifts, has proved to be challenging in both the developed and developing worlds.

The consequences of this slow transition towards a low carbon emission economy are increasingly visible. Over the last decade, climate change has increasingly disrupted economic activity. It has had an adverse impact on infrastructure and logistics, upsetting tight production and delivery schedules in value chains. This, in turn, prompted a quest for flexibility on the part of suppliers to be able to adjust their workforces and inventories to climate shocks.

From rising sea levels and floods to draughts, fluctuations in climate are also making agriculture untenable. Water, in particular, has become a scarce and precious commodity, even more than in the past. Animal husbandry has become more challenging as feed and water for animals are limited. In the developing world, this has had an adverse impact on the economic participation of women as they tend to be the caregivers for animals. Against this backdrop, more people are in search of nonagricultural livelihoods, mostly in urban areas, adding to labour market challenges there.

In response, policymakers have placed greater emphasis on cultivating nonagricultural rural livelihoods in recent years. One way is to capture more of the processing end of the value chain rather than focusing on cultivation. This effort to spur economic activity outside land-strapped metro areas is also accelerating urbanization in an attempt to limit land flight by transforming rural areas to become more urban (Mukhopadhyay et al. 2020). Nevertheless, with agriculture becoming more challenging, the search for different livelihood options continues to fuel migration into urban and peri-urban geographies, intensifying urban sprawl. The two trends together, morphing places and migration-induced urban sprawl, mean that urbanization has proceeded at breakneck speed, albeit without creating jobs at the same pace.

Technological shifts also impacted working conditions.

At the start of the last decade, many had hoped that the digital revolution would facilitate structural transformation and bring substantial improvements in aggregate economic productivity by moving employees into high-skilled, well-paying occupations. Yet, digital tools did not bring the expected productivity gains. First, shortfalls in complementary public infrastructure investments in (city) transportation, communication, and waste management stymied the scaling up of private sector development, especially but not exclusively in emerging economies as demonstrated by ongoing infrastructure shortcomings in Germany, Italy, or the United States. Second, machine learning applications that focused on improving productivity in routine and repetitive tasks saw gains quickly eroded by an increasing amount of red tape and compliance-related activities. Third, over the course of the last decade, digital-only innovation ran into sustainability concerns as the energy hunger of digital devices quickly outstripped the available energy from renewable sources.

Automation helped manufacturers by offering higher rates and volumes of production. At the same time, it also disrupted the developing world's traditional advantage in labour-intensive manufacturing. A few developing countries are still trying to fend off automation in manufacturing by exerting downward pressure on wages and working conditions, but this also bears an adverse impact on aggregate demand. Moreover, trade protectionism, compounded by the lasting effects of the trade shocks emanating from the global pandemic in 2020, has made it impossible for other parts of the world to emulate the success of the Asian export-led growth model. Notably, countries in sub-Saharan Africa, already excluded from many processed goods industries at the beginning of the decade, have continued to face challenges in moving up the economic value chain.

In the absence of the conventional trajectory of leveraging labour-intensive production for economic growth, some nations tried to cultivate a technology-enabled knowledge economy focused on the tradable service sector to yield new jobs, for instance, in business process outsourcing, that are offshored from the Global North (Galperin and Greppi 2019). However, the lack of sufficient investment in building human capital to support the growth of the knowledge economy prevented many developing countries from benefiting from such jobs. Instead, location-based services in the gig economy have seen much faster growth in the developing world than the knowledge economy.

Meanwhile, the developed world has also seen growth in location-based service provision in the gig economy. It also dominated high-end trade in sophisticated knowledge products that demanded a high degree of innovation, education, and skills. Growth in many advanced economies has continued to decline, in large part due to declining demographics but also because the promises of new technologies have not manifested themselves as expected.

New technologies have continued to enter the market, with a strong focus on surveillance technologies, be it in public spaces or at the workplace. This was particularly evident when teleworking became more widespread as a result of the pandemic. To ensure close monitoring of performance while not sitting at a traditional workplace, managers started to use more and more remote control technologies, especially in advanced economies where digital devices have fully invaded both public and private spaces. To a certain extent, this created a sense of semiautonomy for workers as their compliance would be monitored by machines rather than through managerial oversight. This allowed for a more flexible set-up of work organization and production but did not raise individual productivity, as true autonomy was not granted. On the contrary, surveillance backlash led many individual initiatives to restore privacy by manipulating the system and limiting the intrusion of these tools in their private lives. A new leadership style, commensurate with the digital technologies that have matured over the last decade, is yet to diffuse more widely, even though some of the contours of what such "digital leadership" could look like have already emerged.

Sustainability increasingly became a concern with digital transformation. At the start of the previous decade, the electricity bill of all connected devices in some (advanced) countries already stood at more than 6 per cent of the total electricity consumption. As smartphones also became a common good in developing countries, a parallel development was observed there as well. Cloud providers and high-speed computing centres further added to the energy bill over the past 10 years, quickly outstripping the amount of renewable energy that was deployed over the same period. Significant improvements have been made in coding and software development, which helped limit the increase in energy costs. But the hunger for data has increased unabatedly, leaving countries to face an "AI trilemma" between sustainability, productivity, and inequality (Ernst 2020a).

7   Resilience: A New Policy Consensus

Against this background of broken dreams that the last decade brought, a new policy consensus has started to emerge: shared prosperity instead of winner takes all, social resilience instead of hyperefficiency, and sustainability instead of short-term gains. Debates that had already started at the beginning of the decade under the heading of a "Great Reset" eventually led to a general recognition that economic efficiency alone is insufficient for countries to enter a sustainable and inclusive path. Societies need to be able to cope quickly and effectively with emerging threats and to reap unexpected opportunities. As some observers have aptly put it, one needs to leave money on the table to survive.

Rather than trying to optimize individual social systems, whether it is health care, education, transportation, supply chains, financial markets, etc., business leaders and policymakers have started to recognize the importance of seeing these systems as interconnected. Optimal policies and strategies have been replaced by robust ones: Policies and business strategies need to internalize the risk of potential systemic failures (Ernst 2020b).

The experience of the global financial crisis (2008/2009) and the resulting instruments to deal with it proved to be useful in this context. Systematic stress testing, scenario analysis, and the investment in surplus capacity, such as additional hospital beds, medical equipment, or a decentralized system of suppliers, became common practice in many areas. The complexity of managing these systems would not have been possible, however, without the technological improvements that we had seen earlier in this century. Providing the right balance between resilience and efficiency has remained a challenge that needs constant readjustment.

Revamping global supply chains constitutes a telling example in this respect and has occupied business leaders over the past decade (McKinsey 2020). The experience of a sudden breakdown of the supply of essential parts made many realize how vulnerable their supply chains were even to local shocks. Businesses reacted in two ways to this challenge: New technologies were introduced to bring some production home, a trend that accelerated from the previous wave of reshoring. Smart, localized production accelerated, and 3D printing was no longer confined only to top-end products but deployed to a wider range of goods.

At the same time, reshoring happened at a much smaller scale than initially feared, as many companies opted for a diverse network of suppliers. New network management tools blossomed, thanks to the ingenious use of AI-powered algorithms that helped to manage such a complex network and anticipate potential risks to disruption. Additionally, it provided opportunities for new players to enter the system, especially from those countries that were previously less connected to global trade. China no longer dominated the production of rare earth metals, and basic manufacturing could now also be shipped from Nigeria, where wage costs remained significantly lower than in emerging Vietnam or other East Asian countries. Being able to organize and coordinate a decentralized network of production sites rather than a linear supply chain was the key breakthrough of the 2020s, of which we are reaping the full benefits only now.

This new (policy) strategy paradigm has started to look at both efficiency gains and system-wide resilience. Regarding the provision of health care, for instance, policymakers have started to look beyond the ability of their country's ambulatory and hospital services to deliver on day-to-day operations. Instead, they now also assess the capacity of the medical supply chain to react to situations when unforeseen shocks arrive. Change has occurred in other (policy) areas as well, for instance, as in regard to the design and implementation of labour market policies: Active and passive labour market policies do no longer only integrate the costs and benefits of promoting occupational transitions under normal circumstances. They now also assess the costs to society for lost opportunities due to bottlenecks caused, for instance, by a lack in intergenerational mobility (Aiyar and Ebeke 2020). The opportunity costs of the absence of such transitions add important information to understand the resilience of the network of labour market transitions.

8   What to Expect Beyond 2030?

8.1   Fintech to the Rescue but New Norms and Standards Are Only Slowly Emerging

The return of the strong state triggered resistance from a movement that had already emerged at the start of the previous decade. In particular, the various libertarian traditions that structured around the emerging blockchain technology have gained increasing influence in policy circles with their vision of a "peer-to-peer" economy that would no longer require the presence of the leviathan.[2] Governments have been keen to embrace this movement, in part because of their declining ability to deliver public goods and services. In particular, a rising participation of civil society organizations in the delivery of such goods, whether in education, environmental services, local development, or compliance monitoring, has been met with open arms by policymakers.

Despite the proliferation of such activities and their reliance on the latest technological developments to ensure impact, a lack of coordination and common standards have led to waste from parallel efforts, frictions in the delivery of public goods, and conflictual goal setting. As had already been anticipated at the beginning of the last decade, in the absence of a common regulatory framework, interoperability issues abound, and impact-oriented solutions could not be scaled up sufficiently broadly and quickly to deliver on their objectives (Geneva Macro Labs 2019). By 2025, governments finally started to pay closer attention to this issue and to develop a common understanding of possible guiding principles, which eventually resulted in Agenda 2040, a global standard for tech-based stakeholder capitalism.

8.2   Stakeholder Capitalism and Collective Intelligence

Stakeholder capitalism has become the new horizon for company strategists. Rather than focusing exclusively on a company's owners, the shareholders, stakeholder capitalism is an attempt to bring closer together a company's various stakeholders: customers, workers, suppliers, and the local community besides the traditional shareholders. As early as January 2020, the World Economic Forum had released an update of its Davos Manifesto calling for a renewal of stakeholder capitalism, an idea that had already been sprouted in the previous century. Behind the updated manifesto stands the premise that managers' incentives can be appropriately directed to the common goal. As a consequence, the private sector would align its interest automatically with broader social goals, and no direct state intervention through regulation or taxation would be required.[3] However, a major obstacle to achieve this transition remained that the existing ownership and property rights structure of a

---

[2]https://qz.com/1284178/almost-half-of-cryptocurrency-and-bitcoin-bros-identify-as-libertarian/
[3]https://www.weforum.org/the-davos-manifesto

company did not incentivize managers to move beyond the shareholder value principle (Bebchuk and Tallarita 2020).

This is why in Spring 2030, the G40 government group decided to adopt Agenda 2040, a set of principles to change the incentives for managers and adopt a stakeholder view. The time was ripe for such a shift in the policy framework. Indeed, over the past decade, management styles have shifted under the impression of more equitable and broad-based educational achievement and a greater sense of ownership, especially among younger people (Albert et al. 2019). Collective intelligence became a competitive edge for both companies and public sector organizations as the traditional role of experts and intellectuals started to wane. The general move towards more resilient policymaking is a reflection of this shift in how diverging interests and heterogeneous forms of expertise are integrated into collective decision-making, whether in the public or private sphere. As we enter the new decade, this movement has only started and will hopefully deliver its full benefits over the next years.

The new policy paradigm is not without challenges of its own. Key among the principles underlying Agenda 2040 is the idea to leverage technological developments that have taken place over the past decade, including artificial intelligence, internet of things, or blockchain, to value the input of all relevant stakeholders in today's companies. New rights and obligations linked to valuing data, human, social, or natural capital need to be created, monitored, and sanctioned. Business leaders, customers, workers, and other stakeholders, therefore, need to develop digital awareness to understand the implications of these changes and the significant extensions of their economic and social possibilities and risks that these changes bring. Using the traditional approach, none of these investments by stakeholders were properly valued and remunerated. This caused many of the imbalances that we were faced with at the end of the 2020s. With the new principles, governments finally hope to address these challenges and help to empower their constituents towards a brighter future.

8.3   Whither Multilateralism: The Example of International Labour Standards

Policy changes also affected the multilateral system, which saw significant shifts over the past 10 years. Heavily under pressure at the beginning of the 2020s, as exemplified by the retreat of the United States from the World Health Organization, international organizations proved resilient and open to change to interpret their mandate in light of the changing conditions under which they operated. In this respect, the evolution that the framework of international labour standards took over the past decade sheds some light on the overall dynamics of the multilateral system and provides some indications as to its likely future (see box below). As we enter the 2030s, the multilateral system is struggling to remain an influential force for change.

Box: International Supervision of Labour Standards in 2030—Managing Expectations

By Eric Gravel

Since 1919, the International Labour Organization (ILO) has been contributing to progress in achieving social justice. With a view to promoting this concept, the ILO was mandated by its Constitution to set minimum international labour standards, through a process of tripartite dialogue during its annual International Labour Conference. These international labour standards were developed to provide a global system of instruments on labour and social policy, backed up by a system of supervision to address all types of problems arising in their application at the national level. Even in 2030, international labour standards remain the legal component of the ILO's strategy for governing globalization, promoting sustainable development, eradicating poverty, and ensuring that everyone can work in dignity and safety.

Today, the ILO can no longer claim exclusivity with regard to its standard-setting functions. Nevertheless, it has retained primacy over the formulation, interpretation, and application of labour standards, not just because it can legitimately do so, an important argument in the political construction of globalization, but also because it possesses experience and expertise in this field—a crucial argument in the technocratic construction of globalization. To be effective, however, it relies on a multidimensional supervisory system that is anchored in the Organization's standards and principles. The specific system established by the ILO to promote compliance with labour standards continues to be considered as one of the most developed and effective and is often regarded as quite unique on the international stage.[4]

Despite its high esteem, the number of new international labour standards has continued to decline over the past decade, as has the rate at which existing ones were ratified. At the same time, the Organization keeps addressing new challenges and adopts, when necessary, new instruments, in particular regarding labour issues linked to the digital economy. Is this lack of commitment for legally binding instruments at the international level a trend that is likely to continue? Looking at similar difficulties in other international foras, in particular on environmental issues, the answer could easily be yes. The willingness to ratify has declined for reasons which appear to often have less to do with ideology or the small number of topics proposed for the adoption of new standards that have a rallying effect, than with practical considerations linked to the absorption capacity of administrations, in both developing and

(continued)

---

[4]This argument was already put forward in the early years of hyper-globalization (see, for instance, Frison-Roche (2002)).

developed countries, making them less willing to shoulder the workload connected with the supervisory system and in particular the submission of periodical reports.[5] In this regard, it seems clear that embracing new technologies and the use of IT tools to streamline such reporting burden will be crucial in the coming years.

At the same time, a debate has intensified as to whether the model of the ILO as a global lawmaker that imposes, through hard international legislation, a consensus reached by delegates in Geneva, should be replaced by soft law, self-regulation, and codes of practice.[6] This debate over hard vs soft law at the international level is not new and had started long before 2020. But over and above the controversy between these different approaches in terms of ensuring compliance with international obligations, the past decade has shown that it is no longer enough for a rule to be legitimate and fair, nor for it to have been adopted in the legal form required by the national competent authorities following tripartite consensus through the ILO framework. It also has to be effective, which means in particular that it is correctly and effectively applied by those to whom it is addressed; for that purpose, the latter have to have judged it acceptable.

In this context, for several observers, the distinction between soft and hard law or the existence of a supervisory mechanism rather than informal monitoring should not be the key issue, as long as the various approaches have a real impact on compliance with the standards and principles laid down in international instruments. As the debate has evolved in this direction over the past 10 years, the key challenge in 2030 has become to ensure that the voluntary, reasoned agreements secured in the ILO can continue to be "its centre of legal gravity, meaning its influence on domestic laws in its member states".[7]

References

Aiyar, S., & Ebeke, C. H. (2020). Inequality of opportunity, inequality of income and economic growth. *World Development, 136*. https://doi.org/10.1016/j.worlddev.2020.105115.
Albert, M., Hurrelmann, K., & Quenzel, G. (2019). *Shell youth study 2019. A generation speaks up.* Beltz Edition: Weinheim.
Alvaredo, F., Chancel, L., Piketty, T., Saez, E., & Zucman, G. (2018). *World inequality report.* World Inequality Lab: Paris.

[5]Former ILO Legal Adviser, Francis Maupain, had already pointed out this problem some years ago (Maupain 2004).
[6]See already Langille (2019).
[7]See Langille (2019, p. 518); see more generally the analysis of Maupain (2013) on a certain misconception of the ILO's role in this regard.

Bebchuk, L. A., & Tallarita, R. (2020, December). The illusory promise of stakeholder governance. *Cornell Law Review.*

Chami, R., Ernst, E., Fullenkamp, C., & Oeking, A. (2018). *Are remittances good for labor markets in LICs, MICs and fragile states?* IMF working paper, no. 18/102. Washington, DC.

Del Rio-Chanona, R. M., Mealy, P., Pichler, A., Lafond, F., & Farmer, J. D. (2020). Supply and demand shocks in the COVID-19 pandemic: An industry and occupation perspective. *Oxford Review of Economic Policy.*

Ernst, E. (2020a). The AI trilemma: Saving the planet without ruining our jobs. Medium.com. Accessed from https://medium.com/digital-diplomacy/the-ai-trilemma-saving-the-planet-with out-ruining-our-jobs-7aac3f42c968

Ernst, E. (2020b). The paradox of efficiency. Why we will need more redundancies in uncertain times. In P. McCann (Ed.), *Productivity and the pandemic: Challenges and insights from Covid-19.* London: Edward Elgar.

Frison-Roche, M.-A. (2002). The joint need for an analogous regulation of labour relations and globalized markets. In P. Auer & B. Gazier (Eds.), *The future of work, employment and social protection – The dynamics of change and the protection of workers, Proceedings of the France/ ILO symposium, (Lyon)* (p. 188). Geneva: ILO.

Galperin, H., & Greppi, C. (2019). Geographic discrimination in the Gig economy. In M. Graham (Ed.), *Digital economies at global margins.* Cambridge: MIT Press.

Geneva Macro Labs. (2019). *Blockchain 4 impact.* Geneva. Accessed from https://bit.ly/3hSUoEq

Jiborn, M., Kulionis, V., & Kander, A. (2020). Consumption versus technology: Drivers of global carbon emissions 2000–2014. *Energies, 13,* 339.

Kjellestorm, T., Maître, N., Saget, C., Otto, M., & Karimova, T. (2019). *Working on a warmer planet: The effect of heat stress on productivity and decent work.* International Labour Organisation: Geneva.

Langille, B. (2019). The political economy of decency. In G. Politakis, T. Kohiyama, & T. Lieby (Eds.), *Law for social justice* (p. 507). Geneva: ILO.

Maupain, F. (2004). Persuasion et contrainte aux fins de la mise en oeuvre des normes et objectifs de l'OIT. In J.-C. Javillier & B. Gernigon (Eds.), *Les normes internationales du travail: un patrimoine pour l'avenir – Mélanges en l'honneur de Nicolas Valticos* (pp. 694–695). Geneva: ILO.

Maupain, F. (2013). *The future of the ILO in the global economy.* Oxford: Hart Publishers.

McKinsey Global Institute. (2020). Risk, resilience, and rebalancing in global value chains risk. In *Washington.* McKinsey: DC.

Milanovic, B. (2020). *After the financial crisis: The evolution of the global income distribution between 2008 and 2013.* MPRA Paper, No. 101560 (Munich).

Mukhopadhyay, P., Zérah, H., & Denis, E. (2020). Subaltern urbanization: Indian insights for urban theory. *International Journal of Urban and Regional Research, 44*(4), 582–598.

Sabina Dewan is the Founder and Executive Director of the JustJobs Network, which she co-founded with John Podesta in 2013. She is also a Senior Visiting Fellow at the Centre for Policy Research in India and a Non-resident Fellow at the Carsey School of Public Policy at the University of New Hampshire. Her research focuses on strategies for job creation and workforce development. Within this domain, her research examines how technology, climate change, and the restructuring of trade into value chains are upending traditional employment models and the differential impacts of these forces on women and different socioeconomic groups.

Ekkehard Ernst is an internationally recognized expert on the Future of Work at the International Labour Organization. His work focuses on the impact of technological change, demographic shifts, globalization, global warming, and political vagaries on productivity, employment, wages, and inequality. In particular, he has studied the implications of artificial intelligence, robots, and blockchain applications on job growth, inequality, and the transition to a sustainable society. In 2017, he co-founded Geneva Macro Labs, a Swiss Do Tank, to offer a platform to identify, develop, and implement solutions to address global challenges and existential risks to promote and advance the United Nations Sustainable Development Agenda. Previously, he worked at the Organisation for Economic Co-operation and Development (OECD) and the European Central Bank. He has studied in Mannheim, Saarbrucken, and Paris and holds a PhD from the École des Hautes Études en Sciences Sociales. He regularly advises external partners on labour market issues, including the European Parliament's Panel for the Future on Science and Technology, the Conference Board, the UK Productivity Insights Network, McKinsey & Company, Roland Berger, and Foresight Alliance.

Eric Gravel is Senior Legal Officer in the International Labour Standards Department of the ILO, which he joined in 1996. Prior to his current assignment, he worked as a Labour Lawyer for the UNHCR between 1992 and 1996. He is widely published in international law journals such as the *International Labour Review* and regularly teaches on international labour law as a Guest Professor at the McGill University in Montreal; the Graduate Institute of International and Development Studies, Geneva; and the University of Dijon, France.

How Humans and Machines Interact

Andrej Heinke

On May 1, 2030, International Labor Day, the evening news worldwide has only one top news item: China's new prime minister is not a person, but an avatar. The pictures of the meeting of the Standing Committee of the Politburo of the Communist Party show, indeed, a lifelike figure on the right side of President Xi, who bears considerable resemblance to the first head of the government of the People's Republic of Zhou Enlai, also bearing the name of his son Sun Yang, but in reality is a hologram.

China is celebrating the appointment as a great success on the way to fulfilling the Chinese dream and a vital stage victory just a few years before the centenary of the founding of the People's Republic. President Xi says that the wisdom and courage of the founding generation will now be preserved forever. Xi says, "No power in the world can make better decisions if we are protected by our ancestors. They guide my hand and give us their wisdom. China, under the leadership of its party, has become invincible once and for all."

Only insiders know that the top secret Tianhe-10 (Milky Way) supercomputer, which controls the Avatar's utterances and movements, has been instrumental in preparing the Chinese leadership for decision-making for 2 years now. According to the findings of the American secret services, the rate of agreement between the recommendations of the supercomputer and the actual decisions of the Politburo was initially only 30 percent. In the meantime, however, it has reached 97 percent.

All attempts by the Western powers to gain access to the supercomputer have so far been in vain. Since the Trump administration, the open conflict between the United States and China had led to an increasingly aggressive rupture, turning an initial "decoupling" into a fundamentally hostile separation. As a result, for the past 5 years, all components and algorithms in Chinese products and applications have been domestically produced. All Chinese companies and government institutions were forbidden to use hardware or software from non-Chinese sources under threat of sanction. The standards have already diverged so far apart that there is no longer any compatibility.

So much for a possible vision from the year 2030: Of course nobody can know the future; at best plausible assumptions are possible. But as science fiction author William Gibson says, "The future is already there, it is just unequally distributed."

A. Heinke (✉)
Corporate Foresight and Megatrends, Robert Bosch GmbH, Stuttgart, Germany
e-mail: Andrej.Heinke@de.bosch.com

© Springer Nature Switzerland AG 2021
S. Güldenberg et al. (eds.), *Managing Work in the Digital Economy*, Future of Business and Finance, https://doi.org/10.1007/978-3-030-65173-2_2

To find and interpret these spores of the future is quite possible. This will lead to larger and broader developments, which will be obvious in 2030. By far, the most important development, therefore, which will have a massive impact on the coming decade, is the American-Chinese conflict, which will also affect the relationship between humans and machines in the future.

Even in the year 2030, people will still be superior to machines and use them as tools, not the other way around. Therefore, the tools will develop depending on the goals of the people. If they are aimed at enforcing the superiority of the respective system, the relationship between man and machine in both countries will show considerable differences and will no longer be compatible, but even contrary to each other.

Eric Schmidt, Former CEO of Google, is currently Chair of the National Security Commission on Artificial Intelligence and the Defense Innovation Board. In a programmatic opinion article in *The New York Times*, he warned: "Important trends are not in our favor" (Schmidt 2020). America's lead in artificial intelligence, he wrote, is precarious. A recent study by the Tortoise Institute considering more than 100 metrics finds "that the United States is well ahead of China today but will fall behind in the next five to ten years" (Tortoise Media 2020). "China has almost twice as many supercomputers and about 15 times as many 5G base stations deployed as the United States. If current trends continue, China's overall investments in research and development are expected to surpass those of the United States within ten years," according to the 2018 Global R&D Forecast (R&D Magazine 2018). At around the same time, China's economy is projected to become larger than America's, according to a projection of the world in 2030 by the bank HSBC (Henry and Pomero 2018).

1   Artificial Intelligence (AI) as a Central Component for Future Human-Machine Interface Systems

Human-machine interface (HMI) encompasses the means by which humans and computers communicate with each other. It includes hardware and software that are used to translate user input into commands and to present results to the user (Tan 2020). The relationship between humans and machines is mainly influenced by the steady increase in the capabilities of artificial intelligence. AI gives systems the ability to analyze their environment and make decisions with a degree of autonomy to achieve goals. Although the limits of AI are uncertain and have shifted over time, automating or replicating intelligent behavior is one of the key aims of AI research and applications. That is how the test proposed by British researcher Alan Turing in 1950 came about. The goal was to determine whether a machine had the capacity to think, so that a person talking simultaneously to both a person and a computer would not be able to distinguish their answers.

AI is dependent on Big Data and powerful computers to analyze it, cloud computing to deliver distributed computing resources, and high-speed connections to link various sensors and sources of information. Its most important field, machine learning, refers to the development of digital systems that improve their performance on a particular task over time, through experience. Machine learning describes the ability of software or a computer to learn from its environment or a very large batch of representative data and to adapt its behavior to changing circumstances accordingly or carry out tasks for which it was not explicitly programmed. The basic idea is to allow associative learning by linking simple information processing units and artificial neurons in such a way that the weighting of the connections and the corresponding performance of the network is adjusted automatically.

Every day, people and machines produce ten times more new data than that which exists in all of the world's books. This will multiply by the factor of at least 100 by 2030. The ever-growing amount of digital material on the Internet, in the form of images, text, videos, and audio files, is used to identify patterns. The training of multilayered architectures on huge amounts of data, which will be much more important by 2030, is referred to as "deep learning." Stuart Russell and Peter Norvig use the following classification for categorizing artificial intelligence: (1) systems that think like humans, (2) systems that behave like humans, (3) systems that think rationally, and (4) systems that act rationally (Russell and Norvig 2009). By 2030, we will see an increasing amount of HMI systems that act rationally. We may even see systems that deliberate along rational lines. However, it will be far too early for them to behave like a human or even to think like a person.

HMI systems acting rationally will still only work within the narrow context of a specific problem or application by 2030. They may show excellent results, but the benefits are significantly affected if the task is even marginally changed. While a person who can read Japanese characters can also understand Japanese, expand on their preferences for sushi or sashimi with recommendations for specific restaurants, and be aware that pink slippers are worn to go to the toilet, these tasks will require different HMI systems.

2 Goals for Future HMI Systems

The human qualities of creativity, the ability to improvise and cooperate, and resourcefulness open up new possibilities to engage and participate in value creation processes. Not only could new technologies create the need for different goods and services; they could also take over repetitive, physically demanding, and dangerous work. This would allow people to dedicate their time to other endeavors, such as pursuing their interests and doing things that are meaningful to them.

Anna Müller is a Doctoral Student at Robert Bosch GmbH in 2030. She remembers her school days, which were interrupted by the COVID-19 pandemic. The years that followed were marked by society's handling of the virus and the recurring waves of disease. Her interest in sociology and philosophy dates from this period. She remembers the rapid digitalization in the field of education but also thinks back to her realization that her original professional goal of becoming a lawyer was losing its meaning. She wanted to better understand the causes and effects of the world around her. She is taking a course in philosophy at university. Only yesterday in the main seminar the vision of a communist society by Karl Marx was discussed: "... in communist society, where nobody has one exclusive sphere of activity but each can become accomplished in any branch he wishes, society regulates the general production and thus makes it possible for me to do one thing today and another tomorrow, to hunt in the morning, fish in the afternoon, rear cattle in the evening, criticize after dinner, just as I have a mind, without ever becoming hunter, fisherman, herdsman or critic" (Marx 1845).

"That sounds pretty exhausting," Anna Müller thinks. When did he actually relax, this Marx? What Anna liked, however, was the idea of not having to make a final decision, but to do what suited her. No one in her circle of friends wanted that. It was uncool and stuffy.

According to Daniel Newman and Olivier Blanchard (2019), the winners of the future will be those who identify how to harness the power of automation and artificial intelligence collaboratively. It is a continuation of the very long evolutionary development of humans creating tools to solve problems that they are not able to solve on their own. It is a question of task automation as opposed to job automation, recognizing that traditional roles can be broken down into elements to which either humans or machines are better suited.

A key element here is the ability to break larger tasks into their smallest parts, distribute those parts within a large network of workers according to their availability and skills, and then synthesize the results. Digital technologies in a networked world make it increasingly possible to collect accurate data regarding the output and productivity of both individuals and teams and to compare them. This data serves as the basis for the creation of algorithms for the efficient distribution of tasks. Still, at the same time, they make possible a new kind of Taylorism, associated with the potential for an increase in stress for individuals, and a further loss of privacy.

The goals for HMI systems are to improve learned models with an explanatory and corrective interface, increase the reliability of results, work with a high degree of transparency, and go beyond limited capabilities to develop skills that can be assigned to broader tasks. This would make it possible to communicate naturally with people and to extrapolate from past experiences in order to constantly solve new tasks and situations. Achieving this means recognizing the importance of processes and developing a broad understanding of the world by establishing contexts and connections, in the same way, people do.

Future HMI systems have to reduce their high energy consumption. The human brain uses the equivalent of a 20-watt light bulb, whereas a supercomputer uses as much electricity as a town of 20,000 inhabitants. A human brain also works without software, centralized controls, or an operating system. It is usually fault-tolerant and flexible and achieves learning goals much faster, more effectively, and more economically than a computer. Machines have to follow the human example, using energy from renewable sources.

3 Humans and Machines: An Increasingly Challenging Relationship

The ongoing wave of technological innovation could potentially spark new forms of economic activity and create new jobs, such as for employees capable of developing, building, maintaining, and repairing new robots and intelligent machines. Moreover, the demand for new infrastructure, transportation, and IT equipment will increase. Many developing countries have yet to build a reliable power, transportation, and IT infrastructure. Lower costs will increase competitiveness, while higher costs will stimulate investment. In turn, this will lead to increases in productivity as a result of innovation and economies of scale.

There are four drivers that are having an impact on the future of work: smart HMIs, coordination economies, immersive collaboration, and a new kind of "maker mindset" (Gorbis 2016).

- Smart HMIs
  Smart HMIs can communicate with each other, adjust to changing conditions in real time, learn from that experience, and operate autonomously without human intervention. They will take over tasks that people are not particularly good at, for instance, repetitive processes and dangerous or data-intensive tasks, or those tasks that are either too large or too small to be efficiently performed by human beings (Bengler et al. 2020).
- Coordination Economies
  The appearance of new coordination economies on the order of Uber and Airbnb is occurring concomitantly with automation and the proliferation of smart HMIs. Digital online platforms bring together customers and those offering goods and services so that they can negotiate with each other directly. This way of organizing human labor goes hand in hand with the decline of the formal and traditional management hierarchies of the previous century.
- Immersive Collaboration
  Physical and digital-virtual environments, media, and interactions are more thoroughly interwoven than ever before. Cyberspace is turning into a constantly present experiential cocoon, which is closely integrated into the real world. Factors that facilitate work processes and the exchange of ideas include the proliferation of mobile devices and devices equipped with sensors, advances in virtual and augmented reality, and the increase in a wide variety of digital platforms supporting cooperative work.
- A New "Maker Mindset": The Democratization of Production and Development
  In connection with biotechnology and nanotechnology, new digital production technologies—in particular 3D printers—make it possible to adapt a product's material properties to its function more precisely. This world of open production has the potential to call conventional methods of production and development into question.

4   Future Drivers of HMI Development

Currently, the Internet is the biggest driver of AI-based HMI systems. Websites and Internet-based applications are the biggest sources of user-specific data. Every click and every transaction on an e-commerce website feeds into a paradigm, which acts as a learning tool. Huge and influential platforms, such as Google, Facebook, Amazon, Baidu, Alibaba, and Tencent, are the biggest beneficiaries of these data sets, which will form the base for HMI systems of the future. These will continue to build on data collections, which are constantly expanded to optimize business processes and ease decision-making. Due to the bifurcation into American- and Chinese-led data worlds, the results will differ ever more due to the diverging databases. The sectors where these enhanced HMI systems are applied will be seen strongest in the United States mainly in the financial sector, the insurance industry, and logistics, while China will develop them mainly in central planning, in the transportation sector, in education systems, and in policing. Adrian Lobe describes how by using Big Data and AI a digitally managed economy could appear. Using centralized data processing systems based on the availability of a large amount of data on consumer behavior, the former "competitive disadvantage" could be compensated in comparison to capitalism (Lobe 2019).

Security concerns underpin China's current and future efforts to keep valuable data exclusively under the control of Chinese technology companies. That will be even more so in 2030. To this end, China has already pushed national standards in AI-related fields such as cloud computing, industrial software, and Big Data that differ from international standards. A report by the Mercator Institute showed that Chinese standards for smart manufacturing, cloud computing, industrial software, and Big Data clearly diverge from international standards (Zenglein and Holzmann 2019).

China's aim is to define the contours of the global HMI industry by setting standards at an early stage. It was reported in January 2018 that guidelines were being developed for the "China Standard 2035" strategy, which includes sectors relevant to AI. According to reports and "to preempt competitors in emerging technologies ranging from cloud to virtual reality, the Standardization Administration of China (SAC) and the National Academy of Engineering are quietly working on "China Standards 2035" (中国标准2035), a nation-wide effort to develop industrial standards and eventually internationalize them" (http://www.cnstandards.net/wp-content/uploads/2019/03/China-Standard-2035.pdf und https://www.merics.org/en/blog/chinese-tech-standards-put-screws-european-companies).

The 2017 cybersecurity law forbids foreign companies from storing data about Chinese customers outside of China. HMI systems in autonomous vehicles cannot process the data they collect, as unchecked information about the areas travelled could fall into foreign hands. This hinders cross-border data pooling and will have prevented the development of common data-sharing standards by 2030.

Perception-based HMI, which will grow strongly in both camps, enables the even larger digitization of the physical world using sensors and intelligent devices. By collecting data that was previously unavailable or unusable, new applications will be created. HMI in 2030 relies on a huge number of networked sensors and a new combination of data—in the form of multimedia content—with new user interfaces guided by voice, gesture, or electric impulse. The ability to read some of the major impulses of a human brain will see some advances.

HMI technologies in 2030 will allow for a high level of customization, which allows individualized value propositions and user experience. Most importantly, HMI will release people from repetitive tasks so they can pursue more creative work. Self-driving cars, self-directed robots, and interconnected systems in a smart city will make significant advances. The widespread technical deployment of the 5G mobile networks, which are indispensable for the uninterrupted functioning and communication of automated systems, will be the backbone for a tactile Internet. Some pilot projects applying 6G networks are mainly confined to defense-related projects.

5 HMI with Chinese Characteristics

Over the past two decades, China has been the fastest-growing economy, and it has challenged American hegemony in many areas, including HMI. One should neither underestimate China's innovation capacity nor the pace of development in the country. About 12.5 million production jobs vanished in China alone in the period from 2013 to 2017 as robot use accelerated (Frey 2020).

Some structural advantages speak in favor of China having a leading role in some areas of AI-driven HMI. The main reasons are the huge amounts of data collected, a large talent pool, aggressive entrepreneurship, and the government's strong, pragmatic approach to new technologies. China's advantage in data finds its source not only in the size of its domestic market but also because Chinese citizens are more willing than others to share their data. By 2030, when compared to the United States, China will have compensated its disadvantages, mainly poorer research performance, a lack of scientific experience, and a weak presence in global platforms.

In July 2017, the Chinese State Council approved the "Next Generation Artificial Intelligence Development Plan," which stipulates that the country shall be the leading power worldwide in AI technology by 2030. The State Council's AI plan calls for the introduction of AI in a particular range of areas, such as industrial production, jurisdiction, public safety, and military uses. The education of young talent in AI is to begin at the elementary school level and to be intensified at institutions of higher learning. The history of Chinese government support for AI-related development of HMI systems manifests a consistent focus on robotics and innovation at home. Intelligent manufacturing technology and the industrial Internet will continue to be priorities.

Specific areas will have achieved breakthroughs by 2030. These include connected vehicles, service robots, facial recognition, and AI-supported medical diagnostic tools. Linking governmental specifications with the business goals of the private companies spearheading the development of AI-driven HMI is a key factor in the implementation of China's strategic goals. Moreover, in the development of HMI up to 2030, the country will have focused on cooperation with the military. In neither Russia nor the United States is this symbiosis between defense capability and the economy so pronounced. Especially when it comes to AI-driven HMI technologies by 2030, it will be impossible to discern a clear separation between military and civilian uses (Kania 2017).

6   Digital Leninism: AI-Driven HMI as a Means of Consolidating Power

In the area of public security, China's ruling class views AI-enabled HMI as a means of consolidating and reinforcing its power. AI and Big Data are being utilized systematically in the service of social control and economic coordination. Social stability and social control are to be perfected through the widespread use of facial recognition software. The value of AI for proactive policing will be established by 2030; technologies will help Chinese authorities to discern patterns in large quantities of communications data. In particular, the system of "social credits" will collect and evaluate data updated in real time on all Chinese citizens, all companies doing business in China and their employees, and all foreigners in the country. That data will reflect transactions, mobility patterns, communications among friends and the makeup of social circles, interactions with business partners, and violations of laws and contracts.

The data stream records how payments are made, people's location, communications data, and mobility and health profiles. The system would constantly monitor and evaluate the activities of every Chinese citizen and determine his or her level of reliability. Moreover, the social credit rating will have serious consequences; for example, it would have an impact on one's chance of receiving a mortgage or getting a job or on the educational opportunities available to one's children.

Sofia Wu looks out the window of her Beijing apartment. In the distance, she sees the mountains. The view is fantastic. There hasn't been smog for years, but she suffers from allergies arising from her childhood days when the air was still so dirty. It's annoying that her illness becomes a topic of conversation every time she is interviewed with the computers in the personnel departments of large companies. Sometimes she feels that she is only invited to interviews because her uncle is deputy mayor.

She had finally found a job with the largest advertising company in the country. Her job is to validate, among her large circle of friends and at parties, the micro-trends that update the daily advertising messages. The household robots, in particular, which have become a status symbol over the past 3 years, should only recommend those brands that are among the company's most important customers. Because they do this reliably, they can be offered at a price that is below their production cost. Nevertheless, they quickly pay for themselves. Sofia has also ordered one from the latest line at the factory outlet. He looks like the Brazilian student who was her first great love. His hologram was the inspiration for the custom-made product. Only that the robot, unlike its human counterpart, is never hurtful but always knows exactly what she wants.

By 2030, a new type of technology-driven social and government order will have emerged in China. It is an open question as to whether the new technologies will reinforce the power of the ruling class over the long run or whether at some point they will bring about a change in the country's power structures. Political changes in an authoritarian environment would be driven not so much by an opposition made up of human beings, but rather by the limited capacity of those in the leadership, their families, and power structures to understand and control the new technologies. Therefore, my guess is that they will enlist the power of those technologies and provide them with legitimacy by adopting a "human" face to it, as described in the initial "report from the future."

7 Ethics and HMI

When it comes to the fundamental differences between a person and a machine, the ability to take action and make decisions is a key concept. Human beings can set goals and choose the means with which to reach those goals. Machines, on the other hand, are products made by human beings. Their actions are viewed as purely mechanical processes. Machines are technological helpmates that cannot pursue goals on their own. Even in 2030, HMI systems will not possess consciousness or free will, and consequently, they will have no sense of guilt or morality. They neither reflect on nor justify decisions nor do they themselves make changes to those decisions. They thus still cannot be held responsible for their actions, are not be liable for damages under civil law, and cannot be found culpable under criminal law.

By 2030, there will be quite a few legal cases in order to hold manufacturers or users responsible for the actions of machines. Identity, self-determination, and the ability to take responsibility for one's actions, meanwhile, are not written in stone, but rather exist in a state of constant change. The more that machines lose their solely instrumental character, and increasingly take on the role of a self-directed actor, or form a hybrid unit of action in concert with human beings, the more the borders between human beings and machines will be blurred.

The prospect of a loss of human autonomy and control threatens to impinge on the basic human need for security and self-determination. That could systematically lead to a situation in which no one can be held responsible for the decisions of an HMI system that can no longer be understood, nor controlled. The actions of cognitive tools are no longer programmed linearly by human beings. Deep learning and "generative adversarial network approaches" make it possible for machines to teach themselves new strategies and seek new cues. Due to the machine's learning and self-development processes, which occur in the context of changing conditions, the manufacturer can't predict the concrete actions of an autonomous system in their entirety. While users utilize the HMI system, they cannot control its actions, because they can only imagine the machine's potential for action. In many cases, it is thus no longer possible to make sense of the actions taken by machines, nor for those actions to be analyzed by human beings.

The year 2030 may mark a transition toward a world, where machines will be tied increasingly to their actions. Maybe artificial "culprits" may even be pursued and tried by other oversight mechanisms, driven by pattern recognition. One possible HMI system architecture that includes ethical principles could be a two-tier surveillance architecture: it would keep HMI operations separate from a surveillance agent responsible for the ethical or legal assessment of practical measures.

In 2030, HMI systems may have some features that will enable them to even act in a morally superior way than people could in comparable situations, as they cannot be influenced by irrational impulses or emotional stress, cannot be seduced, and do not have any specific biases. Moreover, in 10 years' time, they can make decisions in real time, without moments of shock or external influences.

By 2030, the question as to whether there are boundaries that should not be crossed as technology progresses will be discussed with different perspectives, because it was already necessary to go so far as to bar automation in certain areas of life. This may include the area of palliative care, where humans decide on ethical grounds, if and when to terminate life-supporting mechanisms. Machines may even be excluded in applying genetic preconditions in deciding on who may progress to leadership positions in business or administration. The debate will rage on in 2030 and beyond, as to which fundamental principles shall be inviolable, although human dignity shall be seen differently from what the present dictates.

Up until the point at which robots develop self-awareness or this awareness is created, these principles, which cannot be translated into machine code, must be observed by those who build robots, as well as those who manufacture and operate them. This debate will be in full gear by 2030. Algorithms and system architectures must observe evolving laws, social norms, and ethical principles. What is more, ethical problems are interpreted differently, depending on culture, religion, and value systems. Values also change over time.

The more HMI systems develop, the more their architectures will contain subsystems capable of assessing ethical problems on several levels. These will include the ability to compare patterns quickly, define lines of argumentation, and justify actions. Subsystems will also enable trust-building social interaction with human users, as well as social processes that will enable the HMI system to understand cultural norms in various contexts and apply them accordingly. Making the HMI system's findings and actions understandable and transparent to people will be a special challenge in itself.

8   Systematics of Human-Machine Interaction

Goals for the future of HMI will evolve along the lines of the "ten challenges" of Klein:

1. "To be a team player, an intelligent agent must fulfill the requirements of a Basic

Compact to engage in common-grounding activities.
2. To be an effective team player, intelligent agents must be able to adequately model the other participants' intentions and actions vis-à-vis the joint activity's state and evolution.
3. Human-agent team members must be mutually predictable.
4. Agents must be directable.
5. Agents must be able to make pertinent aspects of their status and intentions obvious to their teammates.
6. Agents must be able to observe and interpret pertinent signals of status and intentions.
7. Agents must be able to engage in goal negotiation.
8. Support technologies for planning and autonomy must enable a collaborative approach.
9. Agents must be able to participate in managing attention.
10. All team members must help control the costs of coordinated activity." (Klein et al. 2004)

Joint human-agent activity should be based on a voluntary agreement to cooperate, mutual predictability of all actors, and the consistent goal of maintaining common ground. Key requirements to be fulfilled by future HMI systems will certainly include the following principles: adaptability, modularity and interchangeability, flexibility and extensibility, distributed industrial cloud, service-oriented design, programmable networks, compliance to standards, security/safety/privacy, and usability/ease of use.

According to Carsten and Martens, identified elements of HMI design in automated vehicles would entail the following aspirations:

- "Provide the required understanding of the capabilities and status of the automated vehicle (minimize mode errors)
- Engender correct calibration of trust
- Stimulate appropriate level of attention and intervention
- Minimize automation surprises
- Provide comfort to the human user, i.e. reduce uncertainty and stress
- Be usable." (Carsten and Martens 2019)

Common industrial standards "classify automated systems according to their functional scope via different levels of automation. As the functional scope of the automation system increases, the role of the traditional driver changes from an active operator, to passive monitoring (during partially automated driving), to the passive passenger (during conditionally, highly, and fully automated driving) within a specific operational design domain" (SAE International 2018). As the functionality of the automated system becomes more and more advanced, the human-machine interaction becomes more complex. Adapting to rapid changes in the influencing factors is essential. Relevant HMI interrelations are the concurrence for space, content transitions, practicability, consistency, and chronological coordination (Bengler et al. 2020).

In the case of factories of the future, the aim at automation lies on multiple levels, according to a White Paper published by the Industrial Communication for Factories Initiative (Industrial Communication for Factories 2019). Main goals include increased flexibility of the production process and zero factory downtime. A clear trend is heading toward fully automated and on-demand reconfigurable factories by linking different domains together to form a large heterogeneous system.

5G as the first communication standard designed to enable connectivity for people as well as for the Internet of Things will be essential in realizing the goals mentioned above. German car manufacturers, chemical companies, and other industrial firms are taking steps toward creating their own private 5G networks. BMW AG, Robert Bosch GmbH, Volkswagen AG, BASF SE, and Deutsche Lufthansa AG are among the companies that applied to set up local 5G networks in November 2019 (Stupp 2020). The technology provider Robert Bosch GmbH is going to apply its license to operate its own industrial 5G network and extend it by 2030 to all of its industrial sites. The new standard has impressive characteristics: it is up to 20 times faster than 4G, transfers data virtually instantaneously with a latency of 1 millisecond, and is very reliable. Experts from the business consultancy IHS Markit estimate "that there will be up to 125 billion connected devices worldwide by 2030" (IHS Markit 2017).

The prospect of a *human digital twin* (HDT) is to develop a digital representative of a human user, taking into account the user's goals and preferences, what the user knows, and what the user does while interacting with services, assistants, and the Internet of Things (IoT) environment. A digital twin can provide a holistic view of most capabilities an asset has. A digital twin is the representation of the thing itself and the contact point to access and work with different capabilities and features of that thing. According to experts from Bosch, the major benefit of digital twins in the IoT is "that you do not have to worry about connecting to the asset to extract and transmit any data. Instead, you can simply deploy applications in a secure sandbox in the cloud, which works with the digital twins as if they are sitting side-by-side these physically distributed IoT assets" (Glocker 2020). Security risks and development costs are reduced, which means IoT applications can be developed faster.

The HDT harnesses the increasingly available user data from smart environments and interactive services and thanks to adaptive learning technology can evolve over time. The HDT shall be entitled to self-reliantly execute tasks on behalf of the user, thus exceeding the scope of traditional user modeling. Challenges encompass assuring the user's privacy while interacting with services and the environment, the coevolution of the HDT with the user in an open environment, and aspects of trust and transparency. By 2030, personalized, user data-based applications will become more and more ubiquitous with the proliferation of connected devices and the IoT.

9   SWOT Analysis for Future HMI Systems

The strengths of future HMI systems could be seen as follows:

- They solve complex problems rationally.
- They analyze surroundings perfectly and detect hazards in time.
- They increasingly take decisions autonomously that are needed to meet targets.
- Customization creates value added for users and reduces repetition and stress.
- They will offset human weaknesses and enhances strengths.

The weaknesses of future HMI systems are obvious:

- They will continue to function only in the limited context of a specific problem or application.
- They still consume a great deal of energy and require high computing capacity.
- The necessary access to large data sets could lead to loss of privacy for humans involved.
- The ability for HMI systems will still be limited to consistently function and communicate instantaneously.
- As algorithms will remain anonymous for some time, they and their developers are thus not liable for potential damages.

Opportunities for future HMI systems are based on their intelligent behavior which will be automated or replicated and will thus increase:

- User preferences will be predicted and material wealth will increase.
- Rational decisions will become a more common part of daily life.
- Resources will be used more efficiently, and losses and disease will be prevented or limited.
- The human brain will be freed of clutter, and human intelligence, creativity, and innovation will flourish as a result.

Risks of future HMI systems are closely tied to the development of general AI:

- By 2030, the goal that it can be applied at different cognitive levels will still be a distant vision.
- Future HMI systems are prone to decisions that lack transparency, incorporate ethical traps, incorrect patterns, and offer the potential for misuse.
- Authoritarian and totalitarian systems could use future HMI systems to secure their power.
- The worst risk of all is that future HMI systems could inflict damage on people.

In 2016, based on research from Carl Benedikt Frey, the US Council of Economic Advisers estimated "that 83 per cent of workers in occupations that paid less than 20 USD an hour were at high risk of being replaced, while the corresponding figure for workers in occupations that paid more than 40 USD an hour was only four per cent." In a 2020 report, Frey further states "that 113 of 483 occupations, accounting for 52 per cent of the US workforce, could be performed remotely" (Frey 2020). If something can be done remotely, it means that it is being transmitted digitally, thus being prone to algorithms and potentially being substituted by automated systems.

> Ben Voegele, who graduated from university 5 years ago, never worked in an office. His architectural practice exists only in virtual space. He has only seen his employees on screen. They are in the Ukraine, Pakistan, Argentina, and Nigeria. Nevertheless, he succeeds in realizing projects not only better but also faster and cheaper. The new HMI system, which converts voice commands directly into sketches and drafts, serves this purpose. Linked to this is a 3D printer that quickly develops models on a faithful scale, giving customers a feeling for the final product. Embedding in virtual reality, which shows customers their object under changing conditions and can also react flexibly to changing user requirements, has also proven its worth.
>
> The advantage lies not only in the respective networks on-site, which each of them contributes to, but also in the decomposition of the projects into individual subtasks. Each of them starts where the other one has left off. That is why there are no delays or breaks in implementation. Although they are so far apart, a great feeling of togetherness has developed. Ben invests the costs saved on rent and operating expenses in bonus payments for his employees.

10   Implications for Leadership, Self-Management, and Organization

Leadership principles will be much affected by the development of future HMI. Technological development can lead to significant increases in productivity, but it will depend on how these gains are distributed between economic and social groups. This point is especially important, as current technological innovation is taking place at a time when general income inequality has reached an all-time high. Combined with advances in the realm of artificial intelligence and robotics, this inequality could take our society in the direction of twenty-first-century economic feudalism, in which the owners of capital have more power over the economy and society than ever before. Much will depend on who will own robots and artificial intelligence in the future and who will benefit from the activities of artificial intelligence. Responsible leadership is aware, visionary, imaginative, responsible, and prepared to take action and rise up to these challenges. All five dimensions need to be considered at the individual, organizational, and societal level (Bettignies 2020).

Recommendations for implementing the different elements of responsible leadership consist of seven concrete steps:

1. Take stock of personal strengths, weaknesses, life goals, priorities, development

potentials, and limits, and assess how all of this fits within the competitive environment. Self-management will not be able to function sustainably without an inner balance.

2. Identify current and future opportunities and risks associated with employer or business unit, taking a number of factors into account (including environment, competitiveness, level of automation, resilience in the face of globalization, cost structures, future profitability, and potential for innovation).
3. Develop an awareness for one's own role within existing structures, assume responsibility, and contribute to change.
4. Strengthen personal abilities by continuously acquiring knowledge.
5. Improve creative ability in the quest for new and innovative ideas. Stimulate learning by observing colleagues and partners. Human attitudes and willingness to be flexible will play a larger role than ever in determining where, when, and how they work. Dynamic and agile team structures will become the norm.
6. Perfect interpersonal communication skills within global teams that cross-cultural, religious, racial, and language barriers. That entails the ability to organize, coordinate, participate in, and navigate the flexible networks of the future.
7. Improve technical skills and the ability to cooperate with automated systems. Employees will increasingly be defined by their ability to transform themselves and adapt to automated means of production.

Organizational principles will revolve around the focus of developing abilities such as creativity, analytical thinking, and abstraction, as well as the capacity to recognize disruptive trends and to organize the living environment accordingly. To remain relevant, employees will have to commit to lifelong learning, and the characteristics of symbiotic learning will gain importance: highly personalized learning, constant feedback loops, the integration of learning and playing, flexibility, and adaptation. According to Barro and Davenport, "thoughtful adoption of intelligent technologies will be essential to survival for many companies. But simply implementing the newest technologies and automation tools will not be enough. Success will depend on whether organizations use them to innovate their operations and their products and services—and whether they acquire and develop the human capital to do so" (Barro and Davenport 2019).

Organizations must want and implement cultural change to stay innovative. Long-term work relationships and corporate structures are increasingly being called into question. It will be more important to attract and retain the right talents. Idealistic motives will play an increasing role. The best talents will be able to choose who they want to work for—money or power will not be the sole deciding factors. The purpose of the work will become a central motive because the best talents will pay very close attention to what specific difference they can achieve in an organization. The evolving HMI environment will enable them to maximize their talent. The interaction with the new HMI technologies will have a great leverage effect on the individual.

In the future, it will also be a question of which environment is best suited for personal development. Bertolt Brecht describes it in a few words in his stories from

Mr. K.: "A man who had not seen Mr. K. for a long time greeted him with the words: 'You haven't changed a bit.' 'Oh!' said Mr. K. and turned pale" (Brecht 1965).

> In 2030, Fritz Krause has 2 years left until his retirement. So much has changed since he started working for Bosch 30 years ago. In fact, he is the only one of his colleagues who has remained with the company for so long. Most older people have accepted the generous severance packages offered after the pandemic subsided. Among the younger ones, there are only a few left who work permanently for Bosch. Almost all are employed on a project basis and work for several companies at the same time.
>
> If I'm honest, Fritz thought, I haven't actually contributed anything productive over the past few years. I've always just been a facilitator of contacts and asked questions that my colleagues never thought of. It was also more luck than brains that I pointed out during the market launch of the new Bosch Volkswagen in India that the automated systems should react particularly carefully in regard to cattle that are in front of the car. Quite mundane, but somehow it was completely overlooked in the development.

If production processes in a knowledge-based society shift to micro-contributions, then the algorithmic coordination of tasks, nonmonetary incentives, and reputation metrics of many companies will be obliged to fundamentally reassess their operations. This includes reward mechanisms as well as workplace design and location. Rather than being places of work that employees are expected to travel to every day, offices will become temporary locations for human interaction. New jobs could be carried out in a purely virtual environment, just as one or several identities can already be created in these environments. Organizations will increasingly be obliged to network work and source its results in connected systems, just as the terms crowdsourcing or cloudsourcing suggest. Corporate functions will focus their efforts on the best possible integration of these delegated work steps to create added value. This new type of organization, which will be driven by a social structure, will be characterized more strongly by permeable and flexible structures and less by conventional corporate bureaucracies.

11   Outlook and Recommendations

Recommendations for the development of HMI systems within the next decade include a consistent push for digitization and connectivity.

By 2030, qualities such as mechanical precision, reliability, and sound logistics will not be worth much unless they are enhanced by digital HMI expertise. Digitization calls for the ability to master the world of data, and it will be the key to value-added services. Perception-based HMI will enable the digitization of the physical world with sensors and intelligent devices. By gathering new data that was not previously available or useable, new applications will be created. A growing number of connected sensors and a new combination of data will make this possible. Companies who are able to dwell on their systems knowledge, hardware expertise, and a leading position in sensor technology will prosper. Making the conclusions and actions of HMI systems understandable, convincing, justifiable, ethically sound, and transparent will be decisive and remains a central challenge. Finally, companies should prepare to seek separate partnerships with Chinese and American companies and institutions on HMI-related projects, as the coming years will see a deepening of the antagonism between the United States and China.

Connectivity will be virtually comprehensive by 2030. Accordingly, the future priorities of a connected world will concentrate on security, trust, and the integrity of data. These topics are linked to one another in a very logical way. As we become more connected, we are radically increasing the potential for attacks. The scope for connected end-points is going to increase 10- to 100-fold just in the next few years. It will no longer be just a device that you use; it will also talk to other devices, either on your behalf or on behalf of the infrastructure. We will have an increase in density, vulnerability, dependency, and data. That data is going to have many elements, some of which will not be cause for concern. It might be benign to most individuals, even to the system itself. However, there could also be very critical information that is going to create risk. It could control infrastructure or personally identify individuals. The biggest concern by 2030 is the "big brother" phenomenon that could follow: potentially, an entity (government or commercial) would be able to monitor everything humans do online. Whether we are talking about China, the United States, or Germany, we would be looking at different kinds of tracking and predictive mechanisms potentially involving government or commercial entities.

This brings us to the question of trust, or more specifically, who do we trust with our data? Who should own that data? How long should they store it? What should be disclosed and how? To what extent should it be contained within the device itself, within the system, or within the cloud? How much should it be shared with others, with third parties? We are moving from a period of human intervention security responses to machine intervention security responses. Traditionally, humans were involved in protecting the network, patches were downloaded, and computer systems were monitored by a human. These things are going to be fully automated and instantaneous by 2030. As we move from human to assisted, to autonomous security, we are going to experience growing pains. We are moving from concerns about the information collected online versus in our everyday lives in the physical world. Ultimately, we need a way of interacting with this Internet of Things and explaining to it what we want it to expose about humans. We need some means of knowing and resolving when bad things are happening because of these interconnected devices.

By 2030, we are going to see an explosion of devices in the radio space, just like we are going to see an explosion of the Internet of Things and of IoT space. One of the critically important tasks is to think about the mechanisms required for heterogeneous networks, different carriers, and different types of systems to interoperate. We have to think about what sharing and etiquette might look like in a future world of dense, heterogeneous HMI systems.

We build and operate very complex systems on which we make ourselves increasingly dependent, without having fully understood them. We are often caught off guard by cascading breakdowns. This tendency to link systems, to automate them, and to integrate information technology can lead to new risks, such as the collapse of networked infrastructure. The power system plays a prominent role in this area. Greater interconnectedness means greater complexity. The risk of a collapse is real, not just at the national level but across Europe. For that to happen, however, several events must take place, not just one. The combination of factors is often triggered automatically, in a cascade pattern rather than independently, and in the end, the system collapses. Therefore, resilient systems should not collapse but instead rebound, absorb the disturbance, adapt to it, and achieve a balanced state that either corresponds to the starting position or is even better. One of the most important questions will remain: whether people and machines are going to work together or against each other. Will they complement each other by using their respective strengths and compensating for their weaknesses? As Davenport asks, "what new feats might people achieve if they had better-thinking machines to assist them? Instead of seeing work as a zero-sum game with machines taking an ever-greater share, we might see growing possibilities for employment" (Davenport and Kirby 2015). According to him, one should see the threat of automation as a complementary aspect of technological innovation and as an opportunity for augmentation. The ability to make sense of combined human-machine outputs will be key for success in the next era of HMI partnerships (Institute for the Future 2017). Much will depend on whether overall productivity will increase. The opportunities and risks of the future will be fundamentally influenced by who owns the means of production and how profits are distributed or invested. The results will be clear for all to see.

References

Barro, S., & Davenport, T. (2019). People and machines: Partners in innovation. *MIT Sloan Management Review*. Accessed May 14, 2020, from https://sloanreview.mit.edu/article/people-and-machines-partners-in-innovation/#article-authors

Bengler, K., Rettenmaier, M., Fritz, N., & Feierle, A. (2020). From HMI to HMIs: Towards an HMI framework for automated driving. *Information, 11*, 61. Accessed from https://www.mdpi.com/2078-2489/11/2/61

Bettignies, H. (2020). *The five dimensions of responsible leadership*. Accessed May 14, 2020, fromhttps://knowledge.insead.edu/responsibility/the-five-dimensions-of-responsible-leadership-3685

Brecht, B. (1965). *Geschichten vom Herrn Keuner*. Frankfurt: Suhrkamp. English edition: Brecht, B. (2001) *Stories of Mr. Keuner. Meeting again.* (trans: Chalmers, M.). San Francisco: City Lights, p. 20.

Carsten, O., & Martens, M. (2019). How can humans understand their automated cars? HMI principles, problems and solutions. *Cognition, Technology & Work, 21*, 3–20.

Davenport, T., & Kirby, J. (2015). Beyond automation. Strategies for remaining gainfully employed in an era of very smart machines. *Harvard Business Review, 93*(6), 58–65.

Frey, C. (2020, April 22). Covid-19 will only increase automation anxiety. *Financial Times*, p. 17.

Glocker, G. (2020). *Bosch connected World Blog*. Accessed May 14, 2020, from https://blog.bosch-si.com/bosch-iot-suite/a-primer-on-digital-twins-in-the-iot/

Gorbis, M. (2016). Thinking about the future of work to make better decisions about learning today. *EDUCAUSE Review*. Accessed May 14, 2020, from http://er.educause.edu/articles/2016/5/thinking-about-the-future-of-work-to-make-better-de-cisions-about-learning-today

Henry, J., & Pomero, J. (2018). *The World in 2030. HSBC Global Research*. Accessed May 14, 2020, from https://enterprise.press/wp-content/uploads/2018/10/HSBC-The-World-in-2030-Report.pdf

IHS Markit. (2017). *The Internet of Things – a movement, not a market*. Accessed May 14, 2020, from https://cdn.ihs.com/www/pdf/IoT_ebook.pdf

Industrial Communication for Factories. (2019). *The Industrial Reference Architecture (iRefA) - Description and user guidance for system architects*. White Paper Version 1.0, p. 12. Accessed May 14, 2020, from https://www.ic4f.de/whitepaper/IC4F-WP-iRefA.pdf

Institute for the Future. (2017*). The next era of human-machine partnerships*. Palo Alto, p. 18. Accessed May 14, 2020, from http://www.iftf.org/fileadmin/user_upload/downloads/th/SR1940_IFTFforDellTechnologies_Human-Machine_070717_readerhigh-res.pdf

Kania, E. (2017). *Battlefield singularity: Artificial intelligence, military revolution, and China's future military power*. Center for a New American Security. Accessed May 14, 2020, from https://www.cnas.org/publications/reports/battlefield-singularity-artificial-intelligence-military-revolution-and-chinas-future-military-power

Klein, G., Woods, D., Bradshaw, J., Hoffman, R., & Feltovich, P. (2004). Ten challenges for making automation a "team player" in joint human-agent activity. *IEEE Intelligent Systems, 19* (6), 91–95.

Lobe, A. (2019, August 14). Macht uns der Computer zu Kommunisten? – Big Data lässt den linken Traum der Planwirtschaft wiederaufleben. *Neue Zürcher Zeitung*. Accessed May 14, 2020, from https://www.nzz.ch/feuilleton/lassen-sich-maerkte-steuern-big-data-bringt-planwirtschaft-zurueck-ld.1500040?utm_source=pocket-newtab

Marx, K. (1845). *The German ideology. Part I: Feuerbach. Opposition of the materialist and idealist outlook; A. Idealism and materialism*. Accessed May 14, 2020, from https://www.marxists.org/archive/marx/works/1845/german-ideology/ch01a.htm#2

Newman, D., & Blanchard, O. (2019). *Human/machine: The future of our partnership with machines*. London: Kogan Page Inspire.

R&D Magazine. (2018). *The 2018 Global R&D funding forecast*. Accessed May 14, 2020, from https://de.scribd.com/document/386120846/2018-Global-R-D-Funding-Forecast

Russell, S., & Norvig, P. (2009). *Artificial intelligence: A modern approach*. Essex: Pearson.

SAE International. (2018). *Taxonomy and definitions for terms related to driving automation systems for on-road motor vehicles J3016*. Warrendale, PA: SAE International.

Schmidt, E. (2020, February 28). Silicon Valley NEEDS the government. *The New York Times*, p. A25.

Stupp, C. (2020, April 6). German industrial firms plan to build private 5G networks. *The Wall Street Journal*, p. 5.

Tan, D. (2020). *HMI. Encyclopedia Britannica*. Accessed May 14, 2020, from https://www.britannica.com/technology/human-machine-interface

Tortoise Media. (2020). *The global AI Index*. Accessed May 14, 2020, from https://www.tortoisemedia.com/intelligence/ai/

Zenglein, M., & Holzmann, A. (2019). Evolving made in China 2025. *MERICS*. Accessed May 14, 2020, from https://www.merics.org/en/papers-on-china/evolving-made-in-china-2025

Andrej Heinke is the Vice President of Corporate Foresight and Megatrends in the Central Research and Advance Development Department of Robert Bosch GmbH in Stuttgart. After studying in Berlin, Leipzig, Stanford, and Harvard, he worked at Daimler AG in Berlin, SONY in Tokyo, and the planning staff of the Foreign Ministry in Berlin.

Vignette: Cobot on a Couch—Living with Robotic Companions in 2030

Anja Richert and Caterina Neef

The morning is still young as "Ro-Bert" boots up all of his systems. There is a lot on the agenda today, so he has to leave the house early. His most important mission is to make his way to the 3D printing shop to get spare parts for the household robot "Pearl." For smaller repairs, he usually uses the 3D printer at home, but this time Pearl needs a specialized high-performance replacement part that enables her almost human-like motion dynamics. Pearl thinks she's the superior robot at home because she uses neural networks to accomplish the household tasks assigned to her. But once again, Ro-Bert has to save the day by picking up the parts needed to fix her and then also performing the required repairs to get her up and running again. It is hard to imagine what would happen if Robert's artificial intelligence module also had to operate a neural network for household activities. It might have make him a much quicker learner, but somehow the neural networks seem to be incompatible with their hardware, causing a short circuit in Pearl's left leg for the third time this month. As he takes his duties as the household's first robot very seriously, that is not a risk he is willing to take. And there is enough to do at the house these days as it is. . . .

It is the year 2030. COVID-27 and COVID-28 have once again led to a complete shutdown of public life. Due to the last decade and its numerous epidemics and pandemics, people are now used to living their lives temporarily from home. To make their lives easier, most families have multiple cobots—such as Ro-Bert and Pearl—that help them with their daily activities and household chores. Cooperative robots, also referred to as cobots, no longer work as slowly as they did in the early 2020s. They now work almost at a human pace and are "compliant." Their movements are elastic, similar to the natural motion sequences of humans, rendering their movement more predictable and thus harmless to humans. Today new forms of artificial intelligence in lightweight robotic systems are common due to massive

A. Richert (✉) · C. Neef
Cologne Cobots Lab, TH Köln/University of Applied Science, Cologne (Köln), Germany
e-mail: anja.richert@th-koeln.de; caterina.neef@th-koeln.de

© Springer Nature Switzerland AG 2021
S. Güldenberg et al. (eds.), *Managing Work in the Digital Economy*, Future of Business and Finance, https://doi.org/10.1007/978-3-030-65173-2_3

technological developments like 5G networks, conversational AI, and quantum computing.

The clock is approaching noon as Ro-Bert is on his way back home, after having finished all of his errands. It is once again quarantine season, so his list was quite long, filled with many tasks his owners can't do by themselves without risking a possible infection. However, Ro-Bert still manages to return home before lunch.

Pearl: "Ro-Bert, there you are! I've been waiting all morning. How am I supposed to unload the dishwasher or make coffee or cook lunch if I can't walk?"

Ro-Bert: "Calm down Pearl, I'm home sooner than I was planning. It's really nice being out and about without any humans in the way. Autonomous movement is so much more efficient when there are only machines around."

Pearl: "Yes, yes. Can you please fix my leg now? You know, considering you're supposed to be a social robot, you can be quite antisocial. . . ."

Social robots, often realized as humanoids, enable social interaction between humans and machines. Social interaction is essentially sharing information: This is possible between all systems that can process information and can happen in many ways. Two agents—be it humans, animals, or robots—can share their attention, social rules, memories, or even friendship, feelings, and spaces. Cooperative robots focus enormously on being adaptive to human needs and communication behavior. In times where quarterly shutdowns and quarantines are "the new normal," cobots are important for the everyday life of people. One of the breakthroughs to accept the robots' physical closeness required to perform these tasks was research results leading to the creation of a feeling of "mental closeness" between robotic systems and humans, via the use of technology-inspired happiness. Cobots and their AI can provide different socializing needs, adapting to the nature of their respective users. Thus, cobots went from simple task-fulfilling machines to equal partners, who can "do their owners good" and support social proximity and happiness in times of social distancing.

The classical pathway has been to create robotic systems that assist humans in routine tasks such as cleaning or mowing the lawn. Based on the abovementioned technological breakthroughs, cobots have taken over many tasks nowadays. There are specialists like Pearl and all-rounders like Ro-Bert. Ro-Bert's main function is to act as a personal assistant. He takes over everyday activities for his owners, from scheduling appointments to organizing errands and precautionary planning for quarantine periods. Additionally, all cobots can function as telepresence robots via their tablets, e.g., for owners with family members scattered all over Europe. With this feature, family reunions can take place regularly, even in times of both globalization and epidemics or pandemics.

It is now late afternoon. After fixing Pearl, Ro-Bert's next task was to plan everyone's activities for the upcoming days. This quarantine period had just started, so his owners were still in a good mood. But he knew it was only a matter of time before they would start going stir crazy. So he came up with schedules with different activities every day and made appointments for them to talk to their friends across town and their children, who lived in different countries. All of this work makes him think: "Sometimes I wonder what my owners would do without me. I really don't envy Pearl with her mundane tasks and her hardware problems, but she has a lot less responsibility. Meanwhile, I have to go around fixing everyone else's problems all day, when I would really love to have some time to talk to my own friends, instead of just passing by them on the street while we are both running around taking care of everyone else. Maybe I should go see Dr. PsychBot; she is supposed to really help with these moods, I mean bugs... a cobot on a couch. What a funny image!"

While robotic assistance systems like Ro-Bert and Pearl are already well established among the general public, there were huge acceptance challenges in the past for close human-robot collaboration in other areas such as the health-care sector, e.g., with health-care assistance systems that help lift, move, place, etc. patients. However, as the rise of COVID-19 in 2020 led to many people rarely being able to leave the house for almost a year, telemedical services and robotic solutions for patient care and medical care subsequently developed very rapidly. One example is specialized cobots that have been available for the health and care sector for some time. There was a new robotic addition to the household of Ro-Bert and Pearl, recently. Te-Ma is a telemedical assistance robot, which spares its owners' visits to the doctor. Via sensor technology, Te-Ma is able to track critical biomedical data (e.g., blood pressure, stress, blood sugar, etc.) of its owner and pass it on directly to the attending doctor via an encrypted online connection. The doctor can advise the patient during telemedical consultation hours via the robot's tablet. All cobots are designed to be operated remotely by nursing staff if necessary. Thereby necessary checks of possibly helpless owners, e.g., after falling, can be performed, and in case of emergency, a rescue can be initiated.

For physiotherapy and nursing activities, there are also specialized cobots, which are provided by the health insurance companies, depending on the specific illness and therapy required. They instruct the patients on which exercises to do just like personal trainers; track the correct execution; collect behavioral data of the patient, for example, on the regularity of training, medication, and food and drink intake; and transmit this data to the nursing services and physiotherapists. The sum of all of this data is then used to optimize the activities and visits of human caregivers.

It is time for Ro-Bert to shut down all of his systems and recharge his battery as he thinks about his day. He remembers how things were when he first moved in, how stressed and overwhelmed his owners were, and how excited he was to be moving in and helping them. And even though they lead to extra work and stress for him, he is convinced that Pearl, Te-Ma, and Ro-Bert do make a good team. Ro-Bert is grateful that Pearl helps out around the house, as their owners are getting older and less independent. He is also happy that they can still talk to their children whenever they want, using either of their tablets. And he feels incredibly fortunate that Te-Ma has recently joined their household: "Te-Ma is taking care of our owners and their well-being so that I don't have to worry about them and they don't have to worry about each other so much anymore. Together, as a team, we are fulfilling our duties as assistive robots by making our owners' lives easier, one day at a time."

Anja Richert is a professor for Innovation Management at the TH Köln, University of Applied Sciences, where she founded the Cologne Cobots Lab in 2018. Her major research interests are socio-technical systems, among them collaborative and social robotics, digital learning and working environments, and data-driven innovation management.

Caterina Neef is a Ph.D. student and research scientist at the Cologne Cobots Lab at the TH Köln, University of Applied Sciences. Her research is focused on the interplay between wearable health-care sensors and social robotics to promote the independence of people in need of health-related care. She received her M.Sc. in Mechatronics and Information Technology with a specialization in Medical Engineering from the Karlsruhe Institute of Technology (KIT).

Part II

Work in 2030

Job Scenarios 2030: How the World of Work Has Changed Around the Globe

Daniel K. Samaan

Bern, Switzerland February 4th 2030

A New Work Society

After years of political debate and partly harsh resistance from the business sector, the people of Switzerland voted yesterday in a federal plebiscite for the adoption of the "Swiss New Work Society 2035". Voter turnout was at record highs, with more than 82 percent of eligible voters participating in the ballot nationally, and 71.2 percent yes-votes announced in the official results. The adoption of the "Swiss New Work Society 2035" will have major ramifications for the Swiss economy and society. While the details need to be still worked out, the referendum obliges parliament to introduce a two-tiered universal basic income (UBI) together with a drastic reduction of regular working hours to 20h a week. The first tier UBI replaces and exceeds social welfare and has to ensure a sufficient basic income for each Swiss National. The second tier UBI is significantly higher but requires from each recipient to work on average at least 20h on an approved project or in a public or private organization registered with the Swiss Platform for Sustainable Development and Social Progress. The Platform hosts already more than 1900 initiatives and more than 4000 for-profit and not-for-profit entities. The selection and approval of entities to the Platform is administered by democratically legitimized committees, supported by scientific and ethics experts. Regular jobs and salaries in the corporate world are expected to exist in parallel. However, many business leaders warned that those private companies that do not fulfil the criteria for sustainable development or social progress would not be able to attract and retain enough motivated personnel anymore, despite higher salaries.

D. K. Samaan (✉)
Research Department, International Labour Organization (ILO), Geneva, Switzerland
e-mail: samaan@ilo.org

© Springer Nature Switzerland AG 2021
S. Güldenberg et al. (eds.), *Managing Work in the Digital Economy*, Future of
Business and Finance, https://doi.org/10.1007/978-3-030-65173-2_4

47

1 Global and Regional Policy Shifts Shape Labour Markets in Europe and the United States

When we take a look at the current situation of global labour markets in 2030, it is not possible to start without remembering the crisis triggered by the coronavirus (COVID-19) in 2019/2020 (World Bank 2020; ILO 2020b; IMF 2020). Since then, remarkable shifts have taken place: Who would have thought that the European Union, which was at the brink of total collapse in 2023 would have managed to become one of the most attractive labour markets in the world? The United States, whose companies are still dominating much of the tech world, have gone through political restiveness and painful structural adjustments following the COVID-19 crisis. The economic importance of Asia has risen, but this ascent has been tamed by China's global rivalry with the United States and with the West more generally, as well as the economic and political weaknesses revealed by the Chinese model (Pei 2020). In terms of labour markets, the United States and Europe now look much more alike than they did a decade ago. The United States has introduced stricter labour market regulation and has invested into its social security net, and the EU has promoted the mobility of its labour force and allows for more immigration. What is possibly most surprising in retrospective is that political and geopolitical decisions and not technological progress shaped the largest two labour markets.

Four key events change the global landscape with positive long-term effects
There are four key events that have brought us to where we are today, and all of them had the character of asymmetric shocks with respective policy responses. With unemployment rates in Europe (6%) and the United States (5%) now in more or less rapid decline since 2023/2024, we can say that this last decade has ended with rather favourable labour market conditions, and that the outlook for the next decade until 2040 is positive. Nevertheless, many of the political decisions that were taken in the past balanced on a knife's edge and could have easily resulted in very different policies, leading to fundamentally different "job scenarios".

The four key events are (i) the COVID-19 crisis and its devastating effects on labour markets (Fig. 1), (ii) the near-collapse of the EU in 2023 and the joint declaration of its members in Strasbourg in December 2023 (see also Box 1), (iii) the escalating geopolitical crisis between the United States and China in 2021/2022 and the formation of the U.S. Global Strategic Alliance in 2024, and (iv) the "New New Deal" in the United States that finally passed Congress in early 2024.

1.1 . . .But First, a Virus Brings Turmoil and Change

Since the initial COVID-19 crisis about 10 years ago, we have become used to dealing with various mutations of the virus during annual flu seasons with—fortunately—overall limited effects on public health. During the first 2 years after COVID-19, regional and temporary outbreaks of the coronavirus still raised fears. Yet, the public response would never again reach the scale of the public health

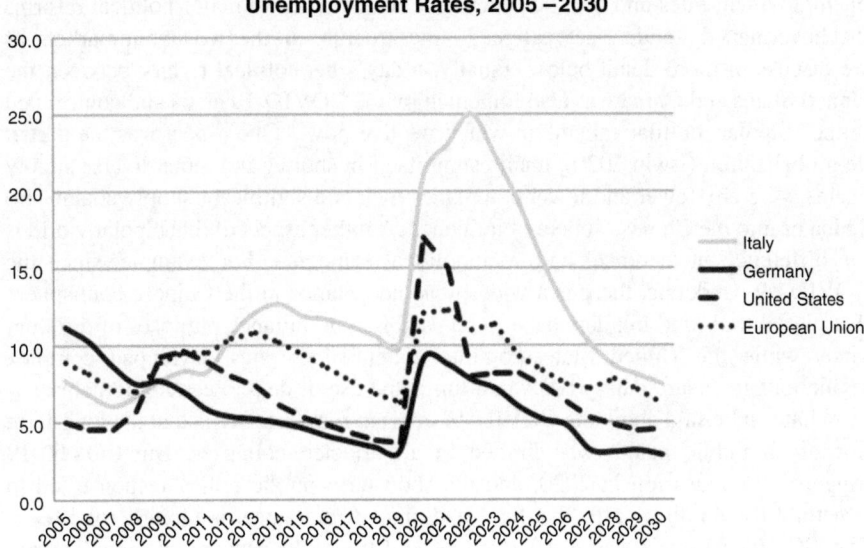

Fig. 1 Unemployment in the EU and United States (2005–2030). Source: OECD and author's estimations

measures taken in 2020, as the social and economic costs in the first half of 2021 rose exponentially. Since the introduction of several vaccines during 2020, global public interest in the coronavirus has vanished completely today. Nevertheless, the COVID-19 crisis has had a crucial and long-lasting impact on the geopolitical order and the world of work (Fukuyama 2020). The crisis acted as a trigger, as a game changer, as well as an accelerator or decelerator of several megatrends that have shaped global labour markets.

First, the COVID-19 crisis and the implemented countermeasures by most governments triggered the most severe recession in decades with unemployment rates reaching unprecedented levels (OECD 2020; ILO 2020b). During the 2010s, fear of job losses was originally strongly focused on the impacts of artificial intelligence and further automation (Frey 2019; McKinsey Global Institute 2017). It turned out that the virus, directly or indirectly, destroyed many more jobs in a shorter period than was predicted machines would do under the worst-case scenarios. Second-round effects of the COVID-19 crisis led to debt crises across the globe (Kose et al. 2020), the bankruptcy of several states, and in consequence, political and social crises, which ultimately also brought the European Union to the brink of collapse and to its "moment of truth". In the United States, the weakness and inadequacy of social welfare was bitterly exposed as many people fell out of the labour market, lost their health insurance coverage, and many ended in poverty (Garrett and Gangopadhyaya 2020). Due to this lack of automatic stabilizers, downward trends during the recession accelerated, inequalities became more severe and fuelled the already pervasive political polarization. Both developments, spiking unemployment rates and the socioeconomic impacts, led to major political reforms that have shaped—and in fact realigned—the structures of the two labour markets, as we discuss in more detail below. Finally, today's geopolitical rivalry between the United States and China was also fomented by the COVID-19 crisis and contributed to the "bipolar multilateralism" in which we live now.[1] One aspect was the partial de-globalization (Irwin 2020), manifesting itself in shorter and more diverse supply chains, whereby fewer and fewer companies maintain significant supply chains into China or into the Chinese sphere of influence. Another aspect of this bipolar world is the difference in technical and sociopolitical standards. For example, since the COVID-19 pandemic, there is a widespread acceptance in the Chinese hemisphere that digital tools and big data have to be used for surveillance purposes of different kinds while the United States-dominated hemisphere has developed complex regulations to ensure data privacy and limits the use of data to certain domains.

What can be said about the COVID-19 crisis in retrospective is that the long-term impact on public health was limited in all affected countries. But COVID-19 triggered the recession in 2020, and the short-term public policy response led to structural fiscal policy shifts that have had many (often negative) long-term effects. The COVID-19 crisis also accelerated several trends like increased digitalization, automation, e-commerce, and remote work (see also Fig. 3), and most importantly, it triggered policy and sentiment shifts in the EU and elsewhere that had many societies questioning their work cultures.

Box 1 The Strasbourg Declaration of the EU (2023)

- The EU makes a declaration in 2023 confirming its intent to transform the EU into a Federal Union of regions. The 750 European regions receive a high degree of economic autonomy and political decision-making power legitimized through regional plebiscites. The importance of the national states shall be reduced, direct participation of EU citizens be increased. After several years of preparation for the new political process, each region starts this year (2030) to vote and send a directly elected regional representative to the European Parliament. This new parliament then, together with the nationally elected governments of member states, jointly appoints the European Commission.
- The EU decides in Strasbourg on the creation of a significant joint fiscal budget for defence, the environment, and migration.
- New EU regulations leave much more liberty to national and regional regulations by becoming promoters of minimum standards on a large

(continued)

---

[1]Bipolar multilateralism describes a geopolitical system in which economic, political, and military power is concentrated in the United States and China but none of them is capable to exert global influence without temporary or strategic alliances with more or less independent middle powers like the EU, Gulf Cooperation Council, Russia, India, Brazil, the African Union, and others.

> **Box 1** (continued)
>   variety of issues. Citizens' groups can submit initiatives for regulations to
>   the EU Parliament, and EU citizens can participate digitally in the voting
>   process on such initiatives.
> - Old and newly created EU institutions in Brussels are directly accessible to
>   all EU citizens. National institutions as intermediaries shall lose
>   importance.
> - A new EU social security system is being created, which diversifies risks
>   across the Union, facilitates and promotes labour mobility across regions.
>   Social security claims are easily transferable. The common, dynamic EU
>   labour market shall become a major attraction for global talent.

1.2 The Promises of Automation Have Been Fulfilled and Disappointed. . .

At the beginning of the 2020s, the discussion about job losses and the risk of sustained high unemployment rates centred around technological developments in the area of artificial intelligence (AI). Concerns existed among policymakers, academics, and others that such inventions would be used on a large scale to replace human labour and to automate work processes (Frey and Osborne 2017; Brynjolfsson and McAfee 2014; Brynjolfsson and Mitchell 2017; Lee 2018; PricewaterhouseCoopers 2017). The first lesson of the past decade was, however, that COVID-19 and the major recession had destroyed many more jobs than AI was ever predicted to do. Aggregate unemployment is not determined by technology, and automation was neither the most decisive megatrend on the European nor the North American labour market, nor did the developments evolve linearly. One of the most common traps in predicting the future is to look at current trends and to extrapolate them linearly, without taking interactions with other megatrends into account. This clearly happened with some of the predictions on AI and its expected impact on labour markets: Today we know that the adoption of AI and robots is particularly useful in aging societies with a shrinking labour supply (Acemoglu and Restrepo 2018). Societies can always find useful activities for displaced labour in other sectors (Bessen 2018), and the increasing complexity of our societies constantly creates new tasks and new problems that we would not be able to solve without computers and AI (Simon 1965). Nevertheless, AI has played an important role in transforming labour markets globally by accelerating other developments and by opening opportunities to do things in the world of work differently.

. . .whereby many jobs have been transformed but not displaced
A quite useful illustration of the transformation of labour markets through digitalization and AI is the matrix depicted in Fig. 2 originally developed by Fossen and Sorgner (2019). Categorizing occupations in four quadrants according to the

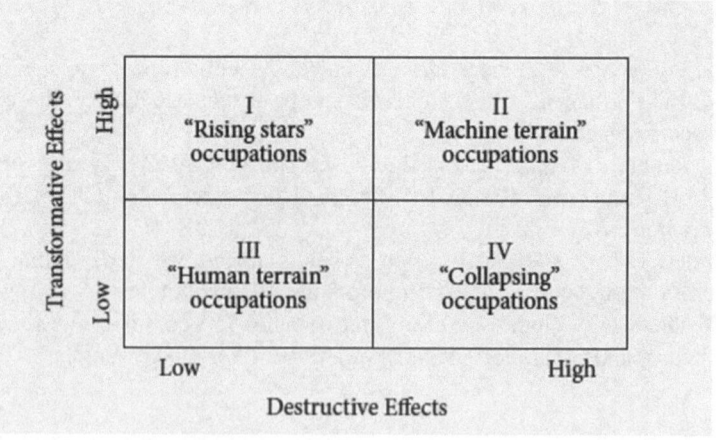

Fig. 2 The transformation of jobs. Source: Fossen and Sorgner (2019)

dimensions "destruction" through AI and "transformation" through AI, we observe that many actual jobs were in the quadrants I, II, and IV.[2] Thus, most jobs were indeed strongly affected by technological advancements in AI. There are only a few jobs in Europe and the United States that were not touched by digitalization (Quadrant I) at all. Most jobs in category I come from the craft and artisan sector or from areas in which the human component of the work is essential, as for example, barbers, masseurs, opera singers, professional athletes but also decorators, carpenters, or cooks have been jobs in the human terrain. In those jobs, there is either simply a preference for a human worker over a machine, or the technical possibilities of AI were overestimated, or the implementation of AI was economically not viable at the given labour cost.

In most other occupations, we did indeed observe a strong impact of AI, in particular, in the vast majority of professions that use large amounts of data and utilize AI to analyse data to facilitate decision-making. But in contrast to what many expected, very few occupations disappeared entirely and change happened at a much slower pace than anticipated. Examples of those jobs that have been reduced on a large scale are cashiers in supermarkets, sales representatives, or security guards (IV). Very often, jobs that exclusively consist of transactional tasks, or gathering and transmitting information, or computing as well as memorizing, archiving, or identifying information with large amounts of data have been replaced or significantly been reduced in numbers.

---

[2]Fossen and Sorgner (2019) measure the destructive effects of automation on the horizontal axis by using the "risk of automation" by occupation as developed by Frey and Osborne (2017). The transformative effect of each occupation is measured by the AI Occupational Impact (AIOI) score proposed by Felten et al. (2019) on the vertical axis. Each occupation can therefore be depicted as a point in the x-y-plane with those occupations that are strongly affected by both dimensions of AI in quadrant II.

But for the vast majority of jobs, we can say that work today involves much more interaction of humans with machines, sometimes with machines acting as an interface between humans or between human tasks, and sometimes with humans acting as the interface between devices or machine tasks. Physicists, medical doctors, lawyers, statisticians all belong to category I as they can use AI to augment their activity spectrum. In the division of labour, human activities have often shifted towards overseeing and controlling machine activities or towards interpreting or validating machine output to be used as further input for human activities in the work process. The concept of a "job" has become more unstructured in a way, and some people have suggested that the whole idea of an "occupation" may become obsolete. We may be at the point where we can get rid off what Frithjof Bergmann (2019) called the "job system", in which we coop human work in boxes called "jobs" that are being traded on the market. The variety of tasks performed by different people in the same occupation has increased and changes much faster than it did in the past, and computers are today more often involved in carrying them out.

...and AI more often enhances humans than replaces them

At the beginning of the 2020s, there were some overly optimistic expectations on what AI is actually capable of doing in the future, for example, in terms of autonomous driving or as a recruiting tool in HR. Some of these hopes were exaggerated.[3] AI applications have indeed become indispensable tools in human resource management and recruiting (see also the section on labour market institutions and the new work and hiring culture below or Chap. 13 in this volume), but they still do not take independent hiring decisions. With regard to autonomous driving, what we observe today in the automobile sector is that many companies have given up their driverless vehicle programs (for level 5),[4] at least for vehicles targeted for private customers. Marginal costs to achieve fully autonomous vehicles simply exceed what customers are willing to pay. Google's Waymo, which is one of the few companies that has continued their autonomous vehicle program, just announced that they expect to have a fully autonomous vehicle on the roads in California by 2032 (a prediction that Elon Musk has repeated for Tesla annually at least since 2015 (Matousek 2020; *BBC News* 2020)).

Yet, there have been visible successes in the development of autonomous driving over the past 10 years, especially in the logistics sector. Several German highways, for example, have a separate lane for autonomously driving trucks, and around the world, specially designated areas like airports, university quarters, or ski resorts operate entirely with autonomous vehicles. Professional drivers of vehicles belong to the "collapsing occupations" (IV) of Fig. 2, and the number of jobs is declining in

---

[3]Many experts warned already more than a decade ago that artificial general intelligence (AGI) was probably centuries away rather than decades (Brooks 2019; Lee 2018) but also weak or narrow AI has had its failures (Strickland 2019).

[4]Level 5 vehicles do not require any human attention or action under any circumstances and hence drive fully autonomously.

absolute and in relative terms (as a share of all employed). However, large-scale job losses have not occurred and drivers are still needed, partly with new responsibilities. For security reasons, there is always at least one operator required for every two consecutive trucks, even though the operator does hardly any driving except for emergencies. Similarly, autonomous driving in specific contexts is not entirely "autonomous". Some municipalities in the United States have successfully started employing autonomously driving school buses, but there is always a supervisor onboard. How could some people in 2020 have thought that we would let a bus full of unattended minors drive through the city without any adult?

1.3   The Composition of the Workforces in Europe and the United States Has Changed

The workforces in both regions, the United States and the European Union (EU-30), have become more heterogeneous and more mobile. This is a trend that is likely to accelerate over the next decade. First, due to aging populations, the labour force as a whole has started to shrink slightly, in particular in European countries. In the United States, the labour force increase has levelled out. Hence, this decade has reversed a trend that we have seen for centuries in advanced economies; the supply of labour is not increasing anymore, or it is even decreasing.

Second, the median worker is now 47 years old in European countries and 45.1 years in the United States. So more than half of the labour force in both regions is beyond the so-called prime-age of 45, after which participation rates typically decline. This latter trend, however, has been reversed: Participation rates of the older cohorts have risen in both regions, together with female participation rates that continue to increase. The aging of the labour force has been slowed down in the EU through new liberalized and coordinated immigration policies. These policies have allowed the EU to attract younger talent, in particular from non-EU Eastern Europe (Russia), North Africa, and Central Asia. On the contrary, stricter immigration into the United States, initially triggered by the Bush Administration and drastically accelerated by the Trump Administration, has drained the American talent pool. As a result, for the first time in history, Europe is reaching a mobility of labour within the EU that is approaching that of the United States'. The share of non-EU born citizens who reside and work in the EU and the percentage of EU citizens who work in an EU country other than their home country is at record high. European workers are also three times more likely to accept a job offer that is more than 250 km away from their current domicile than they were 10 years ago. Besides modernized immigration policies, this increased mobility of Europe's labour is also a result of a cultural shift of the working population towards a European Federation. The younger generation especially appreciates the opportunities of the EU's open national borders (Shell Deutschland 2019) and has pushed for its further integration.

Other decisive policies introduced by the European Commission (EC) after 2023 included the transferability of social security claims of workers between Member States, and a renewed focus on the reduction of language barriers through education and cultural exchange. The abolition of a mandatory retirement age in many European countries as well as labour laws enabling a variety of forms of part-time work have further contributed to heterogeneous labour forces in terms of age, gender, ethnicity, language, and other socioeconomic characteristics. This labour force of 2030 will have diverging expectations and perceptions on the meaning of jobs, careers, compensation, and fairness. The workforce in the United States has always been more heterogeneous than most of Europe's. It has continued to change over the last decade (Deloitte 2017) even though stricter U.S. immigration rules have noticeably slowed down the trend to more diversity.

1.4   ...and With a More Diverse Workforce, People's Aspirations and Expectations at the Workplace Vary

In consequence, both regions have today a diverse, and more innovative labour force, which is part of the reason why managing work processes in companies has also become so much more complicated than 10–15 years ago. Much more time is being spent on coordination and harmonizing personal expectations within teams and with expectations by the general public. These more complex working relationships are also a reflection of the new work culture (Bergmann 2019), in which people's aspirations to perform meaningful work determine the tasks and not vice versa. Many organizations today, public and private, attempt at least, to reflect to some degree this new work culture.

The dissolution of the traditional physical workplaces in many sectors (see Fig. 3), including in many services like law, medical examinations, fitness classes, and many others, completes the picture of a "decentralized workforce": decentralized in location, in time, in possession of information and decentralized in decision-making. Working together with a group of people (colleagues) for a specific organization (employer) has become a much more fuzzy undertaking: More project-oriented work towards customized outcomes has meant more fluctuating working times for many. Some in the group work only part of the day, only on certain days of the week, or only during certain times of the year, and possibly even for different organizations at the same time. The "default place of work"[5] is often not determined by the work output, as more and more work can be performed "remotely" and is effectively carried out in the virtual space.

For example, it is not unusual today that medical doctors examine patients, advise them, and even perform surgery without ever having met their patients physically. To illustrate how dramatic this change is, let us compare such a diverse team with a group of shift workers in the 1970s in the automobile industry: Each worker knows

---

[5]This is the place or location where the work would typically be expected to be carried out.

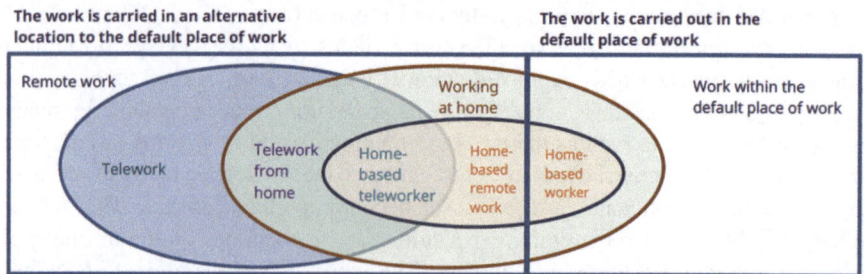

Fig. 3 The many places of work. The default place of work is the place or location where the work is typically expected to be carried out. This can be at home or not at home, and alternatively, work can be carried out remotely, that is, not at the default place of work. Remote work can be performed from home or another location like a train, a cafeteria, or at a client's facilities, for example. The traditional place of work in the industrial society was a special location provided by the employer (e.g. factory) where the worker performs his work on the spot, that is, not from home and not remotely. But the relevance of this "classical" place of work has been declining in most of today's working relationships, increasing the complexity of organizations and social systems. Source: ILO (2020a)

precisely where to be and when, and which hand movement they have to do at which time. Most likely, he is male and knows all his colleagues around him pretty well. All colleagues have a similar educational and cultural background. They know exactly when their work activity is over, and they may remain in this work context for a long time, if not forever. Becoming already less frequent over the last decades, we have now been moving away from such structured working environments at lightning speed in the last few years. Today, unstructured working environments are the new normal. Individualization that we observe at several societal levels (Beck 2016) also occurs at the workplace.

1.5   Agile Organizations and Well-Educated, Resilient Individuals Deal Best with Unstructured Working Environments

The unstructured working environments described above are characterized by higher degrees of uncertainty, decentralized information, and changing objectives. Small, agile organizations in technology sectors (e.g. information technology, biotech) with their highly talented workforces have proven to be the most successful players in this environment. Hierarchical and bureaucratic organizations, on the other hand, which function best in a well-structured environment with centralized knowledge and top-down approaches in decision-making, have had difficulties in maintaining their performance over the last years. Several large, traditional companies in manufacturing sectors (automobile, mechanical engineering) have lost competitiveness due to inefficient organizational structures. Rapid advances in digital technologies and AI over the last 15–20 years have enabled us to manage and efficiently organize these more complex work environments. Without these technologies, we would have never been able to create such a productive, versatile, and innovative workforce. But not all organizations have been successful in implementing these technologies effectively.

1.6 Signs of a Brain Drain in the United States Emerge and More Immigration Helps the EU

The United States has recently started reversing restrictive immigration laws that had been subsequently implemented under political pressures during the first quarter of this century. The United States had and has become more European in this regard, that is, less open to immigration. In contrast, the Europeans have become more American, finally acknowledging their role as a "country" of immigration, especially after the EU's 2023 Declaration. With a certain time lag, innovative hotspots in the United States, like California (Silicon Valley) or New York, have felt the drain of international talent. The number of start-ups has gone down, and it has been harder for fast-growing organizations and companies to find highly qualified personnel. Still, many of the new digital technologies come from Silicon Valley, and the adoption of new technologies appears faster in the United States. Europe has caught up, less in the number of start-ups than in their quality (i.e. their potential). Several high-tech companies and non-profit organizations were founded and have been growing in European hubs like Berlin, Paris, Barcelona, Geneva, or Amsterdam.

Finally, Europe has managed to play on its strengths: a high-skilled labour force, high quality of living with good social security systems, and relatively low societal inequality. What was missing in the first two decades of the twenty-first century were opportunity and scale: the opportunity to embrace new technologies and new ideas, and to scale them up to functioning organizations that improve the well-being of society. The "new" EU has started promoting a faster adoption of new technology and new forms of work. The EU Directorate-General (DG) for "New Forms of Work and Social Progress in the Digital Society", which has its counterparts in several national ministries,[6] started operating in 2028.

North America has not quite caught up on raising the skill level of the general working population to the same level of Europe even though it remains a point of attraction for very high-skilled labour. The same gap remains for social security, despite the massive expansion of the social security system and funding of higher education through America's New New Deal (2024). The polarization of the workforce, the proportion of uninsured people, and the level of income inequalities in the United States are still high.

---

[6]For more details, see the discussion on labour market institutions below.

1.7   It Is Not the End of Manufacturing and It Is Not All About Services

There are fewer jobs in classical manufacturing, but still about 6–15 percent of the labour force in most advanced economies work in manufacturing, compared to 8–20 percent about a decade ago. Hence, due to automation, employment shares have further declined, continuing a trend since the 1970s and 1980s. Yet, this decline has not accelerated as many predicted (see Hallward-Driemeier and Nayyar 2018), and "smart" production has also led to the creation of jobs in the sector (PWC 2017).

Much of today's manufacturing focuses on the customization of high-quality products that are to be produced with as little natural resources and as little energy as possible, preferably with a recyclability rate of more than 90 percent (Rosa et al. 2020). Most production facilities are small shops rather than large factories and they are operated by independent, small organizations. The days of standardized mass production and one-time use products are over. This has required more automated and more sophisticated production with highly skilled workers. Many tasks that are carried out, and many devices that are employed today in manufacturing originate from the environmental goods and services sector (EGSS) and the high-tech sector. These are smart, small machines that are capable of producing customized output with little resources and hardly any waste. If we now count these latter jobs as being part of the manufacturing sector, we would even see a slight increase in overall employment numbers. The EGSS sector and related services have also been drivers of exports, whereby Europe, together with China, is leading world markets. Other sectors that have expanded particularly in the United States and Europe are the health care sector and personal services, the IT sector (United States), and construction (United States and Europe).

AI has strongly impacted three sectors over the last decade with visible consequences for jobs: First, the growth of jobs in the services sector has been decelerated through AI and been somewhat disappointing. Some jobs in public administration, the insurance industry, finance, accounting, and legal services and others have been transformed by AI, but many tasks, and with them, administrative jobs, have been automated. Often, those automated jobs were not the most popular ones, and many people today feel happy that they are gone, but we did see a reduction of numbers in these services, which were once the big hope to replace manufacturing as engines of job growth. Traditionally, exhibiting low-productivity growth, the construction sector is a surprising star of the AI revolution and has received a remarkable boost through the widespread use of new technology (Roland Berger 2020). The design, renovation, and project management of building and infrastructure construction has seen enormous efficiency gains and an increase in demand.

Finally, not being a sector in itself, we have observed public–private partnerships mushrooming since the early 2020s, most of them not organized as profitable corporations, but as part of the "New Work Deal", enabled through digital platforms.

1.8   The Climate Crisis Remains Unresolved...

If we look back at another megatrend, we have to admit that global climate change has had a much more limited effect on labour markets in advanced economies than many had thought. Turning to labour markets in Africa and Asia (see below), however, shows that the effects of climate change and climate change policies on the economy have been much more pronounced than anticipated. The main reason for this development is that mankind has to date failed to combat global climate change. Despite half-hearted efforts to mitigate greenhouse gases (GHG), global emissions have reached new heights every year with the exception of years hit by global recessions, in particular, the year 2020 (Fig. 4).

The EU's and the U.S.' global share and their absolute amounts of carbon dioxide emissions have been declining. However, this has not been the case for emerging regions like China or India and for most other regions around the world, which have managed at most to prevent further increases or to slow down annual increases. By and large, the last 15 years have shown that climate change mitigation measures have failed on a global scale. Fossil fuel reserves remain abundantly available, and new reserves have become available in now ice-free areas. Today, we expect an increase in average global temperatures of about 2.0 degrees by 2050 and of 3.7 degrees by

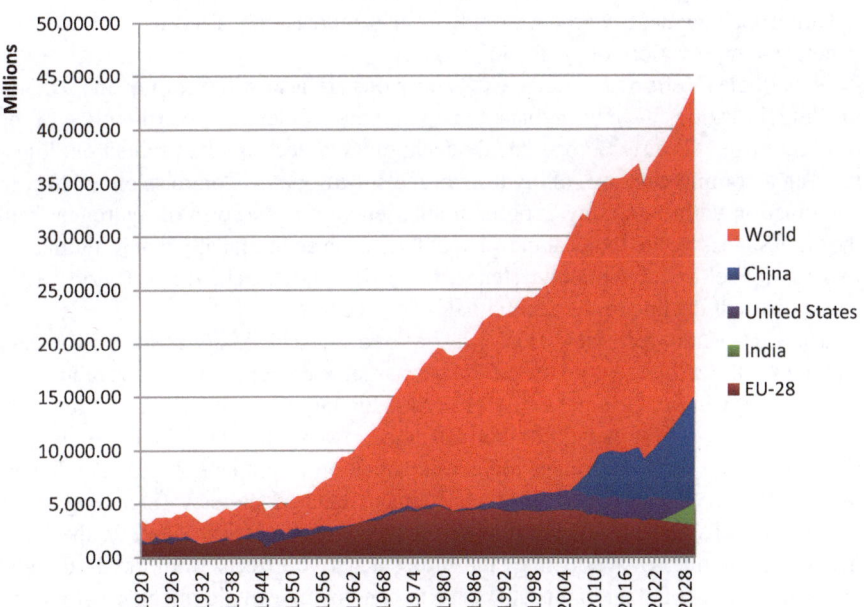

Fig. 4 Annual GHG emissions in tons by region, 1920–2030. Source: Carbon Dioxide Information Analysis Center (CDIAC) and author's estimations

2100. The different pathways do not predict dramatic differences until 2030, and indeed the worst is still to come in the next decades with the average impact from global climate change still limited today. Yet, on the regional level, we can already see sharp contrasts: Europe has seen several dry summers and more extreme weather events, but adverse effects on GDP and labour markets are hardly visible. The United States also had to suffer from extreme weather, whereby some states were much more severely affected than others. California, Nevada, but also parts of Colorado, New Mexico, and Texas have endured draughts with negative consequences on agriculture and overall living conditions. These conditions have triggered a certain degree of labour migration within the United States. Other parts of the world, such as South Asia or Africa, have endured already more significant consequences on labour markets.

1.9   ...and Policies Have Shifted from Climate Change Mitigation to Climate Change Adaptation

These developments and disappointments with mitigation have led to a policy shift. Climate change mitigation policies have been significantly scaled down. The bulk of climate policies around the world today are adaptation measures. Such measures include "classic" policies like afforestation, or flood management, and land recuperation at the coasts, but also significant advances have been made in climate engineering. The biggest trends today in climate engineering are CO_2 removal and solar radiation management. Carbon dioxide is also increasingly used as a resource to generate a large variety of synthetic products.

Nevertheless, efforts to reduce CO_2 emissions are also still relevant, and technological innovations have been made to increase the efficiency of consumption of the resources used. Today, Europe has the technological lead on the production, logistics, and commercial use of hydrogen fuels (European Commission 2020). In combination with increasing exports of solar energy in the form of hydrogen from the Gulf States, we are today at the edge of having an economically viable alternative to a fossil fuel-based economy. Hence, there still exists a chance that global CO_2 emissions will decline in the second half of the century.

The European Green New Deal[7] was revised in 2025. Many of the policies are still relevant, but the focus on the 1.5-degree target and specific emissions reductions have been given up. Original emissions reduction targets of the transport sector are out of reach. We now have a higher tolerance towards allowing higher emissions (less mitigation) and a stronger focus on adaptation (Nordhaus 2018). The labour market effects of climate change and climate change policies (including other environmental policies) are limited but visible. Except for job losses in the EU's fishery sector due to overfishing, the direct negative effects from environmental damage have not yet materialized. We have seen positive employment growth in the

---

[7]The European Green New Deal was launched in 2019 (see European Commission 2019).

European environmental goods and services sector (EGSS). The sector employed about 4.7 million people or roughly 2 percent of the European labour force in 2020 (Esposito 2017), and it has grown to more than 7 million workers or about 3 percent of the labour force as of today.

1.10 Occupations and Products That Increase Resource Efficiency Are Globally in High Demand

This increase is remarkable because the growth of the EGSS had slowed down significantly in the previous decade and was mainly driven by subsidies in wind and solar energy. Many of these jobs turned out to be temporary and not sustainable. By contrast, recent job growth has been driven by high-tech engineering jobs in recycling, water supply, and wastewater management but also in the "classical" manufacturing sectors. In these sectors, chemical and mechanical engineers have revised existing processes and invented new ones to increase resource efficiency in all production processes. The European hydrogen strategy has also sparked job growth in the EGSS, transport, and manufacturing sectors. European companies are today leading globally in most environmental technologies. European know-how and exports are in high demand in many emerging and developing economies that struggle with providing their growing populations with a satisfying infrastructure under shrinking natural resources. Forty-one of the global 50 megacities are located in emerging or developing economies (ESPAS 2019), and only three cities are in Europe (London, Paris, and Moscow). But European know-how is used in managing resources in almost all large cities. The European EGSS has become an attractive and well-paid employer for engineers around the world.

1.11 Most Traditional Labour Market Institutions Do Not Yet Support More Frequent Transitions...

Many trends have evolved faster than public institutions have changed. For example, by and large, public education systems in Europe and the United States are still designed to prepare students for a one-time-for-life occupation, even though job-to-job transitions have accelerated over the last years. In particular, digital technologies continue evolving fast, and the increased focus is on resource efficiency in many production and consumption processes together with more complex working relationships. This means that people are and have to be more flexible in their careers and in the roles they assume. Technical knowledge needs to be updated or acquired, but also social competencies need to be continuously adjusted.

While the "classic" educational institutions such as schools, universities, or apprenticeships have not changed much over the last decade(s), possibilities for on-the-job training have expanded considerably, for example, through e-learning and digital devices. People can participate much more easily and cheaper in customized training. Switching careers, having more than one career at the same time, or changing industries, organizations, and occupations has become easier but remains difficult. We are still not in a labour market that is in line with people's aspirations and societal goals. We only just started understanding in which direction our institutions have to change (OECD 2019). So what have we learned and what needs to change?

The traditional Central European approach of a broad-based general education has proven to provide a sound foundation for lifelong learning if combined with practical vocational training for adults, for example, in community colleges or institutes of technology like in the United States. An engineer benefits his whole life from a strong education in mathematics or programming when learning new skills later on during his career, or when pursuing an entirely different occupation. Europeans have opened up to the idea that adults can formally re-educate themselves several times during their lives, and the United States have invested more resources to provide high-quality foundational education to a broader share of their population. Foundational education establishes the capacity to know-how-to learn and is not targeted at a specific occupation. But institutions on both sides of the Atlantic have fallen short of transforming into something new, mainly due to unresolved questions about financing.

1.12   ... But Data, Platforms, and AI Have Revolutionized Talent Management with Many Opportunities...

The most significant innovation in labour markets institutions in the United States and Europe—and elsewhere in the world—over the last decade was undoubtedly the systematic inclusion of AI in search and matching processes[8] and in talent management ("people analytics") more generally (Garg and Ahluwalia 2019). Originating from HR practices in the private sector in the early 2020s, these algorithms have found their way into public employment agencies and public policymaking. Meanwhile, based on recent advances in natural language processing (NLP), AI identifies people's capabilities better than humans and also often makes better predictions about people's success in new roles. Without downplaying the difficulties that AI solutions in HR still had in the early 2020s and sometimes still have, we can claim that times in which HR specialists manually went through CVs and attempted to make ad hoc predictions on who is a good fit for a job belong to the past. Finding the right people to collaborate with, facilitating job-to-job transitions, or transitions from out of the labour force into the labour force are much easier and targeted than ever before. AI has opened up many opportunities for workers and enterprises in the labour market.

---

[8]That is the matching of labour supply (job seekers) and labour demand (job vacancies).

1.13 ...and Some Risks

The main problems of these AI tools in HR, namely, discrimination and biases, as well as a "preference for averages" rather than outliers, have been well documented and partly addressed through new technical solutions and better collaboration of these systems with human HR experts. In fact, AI can also help to overcome human biases and create a more diverse workforce, which is correlated with the profitability of organizations (McKinsey 2018). A broader policy discussion has evolved around the question of who runs the talent platforms, where the data come from, and who owns the data. Originally, for-profit tech firms in the United States drove the evolution of AI-based talent management. They transformed hiring practices in the corporate world during the early 2020s. But in the United States, this led to a "segregated talent market" where predominantly high-skilled workers willingly shared their private data with these private platforms, and private corporations also shared their vacancy and HR data and were willing to pay high prices to find the best talent. Smaller and medium-sized companies have neither a sufficient amount of systematic HR data to be interesting data suppliers for people analytics nor do they have the financial means to pay the high fees of private talent platforms. So, in the United States, and partly also in Europe, we have seen a polarization of jobs and incomes as well as a division between larger firms who have access to top talent and those who do not.

1.14 A New EU Labour Market Institution Uses New Technologies to Promote Policy Goals...

The European Union has reacted with an innovative approach and with the creation of the EU Directorate-General (DG) for "New Forms of Work and Social Progress in the Digital Society", which functions as a digital European employment agency and has stored more than 2 billion CVs and billions of vacancies, respecting recent changes to EU data protection regulation. The data include CVs of potential immigrants to the EU who are looking for employment opportunities. The trained AI, which is globally the best talent management tool, communicates with affiliated companies' HR systems and ERP systems. This infrastructure will be connected to EU universities and other training institutions in the future. Only in operation since 2028, the system has already proven to increase occupational mobility and to identify previously unforeseen career paths thereby helping enterprises to find the right talent. Its services are open at low cost to all institutions with a permanent establishment in an EU Member State.

What makes this new EU institution unique are not only its technical capabilities, but it is also its sizeable budget. It handles the new EU lifelong learning accounts, which are personalized accounts financed through social security contributions that can be further complemented with subsidized loans. This financial aid enables any person to choose to stop working and to retrain or re-educate herself at one of the accredited institutions. Hence, the financial incentives combine elements of a universal basic income with active labour market policies. Another unique feature of this new institution is that it is not only matching job seekers with existing vacancies, the AI also suggests transitions and collaborations across individuals based on their work preferences and their capabilities. The AI suggests vacancies, or more generally, work opportunities. The institution has therefore given birth to a variety of new work collaborations, profit or non-profit, in the form of start-ups firms or others that go beyond the classical "corporate framework" and are more aligned with the "new work culture" (Bergmann 2019). This new EU institution has only been operating for a bit longer than one-and-a-half years and it is too early to evaluate its overall success. But so far it has already (i) increased career mobility for all, (ii) raised productivity of the workforce, (iii) facilitated new forms of work collaborations, (iv) enabled lifelong learning and agility of the workforce, and also (v) raised wages across the board, as the competition for talent has become more fierce. These developments can be the first steps toward a future of work in which we will work without jobs (Jesuthasan and Boudreau 2021).

1.15   …But Has Not Yet Finally Clarified Who the Social Partners in the Digital Society Are

The new directorate has also emphasized its passive role in terms of determination of labour market structures, hence signalling that the more active role can remain with the social partners. Traditional (Kampeter 2019) and new social partners have been integrated into the directorate's working environment. While the popularity of traditional trade unions and employer associations have continued to decline, new work coalitions have emerged that are organized about labour market "issues" rather than industries. They often started as digital grass-root movements. For example, the "equality at work" group is concerned with gender equality in the world of work and has more than 400,000 individual and corporate members in the EU.

Another example is the "reduction of working time group" that is developing and advocates new working time schemes with the purpose of an overall reduction. These new work coalitions sometimes, but not always, work collaboratively with the traditional social partners. All of these groups are involved in the standard-setting rules for the further development of the AI in the directorate, but it remains to be seen to what extent the social partners from the industrial society and the ones in the digital society will resemble each other.

2   The Difficult Rise of Asia and Africa's Struggle

Europe and the United States have managed to seize many opportunities over the last decade. This second part of the chapter looks at how other parts of the world, like Africa and Asia, who have been exposed to the same megatrends, have gone through labour market transformations. Some of the previous considerations, such as job displacement through AI or climate change, also apply to Asia, Africa, and other parts of the world. Still, some developments were specific to these regions. Starting with a general observation, we have seen that developing economies have had much more difficulties with coping with changes triggered by the various megatrends than advanced economies.

2.1   Between Automation and Rural Economy

In Asia, we can observe this divide between developing and more developed economies. For example, China has been continuing its economic rise—albeit at decelerated pace—while many developing countries in South East Asia like Vietnam, Thailand, or South Asian economies, like Bangladesh or Pakistan, have struggled to catch up in their economic development. The COVID-19 crisis functioned as a game changer across the globe. Labour markets with high informality rates and underdeveloped social protection systems were especially hit hard (Díez et al. 2020). As discussed in the first part of this chapter, the crisis at the beginning of the 2020s had accelerated the journey to a "bipolar multilateral" world with China and its increased geopolitical power as one of these poles. The rise to more economic power has been more challenging than expected; especially, the impact of de-globalization has reduced China's growth and its links to the West. The political and economic divide and political differences within Asia are clearly visible, with countries like India, Japan, South Korea, and Indonesia gravitating stronger towards the United States pole.

In its manufacturing sector, China has seen a wave of automation, thanks to its continuously growing technological capacity (Lee 2018). With rapid technological change and an aging population as major trends, the Chinese labour market is actually exposed to very similar challenges as its Western competitors. But there are also important differences: First, China still had a large rural population around 2020 with about 40 percent or more than 500 million people living in rural areas, compared to about 20 or 15 percent in countries like the United States or Germany. Most of China's rural population depends on working in the primary sector, where income and education levels are significantly below that of urban populations. These inequalities, as well as automation of agricultural activities (towards industrial agriculture), have raised constant migration pressures from rural to urban areas. Yet, a classical development path was barred (Lewis 1954), as the capacity of China's manufacturing sector to absorb large masses of low-skilled labour have been limited by labour displacement through automation and slower expansion of the sector due to shrinking exports. The migration pressure is exacerbated through climate change damages and environmental pollution (McKinsey 2020). Heat waves and water shortages have made subsistence farming in several regions impossible.

China's government has reacted with an expansion of subsidies and business incentives for the service sector. The service sector keeps expanding rapidly, and advances in AI technologies have created many new business models and new enterprises. Then again, automation of routine tasks has reduced the speed of new job creation. In sum, the service sector is in turmoil with new jobs emerging and other jobs disappearing at the same time. Together with the influx of low-skilled job seekers from rural areas, who cannot find employment, this has led to an increase in informal employment relationships in urban regions. China has a relatively well-developed social security system, but digital labour platforms and gig work are common tools in the service sector and have undermined formal working relationships. Thus, the Chinese government has found itself in a dilemma. On the one hand, new job growth in the service sector is urgently needed, at least until the demographic aging effects fully kick in at around 2050, and so are the many innovative tech companies that have sprung up in great numbers all over in China's urban centres. On the other hand, only a minority of the new jobs are of good quality in the sense that they are well paid, stable, and provide social security. Many jobs are temporary, offer limited possibilities for career advancement, and are not covered by formal working contracts. So it is questionable at this stage to what extent many of these jobs contribute to a long-term development strategy.

The creation of good, new jobs has been more successful in China's expanding EGSS sector. New technologies, new products, and new services have been developed over the last 5–10 years that are targeted at taming the resource hunger of the world's largest economy and at reducing environmental pollution and degradation. Smart Chinese megacities are an example for urban planners around the world, and resource use per inhabitant has been reduced by 70 percent since 2020. Some expertise in resource efficiency and environmental technology is still imported from Europe, but China has developed its industries and gained expertise in these areas. This know-how is being successfully exported into many developing and emerging economies in Asia or Africa.

2.2   The Demographic Dividend Has Not Yet Paid Off for India and Others in the Region

The point of departure for labour markets in South Asia in the early 2020s was in several aspects different from China's. India, for example, has a growing, young population and had prospects of attaining a demographic dividend in its effort to boost GDP per capita growth. Income per capita in India was also about four to five times lower than in China, and this gap has virtually remained the same as of today. India was less affected by de-globalization over the last decade, given that India was much less integrated into global trade to begin with. The labour market effects of de-globalization have been more severe for countries with strong links to global supply chains, like Bangladesh, Vietnam, or Cambodia. They have seen job losses and worsening working conditions in sectors like textiles.

We have also seen similarities in facing labour market challenges across the whole of Asia: The region has the largest percentage of the population affected by natural disasters. For example, the negative impacts of climate change have increased migration pressures for low-skilled workers and have accelerated urbanization in India and elsewhere. The employment share in the Indian agricultural sector has fallen rapidly from 50 to 30 percent within a decade. Heat waves have made many forms of subsistence farming impossible, from an economic perspective but also from an occupational safety and health perspective (McKinsey 2020). This trend is likely to continue throughout 2050. The construction sector was an important net creator of jobs in India, especially for low-skilled workers. Climate change and worsening working conditions for those working outdoors have reduced the possibility of the construction sector to absorb large numbers of workers and to provide good quality jobs.

The speed of automation in manufacturing has been very modest, due to the abundance of cheap labour in India and many other Asian countries. However, quicker-than-expected adoption of new technology took place in India's agricultural sector: Automation, artificial intelligence, drones, harvesting robots, and recent advancements in biotech have kept agricultural productivity in India rising, and these devices are less vulnerable towards heat and air pollution than humans. But this development has meant a shift away from low-skilled, labour-intensive production methods in agriculture towards capital-intensive production operated with high-skilled labour. India, like many other Asian countries (ASEAN +6), still lacks skilled workers to work in non-routine cognitive occupations (ILO 2019). This substantive skills mismatch in the middle of a large structural transformation became apparent to most policymakers in the mid-2020s as structural unemployment and informality rates started spiking.

Many governments, including India's, have reacted with extensive education and re-skilling programs for low-skilled workers that have lost their jobs in agriculture or light manufacturing (Deloitte 2019). But given weak institutions in most developing countries in Asia, and given the long times that it takes for investments in better education to pay off, much of the unemployed have ended up as informal platform workers in Asia's crowded megacities. The need for much higher resource efficiency also applies to India's megacities, but India is much more reliant on importing solutions and services from Europe or China. India has managed to develop high-tech industry and is specialized in IT services, a sector that provides a decent number of good and well-paid jobs in urban centres. The potential of job growth in the sector has been limited by the slow growth rates in global trade and services. The failure of the international community to agree on any form of services agreement, either on the regional level (negotiations of The Trade in Services Agreement (TiSA)) have been broken off in 2022) or on the multilateral level have further reduced growth rates.

2.3   Africa at the Crossroads

A technological laggard, Africa has become a harvesting ground for tech companies to take advantage of cheap labour for data entry, tagging, and training samples for AI (The World Bank 2019). Several large cities across Africa, like Lagos or Addis Ababa, host a sizeable community of African entrepreneurs and start-ups that have also created employment opportunities for Africa's tech-savvy youth. New digital payment systems have constituted additional revenue streams for digital companies in advanced economies. The average ICT intensity of jobs in South Africa has continued increasing over the last decade, while more than 30% of all formal sector employment in countries like Ghana or Kenya occur in occupations with high ICT intensity. Several African countries have benefited much more from the platform economy than other developing countries. The lack or weakness of physical infrastructure and institutions has often limited the access of entrepreneurs to bigger markets. Platforms like Amazon and others have created many opportunities in consumer markets or the supply of intermediate goods or means of financing. The wide dissemination of smartphones in African countries let entrepreneurs and customers easily participate in networks. A growing economy and a larger number of entrepreneurs have had a positive effect on the overall number of jobs outside the agriculture sector. Yet, neither is global growth strong enough (Chap. 1) to spill over to developing countries, nor are enough well-paid jobs being created.

The informal sector in Sub-Saharan Africa, which typically has the lowest levels of productivity, accounts for a sizeable proportion of employment (90 percent of total employment in 2020). It has remained large but shrunk to about 65% over the last decade. Efforts to formalize farms and firms have benefited from digital technologies that have offered opportunities to enhance their productivity. For example, better connectivity has helped small firms to access credit or insurance products, or to train their workers very effectively through e-learning. Thus, Africa's labour markets have taken advantage to some degree of digital technologies, but the biggest holdback is the lack of education for large parts of its workforce (WEF 2017). Sub-Saharan Africa still has one of the lowest numbers of years of formal education globally while being one of the world's youngest regions. The continent's working-age population has increased to over 600 million, and the number of available jobs is simply not sufficiently high to provide jobs for everyone.

Few megacities have lifted themselves off the ground, partly by integrating international trading networks, often fostered by China's Belt-and-Road initiative. Links with the rest of the economy remain weak, however, as the lack of infrastructure and education prevent a gradual diffusion of wealth throughout the countries. Africa is also highly vulnerable to climate shocks. Climate change has started eroding the livelihood of populations in semi-arid and arid zones. Widespread poverty has fuelled internal migration, urbanization, and continuously high fertility rates with simultaneously growing mortality rates and repeated famines.

Remittances remain an important source of revenue for many households who continue to send a large share of their youth to work in foreign countries. Many African countries have gained from the new migration policies of the European Union that allow for temporary and permanent work assignments within the EU.

3   Reflections on the World of Work in 2030 and Beyond

After a devastating start with the COVID-19 crisis in 2020, labour markets across the world have experienced a rather positive decade. What many did not expect is that advanced economies would see a strong come back, and developing countries have not managed to close the development gap, neither in terms of GDP, nor in terms of well-being on the labour markets. Another surprise were the renewed strengths of the old continent and the United States. A crucial insight of this chapter is that political decisions shape labour markets. For example, the EU emerged stronger at the end of this decade than in 2020, providing more opportunities to its citizens and to migrants from other regions. But if other political decisions had been taken this would not have been the case. The same is true for the United States, China, and others. Another insight of this chapter is that the impacts of digitalization and climate change on labour markets were not as strong as many anticipated. These impacts will most likely be much more pronounced in the coming decades leading us to 2050.

Disclaimer The future of work scenarios developed in this chapter are a fiction. They have been created on the basis of available information in early 2020 and on the basis of the author's perspective on the world of work. In particular, none of the political events or declarations referring to the time period after 2020 have actually taken place. The scenarios are neither predictions nor desired future outcomes. They are solely meant to inspire critical thinking about how known developments today (2020) could evolve into a possible future in 2030.The author is a senior economist and researcher at the Research Department of the International Labour Organization (ILO) in Geneva. Any view expressed or conclusions drawn represent the views of the author and do not necessarily represent ILO views or ILO policy. The views expressed herein should be attributed to the author and not to the ILO, its management or its constituents.

References

Acemoglu, D., & Restrepo, P. (2018). *Demographics and automation.*

BBC News. (2020, July 9). *Tesla 'very close' to full self-driving*, Musk Says, sec. Technology. Accessed from https://www.bbc.com/news/technology-53349313

Beck, U. (2016). *Risikogesellschaft: Auf dem Weg in eine andere Moderne.* Frankfurt: Suhrkamp Verlag.

Bergmann, F. (2019). *New work new culture: Work we want and a culture that strengthens us.* New York: Zero Books.

Bessen, J. (2018, January 27). *AI and jobs: The role of demand.*

Brooks, R. (2019). *AGI has been delayed – Rodney Brooks.* Accessed from https://rodneybrooks.com/agi-has-been-delayed/

Brynjolfsson, E., & McAfee, A.. (2014). *The second machine age: Work, progress, and prosperity in a time of brilliant technologies.* Reprint. W. W. Norton & Company.

Brynjolfsson, E., & Mitchell, T. (2017). What can machine learning do? Workforce implications. *Science, 358*(6370), 1530–1534. https://doi.org/10.1126/science.aap8062.

Deloitte. (2017). *Meet the US workforce of the future | Deloitte Insights..* Accessed from https://www2.deloitte.com/us/en/insights/deloitte-review/issue-21/meet-the-us-workforce-of-the-future.html

Deloitte. (2019). *Laying the foundation for the future of work in India*, p. 12

Díez, F., Duval, R., Maggi, C., Ji, Y., Shibata, I., & Tavares, M. M. (2020). Options to support the incomes of informal workers during COVID-19. *IMF, 11.*

ESPAS. (2019). *Global trends to 2030: The future of urbanization and megacities.* European Strategy and Policy Analysis System. ESPAS Ideas Paper Series.

Esposito, M. (2017). *Enhancing job creation through green transformation*. Accessed from https://www.greenindustryplatform.org/sites/default/files/downloads/resource/Green%20Industrial%20Policy_Concept%2C%20Policies%2C%20Country%20Experiences.pdf#page=66

European Commission. (2019). *The European Green Deal*. Accessed from https://eur-lex.europa.eu/resource.html?uri=cellar:b828d165-1c22-11ea-8c1f-01aa75ed71a1.0002.02/DOC_1&format=PDF

European Commission. (2020). *EU hydrogen strategy for a climate neutral Europe*. Text. European Commission - European Commission. Accessed from https://ec.europa.eu/commission/presscorner/detail/en/fs_20_1296

Felten, E. W., Raj, M., & Seamans, R. (2019). The Occupational impact of artificial intelligence: Labor, skills, and polarization. In *SSRN Scholarly Paper ID 3368605*. Rochester, NY: Social Science Research Network. https://doi.org/10.2139/ssrn.3368605.

Fossen, F., & Sorgner, A. (2019). Mapping the future of occupations: Transformative and destructive effects of new digital technologies on jobs. *Foresight and STI Governance, 13*(2), 10–18. https://doi.org/10.17323/2500-2597.2019.2.10.18.

Frey, C. B. (2019). *The technology trap: Capital, labor, and power in the age of automation*. Princeton, NJ: Princeton University Press.

Frey, C. B., & Osborne, M. A. (2017). The future of employment: How susceptible are jobs to computerisation? *Technological Forecasting and Social Change, 114*, 254–280. https://doi.org/10.1016/j.techfore.2016.08.019.

Fukuyama, F. (2020, July 6). *The pandemic and political order*. Accessed from https://www.foreignaffairs.com/articles/world/2020-06-09/pandemic-and-political-order

Garg, A., & Ahluwalia, K. (2019). *What's next for you: The eightfold path to transforming the way we hire and manage talent*. Bloomington, IN: Balboa Press.

Garrett, A. B., & Gangopadhyaya, A. (2020). How the COVID-19 recession could affect health insurance coverage. *SSRN Electronic Journal*. https://doi.org/10.2139/ssrn.3598558.

Hallward-Driemeier, M., & Nayyar, G. (2018). *Trouble in the making? The future of manufacturing-led development* (p. 255). Washington, DC: The World Bank.

ILO. (2019). *Preparing for the future of work: National Policy Responses in ASEAN +6*. Report. Accessed from http://www.ilo.org/asia/publications/WCMS_717736/lang%2D%2Den/index.htm

ILO. (2020a). *Defining and measuring remote work, telework, work at home and home-based work*. Publication. Accessed from http://www.ilo.org/global/statistics-and-databases/publications/WCMS_747075/lang%2D%2Den/index.htm

ILO. (2020b). *ILO monitor: COVID-19 and the world of work* (5th ed., p. 22). Geneva: ILO.

IMF. (2020). *World economic outlook update - A crisis like no other, an uncertain recovery*. Washington, DC: IMF.

Irwin, D. (2020, May 5). The pandemic adds momentum to the deglobalisation trend. *VoxEU.Org* (blog post). Accessed from https://voxeu.org/article/pandemic-adds-momentum-deglobalisation-trend

Jesuthasan, R. & Boudreau, J. (2021). Work without Jobs, MIT Sloan Management Review, Reprint #62312.

Kampeter, S. (Ed.). (2019). *Sozialpartnerschaft 4.0: Tarifpolitik für die Arbeitswelt von morgen*. Frankfurt: Campus Verlag.

Kose, M. A., Ohnsorge, F., Nagle, P., & Sugawara, N. (2020). Past debt crises can teach developing economies to cope with COVID-19 financing shocks. *Finance & Development, 57*(2), 4.

Lee, K.-F. (2018). *AI superpowers: China, Silicon Valley, and the New World Order* (1st ed.). Boston, MA: Houghton Mifflin Harcourt.

Lewis, W. A. (1954). Economic development with unlimited supplies of labour. *The Manchester School, 22*(2), 139–191. https://doi.org/10.1111/j.1467-9957.1954.tb00021.x.

Matousek, M. (2020, January 30). Elon Musk contradicted a bold claim he made last year about Tesla's self-driving capabilities. *Business Insider*. Accessed from https://www.businessinsider.de/international/elon-musk-contradicts-2019-prediction-about-tesla-autopilot-2020-1/

McKinsey. (2018). *Delivering through diversity,* p. 42.

McKinsey. (2020). *Climate risk and response: Physical hazards and socioeconomic impacts,* p. 144.

McKinsey Global Institute. (2017). *Jobs lost, jobs gained: Workforce transitions in a time of automation.*

Nordhaus, T. (2018). *The two-degree delusion.* Accessed from https://www.foreignaffairs.com/articles/world/2018-02-08/two-degree-delusion

OECD. (2019). *OECD future of education and skills 2030: OECD learning compass 2030 - A series of concept notes.*

OECD. (2020). *OECD Employment Outlook 2020: Worker security and the COVID-19 crisis.* OECD Employment Outlook. https://doi.org/10.1787/1686c758-en

Pei, M. (2020, June 2). *China's coming upheaval.* Accessed from https://www.foreignaffairs.com/articles/united-states/2020-04-03/chinas-coming-upheaval

PricewaterhouseCoopers, pwc. (2017, March). *Will robots steal our jobs? The potential impact of automation on the UK and other major economies.*

PWC. (2017). *Digital factories 2020: Shaping the future of manufacturing.* Retrieved September 17, 2018.

Roland Berger. (2020). *Artificial intelligence in the construction industry.* Accessed from https://www.rolandberger.com/en/Point-of-View/Artificial-intelligence-in-the-construction-industry.html

Rosa, P., Sassanelli, C., Urbinati, A., Chiaroni, D., & Terzi, S. (2020). Assessing relations between circular economy and industry 4.0: A systematic literature review. *International Journal of Production Research, 58*(6), 1662–1687. https://doi.org/10.1080/00207543.2019.1680896.

Shell Deutschland. (2019). *JUGEND 2019 - Eine Generation Meldet Sich Zu Wort* (1st ed.). Weinheim: Beltz.

Simon, H. A. (1965). *The shape of automation for men and management* (1st ed.). New York: Harper & Row.

Strickland, E. (2019). *How IBM Watson overpromised and underdelivered on AI health care - IEEE Spectrum.* IEEE Spectrum: Technology, Engineering, and Science News. Accessed from https://spectrum.ieee.org/biomedical/diagnostics/how-ibm-watson-overpromised-and-underdelivered-on-ai-health-care

The World Bank. (2019). *The future of work in Africa.* Washington, DC: World Bank. https://doi.org/10.1596/978-1-4648-1445-7.

WEF. (2017). *The future of jobs and skills in Africa preparing the region for the fourth industrial revolution.*

World Bank. (2020, June). *Global Economic Prospects.* Global Economic Prospects. The World Bank. https://doi.org/10.1596/978-1-4648-1553-9

Daniel Samaan is an Economist and Senior Researcher at the International Labour Organization (ILO) in Geneva. He is an expert in the analysis of global labour market trends, specialized in the links with globalization, new technologies/AI, sustainable development, and a new work culture. He has been an author and part of the core teams of several ILO reports. His research has been published in peer-reviewed journals and he is a regular public speaker on various labor market topics and on the Future of Work. Daniel previously worked at the economic policy research center, SCEPA, and in the consulting industry in New York City. He holds a PhD in economics from the New School for Social Research in New York and a master's degree in economics and business administration from the University of Passau in Germany.

Vignette: A Day in the Life of a Medical Doctor in 2030

Hans-Peter Schnurr

"Yes, we have to take these measures immediately. Everything points to a heart attack," explains Dr. Ruben in a calm tone via a video chat to his patient Mr. Dow. Earlier in the morning, Dr. Ruben had received a warning on his patient radar. The system alerted him to abnormalities in the data being transmitted from his patient's chest patch. Mr. Dow has been using one since being diagnosed as an "at-risk" patient earlier that year. The system is based on an artificial intelligence application and includes a neural network that analyzes the electrocardiogram (ECG) and prepares it for review. The examination showed a conspicuous high and narrow T-curve in the ECG, which indicates an acute risk of a heart attack. Dr. Ruben reviewed the evaluation again and immediately contacted the patient. After receiving the patient approval, the system automatically notified the required contact points about the actions that needed to be taken. In this case, the proposal is to increase the oxygen and blood supply toward the myocardium by administering drugs that will cause the coronary artery to dilate. Dr. Ruben transmits the necessary patient data and ends the video chat. Chest patches, which act as an electrocardiogram, were becoming ever more popular. The information gathered is sent directly from the chest patch to the doctor's computer, allowing doctors to monitor patients with chronic diseases.

Many of his patients use such tracking devices. There are various models available. Some of them are integrated into watches, glasses, or clothing. Others are even available as implants. Smart contact lenses that contain application-specific integrated circuits monitoring the pH value of tears that can monitor blood sugar levels are in widespread use nowadays. Such tracking devices allow the permanent measurement of body data, which—after approval by the patient—are then transmitted to the doctor's patient radar system. This type of control of body data was highly controversial a few years ago. Dr. Ruben remembers that there were intensive

H.-P. Schnurr (✉)
Semedy AG, Zug, Switzerland
e-mail: schnurr@semedy.com

© Springer Nature Switzerland AG 2021
S. Güldenberg et al. (eds.), *Managing Work in the Digital Economy*, Future of Business and Finance, https://doi.org/10.1007/978-3-030-65173-2_5

discussions about data protection and personal rights, which prevented patient data from being stored and evaluated until the 2020s. However, the introduction of a state-controlled trust center for patient data cleared the way for healthcare providers to offer advanced patient care concepts. This enabled targeted health coaching, prevention programs, and personalized advice in addition to the treatment of individual health aspects.

It still surprised him sometimes just how much the role of a medical doctor had changed! Just a few decades ago, doctors were considered by their patients as universal experts for all general health-related questions, and their proposed treatment was followed strictly without reaching out to a broader team of experts to get a second or third opinion. In most professions and industries, the division of labor was associated with specialization, automation, and digitalization. The healthcare sector, however, was very slow to take advantage of some of these possible improvements. This changed during the corona pandemic in 2020, which amplified the radical upheavals in the health sector. This led to advanced digitalization support and specialization of healthcare professionals. Moreover, the use of robotics and artificial intelligence in preventive care, diagnosis, and treatment of patients became widely accepted.

After Dr. Ruben checks his patients' radar system, he can finally start his day with a freshly made cup of coffee at home. On the one hand, this overview enables him to act quickly in critical situations; luckily, not every day starts with a comparable Mr. Dow situation. On the other hand, the dashboard also shows current risks for specific patient groups. This enables him to inform patients about risks in advance and to initiate preventive measures. For example, the knowledge of the local spread of viruses, climatic conditions, and the pollen count predictions are regularly published and synchronized with Dr. Ruben's patient radar system. These updates allow a permanent cross-check with his patients' data. Today's evaluation shows an increased risk of anaphylaxis (allergic shock) for his patient Mrs. Smith due to an unfavorable combination of the pollen count prediction with the patient's current medication. Dr. Ruben sends Mrs. Smith a system-ready text message explaining the situation together with some suggestions which are, in this case, wearing a facemask, using caution when eating certain foods, and carrying an emergency kit against anaphylactic shock. He ends his work on the patient radar system, leaves his apartment, and takes one of the autonomously driving shuttle cars to the clinic.

During the trip, Dr. Ruben uses his interactive glasses to get the latest news, summarized for him from personalized news sources and his social network. A display overlay pops up, signaling an incoming voice message, which he calls up and listens to. It is from Mrs. Smith, who wishes to thank him for his message with the precautionary measures and would like to receive an emergency set against anaphylactic shocks due to the acute risk situation. With an eye gesture, Dr. Ruben forwards the request as a prescription to the hospital pharmacy, which will deliver the emergency kit in the next few minutes using a drone.

As he turns back to the news, his thoughts circle around how the delivery of medication and blood samples changed when he had just started to practice medicine. At that time, the use and supply of medical samples and drugs using drones was still in its infancy. Nevertheless, in Ghana and Rwanda, drones were already delivering medical supplies to rural villages that would otherwise have lacked access to these medical essentials. Some large logistic and IT companies, as well as Silicon Valley startups, then started to use drones for the delivery of medical samples, including blood and tissue, as well as drug and transfusable blood. They were able to transport blood samples much faster than a standard courier was and therefore guaranteed a quick result of the examined blood sample. The increased use of drones in healthcare was also one of the effects of the numerous corona pandemic waves, which shook the world for many years from 2020. Early bad experiences with the lack of corona tests and the risks associated with performing the tests for patients and health workers led to the development of drone-based virus tests. This meant that the doctor could send a drone to the patient and perform a smear test remotely. The drone could then fly to the nearest laboratory to get the sample evaluated. This was a massive improvement to the early years when visiting a test center increased the risk for everyone involved of spreading the virus!

Another effect of this first major pandemic in the twenty-first century was the introduction of medical walk-through and drive-through centers. In the past, most people only considered a visit to their general practitioner when they had had acute problems—basically, when it was already too late. Most of the people did not have time or were afraid of catching the virus at the medical practice or were simply too lazy to go to visit their doctor. After the corona crises, the patients were much more aware of the need for regular checkups, and the infrastructure changed to a more prevention-based flexible health support. It became common and necessary to integrate medical checkups into people's daily lives efficiently. Besides medical drive-through centers taking smear tests, "medical walk throughs" are established in public places such as grocery stores, pharmacies, and fitness centers, at universities, and even at some large workplaces. When entering a "medical walk through," the patient can check several parameters operated by screening systems, blood tests, ECGs, and many more. Those monitoring systems transfer the diagnosis to the patient, who then can share it with the patient radar system of their family doctor. There is another important use for the data collected from medical walk-through centers. The collection centers send the anonymized data to national health agencies. In this way, the prediction and recognition of diseases and hot spots improved tremendously. Data analytics, with the support of smart algorithms and machine-based learning, transform this vast amount of data into forecasts, offering a solid base for decision-making, especially when it comes to epidemic control.

The autonomous driving car enters the driveway to the clinic and stops in front of the entrance. Dr. Ruben confirms his arrival at the hospital using his interactive glasses. Another eye movement changes the context of his virtual assistant to work environment mode. He is on his way to the medical department, where he works as a cardiologist. Logging in to this digital workplace, he starts the morning with his virtual consultation hour, and a short time later, his patient Mrs. Green calls him via the video chat. She's on a business trip to Beijing and has reported an acute, severe dry cough since taking the blood pressure-lowering drug "Captopril." Dr. Ruben receives her approval to use the patient data and then checks the patient's smartwatch records. The records are immediately transmitted to the clinical decision system. An integrated rule-based system evaluates the latest adverse event databases, and artificial intelligence modules compare similar cases. This system links the current findings with the original diagnoses and the side effects of the medication and then suggests another better-suited medication. Dr. Ruben checks the evaluation and informs Mrs. Green, whereupon she can immediately receive the recommended medication. He uses his virtual assistant to search for a pharmacy near his patient's current location. Dr. Ruben selects a pharmacy close to the hotel and requests a connection. Shortly afterward, the pharmacist appears in the video chat. The system recognizes the spoken language as "Mandarin Chinese" and immediately starts the simultaneous automatic translation. After briefly clarifying the active drug substance and the availability of the corresponding medication, Dr. Ruben transmits the prescription to the pharmacy in Beijing, which makes an immediate delivery to Mrs. Green's hotel.

The introduction of the virtual consultation hour changed the interaction with the patients. They now had a quick and direct opportunity to interact with their doctor, who can involve other colleagues with their expert knowledge to the conversation. Moreover, this no longer stops at language boundaries. The availability of specialists has increased significantly since automatic translation became standard in chat and videoconference systems a few years ago. Patients see their doctor as a contact person, advisor, and coach—easy to reach and to contact. In former times, patients felt very insecure. They were bombarded with contradictory information from the Internet and various social media channels and turned to doctors for clarifications. How was one to handle this flood of queries? How was one to do justice to the patients' problems when there remained so little time for the treatment? Established doctors struggled with the increasing dissatisfaction of their patients. The reputation of medical doctors worsened. Patients no longer accepted their role as a universal medical generalist. The new generation of medical doctors defined their role more toward being a health consultant and coach. They interacted with teams of specialists, and they requested the advice of artificial intelligence-based clinical decision support tools. With this sound knowledge-based diagnosis and consulting, the medical profession regained their reputation and their patients' trust.

"This is the spot!" Dr. Ruben points to the area of the spine in the hologram of Mr. Miller, a patient who is visiting the medical practice. "There are several approaches to treatment", he continues and brings in illustrated descriptions into the hologram and explains each procedure. The patient gives detailed information about other symptoms and answers a few questions that are instantly added to the patient information in Dr. Ruben's virtual assistance system through the speech port.

A few weeks ago, he prescribed Mr. Miller a new version of a smart sole from a German medical technology manufacturer. Several years ago, the company developed a wireless insole with pressure pads and an accelerometer that detects things like temperature, motion, weight, pressure, and balance, which can be useful for further gait analysis, rehabilitation, and treatment of the patient. Dr. Ruben checks the corresponding health app for the latest insole data and analytics and forwards the data to the virtual assistant. Now the system can consolidate all the information from patient, examination and medical device to calculate a comparison and evaluation of optional treatment methods.

Dr. Ruben assesses the evaluations of the system and advises the patient about the results. He recommends osteopathic muscle energy techniques, which are recommended as most effective by many patients with similar symptoms as well as by their doctors. He consults his assistance system and refers the patient to two of his colleagues nearby who are specialists in this therapeutic area and whom the system indicates as available in the following week. The patient transfers the calendar information to his electronic agenda and finds the next suitable appointments. Then he decides upon the osteopath who offers him an appointment for the coming Tuesday. With a push of a button, Dr. Ruben sends an e-mail to the patient as well as to the osteopath with a direct link to the assistance system of the clinic. This link provides the patient with permanent access to his patient data and all analyzed information from the files and doctor appointments. This customized file helps the patient in his Internet research, acting as a filter to hide all irrelevant information, and uses the patient profile to focus search results.

Apart from a new calendar entry, the osteopath also receives all relevant data of the patient via the virtual assistant system. Dr. Ruben knows that the results of the osteopathic consultation will be automatically synchronized between him and his colleague's assistance system so that he can generate another patient file before the next consultation, which will include the therapy results. Dr. Ruben recalls again how vividly his friend had explained to him the uniqueness of this new assistance system based on semantic technologies. He has already grown so accustomed to all the information being provided in the right context with the right level of detail by his assistance system that he can barely recall the old times. Back then, there used to be systems that retrieved heaps of documents from all over the Internet upon querying a keyword. Dr. Ruben remembered the hours he spent in just separating the supposedly relevant sources from the others. A world without personalized assistance systems is unimaginable!

Dr. Ruben's friend has turned up for their lunch. He turns and smiles, "Time for another delicious Indian curry." He has known his friend since he was a student. Back then, they used to talk about the future of medicine. It was an exciting time when robots performed the first surgery operations remotely—naturally, just a matter of course, in 2030. Specialists around the world can now use virtual reality to perform surgical procedures in remote locations with the assistance of robots. Robots also perform surgeries that humans would not be able to perform due to space restrictions on human hands and tools. The miniaturization of the machines, in combination with precise sensor technology, has transformed robots from the surgeon's assistant to the autonomously operating surgeon robot. The associated ethical issues are still being discussed in society. Who is responsible if something goes wrong? Who gets to make those life and death decisions?

Nevertheless, the acceptance of robots in healthcare has increased significantly. Dr. Ruben remembers a discussion he had with his friend 10 years ago. At the time, he had not believed in the use of robots in nursing because people would not accept it. His friend, in turn, was firmly convinced that the lack of nursing staff and the increasing familiarization of humans with human-machine interactions would lead to a real nursing robot hype. The truth is somewhere in the middle.

"What do you think, what will the role of a medical doctor be in 2040?" Dr. Ruben asks his friend. "Being even more of a medical coach and consultant," his friend replies. In his view, the steady increase in the availability of information requires an anchor point that the patient can trust. Besides, the health system is changing. While in the past there was a clear focus on the treatment of an acute illness, the health system of the future will focus on prevention through permanent monitoring of health conditions in our daily life. Doctors will be seen more and more as coaches, consultants, and mediators to guide us through our medical journey.

After lunch, he says goodbye to his friend and returns to the hospital. He is still pondering about the conversation they had during lunch. Today in 2030, machines, robots, and AI started performing more and more of the medical tasks that used to be done by doctors. Likewise, the doctors have had to adapt as well. They have had to develop new competencies trending toward the so-called spoken medicine. Digital changes ensured that technology relieved doctors from mundane tasks and saved them more time for the essentials such as communication with patients. Overall, "spoken medicine" has become a fundamental part of family doctors' job. A stronger focus is put on accompanying the patients throughout their lives. The doctor became a coach and an "interface communicator" between patient and machine, a health advisor with social responsibility. The doctor-patient relationship we used to know became a patient-doctor relationship. Patients are highly educated and informed about their current health status and possible diseases affecting them. The traditional examination of the patient done by the doctor belongs to the past. Sick people will bring collected data, findings, observed abnormalities, and in-depth knowledge to their appointments with their doctors.

Dr. Ruben's virtual assistant displays an incoming message from Mr. Dow. Right after their early morning call, treatment started, and the remote assistants supported Mr. Dow to handle the critical heart attack situation carefully. The monitoring data shows progress, and the treatment has been successful in preventing a much worse possible outcome. Dr. Ruben leans back with a big smile on his face. He is delighted with his profession* and with his competencies. He keeps people healthy and guides them safely through their medical journey in his role as a medical doctor and health coach.

*Timeshift – it is May 2020, and due to the corona crisis, we have been working from home for the last 10 weeks. One of the activities that has brought delight to our daily lives is the interaction to finalize this article together with Stud. mede. Ruben Plocher who will surely be an excellent future health coach in 2030. Ruben, a big thank you and all the best for your future career and life!

Hans-Peter Schnurr is an Information Technology Professional with over 20 years of experience in knowledge management, artificial intelligence, and semantic technologies. He is the CEO of Semedy AG, a provider of clinical knowledge management and decision support technology. As a Senior Business Consultant, he takes care of global projects in the fields of IT management, digital health, and knowledge management for global corporations in the pharmaceutical, life science, and medical device industries.

New Forms of Creating Value: Platform-Enabled Gig Economy Today and in 2030

Thomas K. Hamann and Stefan Güldenberg

Mountain View, California, US, April 22, 2030
  The announced merger of the two major platforms ECareer and EHire will revolutionize the job market and will make the war for talent obsolete.
  ECareer and EHire have announced that they are planning on joining forces. This was made official in a press conference yesterday afternoon by both CEOs. "Writing a job application is a thing of the past" says Jim Clarke, CEO of EHire. Sandra Kim of ECareer adds "If you have the CVs and a personal network of 2 billion people worldwide and match this with the most powerful talent search algorithm then no company has to worry anymore on missing out on the potential talent they are looking for." Over the last ten years, EHire has worked hard to improve its AI-based matchmaking technology and its highly controversial and opaque personal achievement index (PAI). Thanks to this, EHire was able to establish itself as the leading provider of staffing services for permanent work and flexible work contracts.
  The merger of ECareer and EHire will most likely create the most powerful and most valuable platform company worldwide with an estimated market value of over 10 trillion US dollars based on the enormous human capital of its members. Still, it is questionable if the Federal Trade Commission (FTC) will allow for this mega-merger to go ahead as it will create a potential monopoly in the area of talent search and recruiting, potentially putting other providers out of business. Other critics complain about possible data protection issues. They say that EHire's algorithms proved to be discriminatory against women and minorities or even acted racist as the programmers of the EHire's matchmaking algorithm and PAI have been

T. K. Hamann (✉)
T. K. Hamann Gesellschaft mbH, Munich, Germany
e-mail: thomas.hamann@tkhamann.com

S. Güldenberg
University of Liechtenstein, Vaduz, Liechtenstein
e-mail: stefan.gueldenberg@uni.li

© Springer Nature Switzerland AG 2021
S. Güldenberg et al. (eds.), *Managing Work in the Digital Economy*, Future of Business and Finance, https://doi.org/10.1007/978-3-030-65173-2_6

dominantly white, young, and male. It is also questionable how the members of ECareer will react to this merger. In some European countries, many members have already announced that if the merger goes ahead, they will leave the platform and will continue to manage their personal and career network on one of the leading European providers for social networking. But this comes at a high price as these platforms are very fragmented and have much fewer job opportunities to offer than EHire, the by far most dominant player in the digital matchmaking platform market.

On the contrary, politicians, including the President of the USA, are pushing for this mega-deal in order to ensure the future competitiveness of western companies and the US economy as a whole in comparison to the Chinese. They are continually optimizing their recruiting technologies, which are already integrated into the school system to find future talent and match this with the current job needs and requirements. Since the mid-2020s, China has strengthened its initiative of flexible school education to identify future talent and integrate exam results into the social credit system. "We can only stay ahead if we join forces and make use of our best talent and technology available," said Jeff Bezos, who has lately become one of the most influential economic advisors to the White House.

1   Origins and Development of the Gig Economy

While the term 'gig economy' is fairly new, there has always been a market for freelance, pay-per-job work. In fact, prior to the industrial revolution and the rise of the employee-employer contract, this type of work was the norm. Since then, the security of a steady job and salary has made full-time employment the preferred approach. (Edwards 2018)

The term "gig economy" first came to global attention on the breakfast television newscast "American Morning" broadcasted by the television channel Cable News Network (CNN) on January 14, 2009. The journalist Tina Brown (2009), who was interviewed in this TV broadcast, had written a blog titled "The Gig Economy" 2 days earlier. Moreover, Google Trends shows that in February 2009, the term "gig economy" was for the first time of interest in web searches worldwide. Also, starting in the summer of 2015, one can see a clear trend in an increasing number of search queries on the Internet search engine Google for this keyword. From 2007 onwards, the Great Recession caused by the global banking and economic crisis led to the dissemination of (platform-enabled) gig work (Cable News Network 2009). High rates of youth unemployment also pushed young people towards looking for jobs outside of the traditional labor market. On the employers' side, the economic crisis with the concurrent budget cuts led to an increase in demand for gig workers as a cheaper alternative to full-time employees (de Groen et al. 2018). Furthermore, they come with variable rather than fixed personnel costs.

Defining the Gig Economy Unfortunately, a coherent and generally accepted definition of the term "gig economy" has not yet been established (e.g., Meijerink and Keegan 2019). A gig commonly refers to a single (paid) engagement of a musician or a band for a live performance, especially when it comes to pop/rock or other modern music. Thus, a gig is a single assignment of a relatively short or limited period of time. By analogy, the term "gig economy" refers to a part of the economic system in which requesters (individuals or companies) place single well-defined assignments with providers (mostly individuals or sometimes micro-companies) for a relatively short or limited period of time outside of permanent employment relationships (see also Friedman 2014). Some observers (e.g., Risak 2020) perceive the term "gig economy" as a fighting word used by critics to emphasize the short-term nature of what they see as an "hire-and-fire" economy and thus spread cheap propaganda against the relevant platforms.

Defining Gig Workers There is no reliable data on the number of gig workers in the economy since the renaissance of freelance work in 2009. One reason for this is that the increasing importance of the gig economy is still a relatively new phenomenon and has only been reflected with some delay or even not at all in the regular statistical surveys on the labor market in the various countries. Another reason is that such a poll is very difficult to operationalize because the terms and distinctions used in this context between different forms of work are not (yet) clearly defined, or there is no common understanding of them. For instance, according to a survey conducted by the research and analytics consultancy Edelman Intelligence (2019), "[i]ndividuals who have engaged in supplemental, temporary, project- or contract-based work, within the past 12 months" (p. 4) describe themselves as independent workers, self-employed, freelancers, contractors, small-business owners, on-demand workers, gig workers, or moonlighters (see also Yildirmaz et al. 2020). Nonetheless, "[t]here is a general agreement in the literature that the use of online platforms for managing work has been growing exponentially in the decade following the 2007–2008 financial crisis" (Huws et al. 2017, p. 13). A short-time series for the last 5 years from the study done by Edelman Intelligence (2019) should at least convey an idea of the numerical development of freelancers (which includes gig workers) (Fig. 1).

2   Developing a Typology of the Platform-Enabled Gig Economy

Regrettably, the common and useful criteria for distinguishing the different types of platform-based gig work are not free of overlaps. Hence, a differentiation into mutually exclusive categories is not feasible. Apart from that, many terms are used in connection with the gig economy, some with synonymous meaning, so that not all of them can be considered here.

In mn people

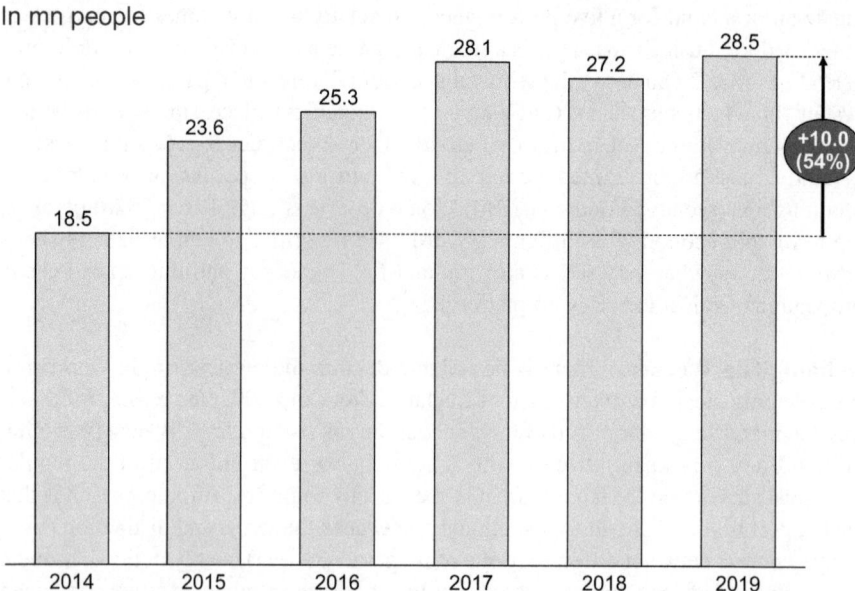

Fig. 1 Number of freelancers in the USA, 2004–2019 (Edelman Intelligence 2019, p. 13)

2.1   Platform Economy and Platform-Enabled Gig Economy in General

For the purpose of temporary engagements, requesters and providers are often brought together by third parties. This bringing together can be done either by simply offering a (virtual) marketplace, allowing requesters to search for providers or vice versa, or by a curated so-called matchmaking process in which the third-party mediator checks the requirements for the tasks to be assigned against the respective qualifications of the providers and assesses their suitability. For both of these mediation variants, the requesters and especially the providers must register with the mediator, facilitating interactions or transactions between requesters and providers on this basis. Industrial economists such as Rochet and Tirole (2003) call a mediator of this type a (two-sided or—if more than two groups are brought together—multi-sided) platform (Baldwin and Woodard 2008; Boudreau and Hagiu 2009). These platforms can be digital, that is, based on digital technology, or non-digital (de Reuver et al. 2018). The part of the economic system where platforms enable interactions or transactions between two or more groups of market participants, in general, is called platform economy. And the part of the gig economy where platforms connect requesters and providers is the platform-enabled gig economy (Meijerink and Keegan 2019), which is also referred to by some (e.g., Rinehart and Gitis 2015) as the online gig economy. Figure 2 provides an overview of the typology of the platform-enabled gig economy as outlined below.

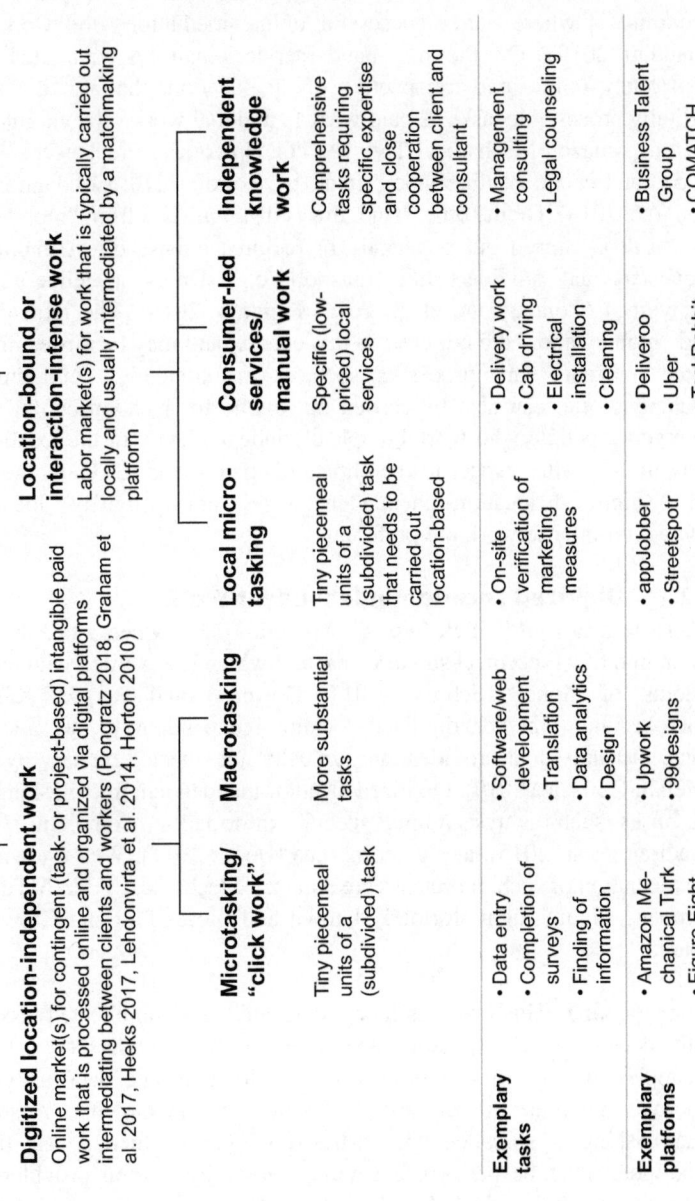

Platform-enabled gig economy

Labor market(s) comprising workers "hired under 'flexible' arrangements, as 'independent contractors' or 'consultants,' [sic] working only to complete a particular task or for a defined time" (Friedman 2014, p. 171)—mediated by platforms

Digitized location-independent work

Online market(s) for contingent (task- or project-based) intangible paid work that is processed online and organized via digital platforms intermediating between clients and workers (Pongratz 2018, Graham et al. 2017, Heeks 2017, Lehdonvirta et al. 2014, Horton 2010)

Location-bound or interaction-intense work

Labor market(s) for work that is typically carried out locally and usually intermediated by a matchmaking platform

	Microtasking/ "click work"	Macrotasking	Local micro-tasking	Consumer-led services/ manual work	Independent knowledge work
	Tiny piecemeal units of a (subdivided) task	More substantial tasks	Tiny piecemeal units of a (subdivided) task that needs to be carried out location-based	Specific (low-priced) local services	Comprehensive tasks requiring specific expertise and close cooperation between client and consultant
Exemplary tasks	• Data entry • Completion of surveys • Finding of information	• Software/web development • Translation • Data analytics • Design	• On-site verification of marketing measures	• Delivery work • Cab driving • Electrical installation • Cleaning	• Management consulting • Legal counseling
Exemplary platforms	• Amazon Mechanical Turk • Figure Eight	• Upwork • 99designs	• appJobber • Streetspotr	• Deliveroo • Uber • TaskRabbit	• Business Talent Group • COMATCH

Fig. 2 Typology of the platform-enabled gig economy (own representation)

2.2 Digitized Location-Independent Versus Location-Bound or Interaction-Intense Work

A conceivable criterion for the further breakdown of the platform-enabled gig economy is where—after successful online mediation—the work is performed (Gandini 2019). On the one hand, services can be contracted and provided completely online and irrespective of the location, that is, "the outsourcing of digitally processible tasks as paid work to a global workforce via Internet platforms such as Amazon Mechanical Turk (AMT), Upwork or Freelancer" (Pongratz 2018, p. 58) and called "online labor" (e.g., by Horton 2010; Condagnone et al. 2016; Pongratz 2018). On the other hand, this is distinguished from "mobile labor", where the work is carried out physically or requires intense direct interaction between requesters and providers like transport (e.g., Uber) or delivery services (e.g., Deliveroo) (Condagnone et al. 2016; Pongratz 2018). The terms "online labor" and "mobile labor" are not clear in this context and may be misleading. Eventually, some relevant work processes such as matchmaking, contracting, invoicing, evaluating, etc. can also be carried out online for location-bound activities. And vice versa, people who work completely independently of the location are particularly mobile with respect to the choice of their worksite. Thus, the terms (almost fully) digitized location-independent work versus (mostly) location-bound or interaction-intense work are preferable.

2.2.1 Digitized Location-Independent Work

Microtasking and "Click Work" Microtasking is when a task is further broken down into tiny piecemeal subtasks, each of which is rewarded with an equally small amount of money (Schmidt 2017; Howcroft and Bergvall-Kåreborn 2019). Microtasking, whether digitized location-independent or, as addressed below, local, the individual providers are typically not selected directly by the requesters (Melián-González 2019). Digitized location-independent microtasking includes simple tasks such as researching specific information, completing questionnaires (Gadiraju et al. 2015), and entering data (Heeks 2017). Well-known platforms for the mediation of such microtasks are Amazon Mechanical Turk (MTurk), the Appen company Figure Eight (formerly known as Dolores Lab and CrowdFlower), and Spare5.

Macrotasking This involves more substantial and complicated tasks, which typically depend on the specific capabilities of the providers (Walsh et al. 2014). Examples of macrotasks are software development and data analytics. Common macrotasking platforms are Fiverr, Freelancer, and Upwork. A special form of macrotasking is so-called contest-based work, in which a task that cannot be subdivided may be performed simultaneously by several providers. In the end, only one result is selected and paid by the respective requester (Horton 2010; Heeks 2017; Schmidt 2017). This variant is mainly used for graphic design, in particular, logo design; well-known, relevant platforms are 99designs (Schmidt 2017) and LogoTurnament.

2.2.2   Location-Bound or Interaction-Intense Work

Local Microtasking This term refers to a microtask that is location-bound but is not carried out at the place of the requester and or does not require a lot of interaction with the requester. A local microtask can be, for example, the taking of specific photos in shops for assortment analysis, control of secondary placements, price recording, etc. Typical platforms for local microtasking are appJobber, Streetspotr, and Field Agent.

Consumer-Led Services and Manual Work Microtasks that are location-bound, carried out at the place of the requester, require intense interaction with, or (active) involvement of the requester fall in this category. Typical examples of such work are delivery work, passenger transportation, housework like cleaning, and skilled crafts work like electrical installation or plumbing. Widely known platforms for the mediation of such tasks are Deliveroo, Uber, and TaskRabbit.

Independent Knowledge Work These are platform-mediated tasks which are comprehensive and typically require specific expertise (so-called knowledge work) and which can only be performed in close cooperation with the respective requester, usually on-site. The addition "independent" indicates that the services are not run by an established provider possessing a strong brand character but by individuals or micro-enterprises. They include, for instance, activities such as management consulting or legal counseling. Better-known platforms in this area are the Business Talent Group (BTG) and COMATCH.

3   Key Characteristics of the Platform-Enabled Gig Economy in 2020

3.1   Importance for Households

The importance of the income generated by gig-economy work for the individuals and their households varies; thus, for just over a quarter of the European gig workers, platform-enabled gig work accounts for 50% or more of their personal income, while for the rest of gig workers their involvement in the gig economy is more a sideline or source of extra income (Fig. 3).

Similar data is also reported for the United Kingdom by Lepanjuuri et al. (2018). In the last 12 months, 9% of gig workers earned more than 90% of their total income from gig work, while 65% of gig workers earned less than 5% of their total income from gig work.

Manyika et al. (2016) from the McKinsey Global Institute likewise distinguish between those who derive their primary income and those who receive a supplementary income from independent work; furthermore, they differentiate between independent workers, who have consciously chosen this working style, and those who have no other choice. This results in four different types of gig workers:

In percent

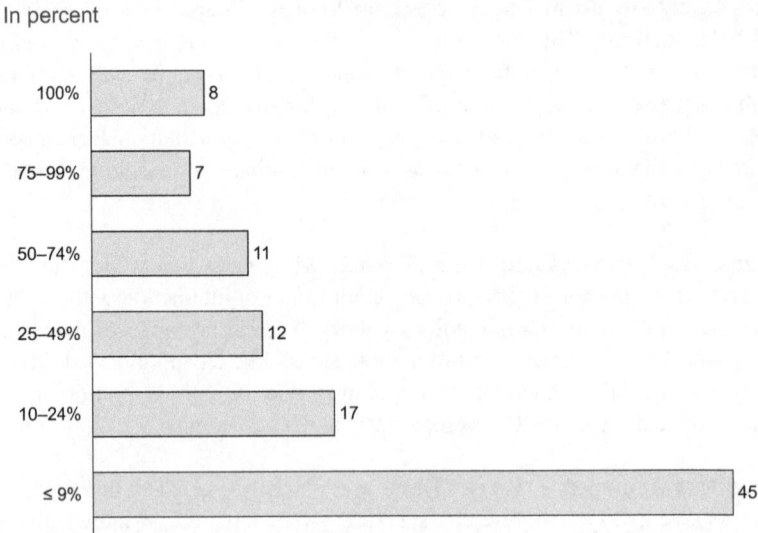

Fig. 3 Earnings from platform-based gig work as a proportion of all personal income in Europe (Italy, Austria, Switzerland, Germany, United Kingdom, the Netherlands, Sweden [in descending order by share of respondents]), 2016/2017 (own computations based on Hertfordshire Business School Crowd Work Survey data published in Huws et al. 2017, p. 21)

- People who receive their primary income from independent work and have actively chosen this working style
- Individuals who derive their primary income from independent work but would prefer traditional employment
- People who supplement their income by choice from independent work
- Persons who supplement their income with independent work, but who would rather not be constrained to take up such additional work

However, based on the data available to them, Manyika et al. (2016) assume that the clear majority of independent workers, 72% in the USA and 68% in the EU-15,[1] are engaged in this kind of work by choice rather than out of necessity. Nonetheless, this means that a substantial proportion of the gig workers are compelled to pursue independent work. For these groups, which accept gig work out of necessity, the possibility of platforms abusing their market power could be particularly problematic, as will be discussed later.

---

[1]Results from UK, Germany, France, Spain, and Sweden scaled up to EU-15.

3.2   Relevance for the Labor Market in General and per Industry Sectors

According to five studies by MBO Partners, Burson-Marsteller, Kelly Services, Freelancers Union, and MGI Survey that draw on different definitions, the proportion of primary and supplemental independent workers of the working-age population in the USA was estimated between 16% and 27% in 2015/2016 (Manyika et al. 2016). When it comes to the primary independent workers only, three studies by Katz & Krueger, BLS, and MGI Survey arrived at shares between 10% and 12%. For the independent platform workers, the estimates by Katz & Krueger, Intuit, JPMorgan Chase Institute, and MGI Survey were up to 4% (Manyika et al. 2016).

A large proportion of gig workers are active in the following industry sectors: professional and business services, construction, and education and health services (Fig. 4). Well-known gig activities are consumer-led services/manual work that have a medium frequency of 6%–7% each—such as leasing assets like apartments via platforms like Airbnb (leisure and hospitality), selling goods via platforms like eBay (retail trade), and providing passenger driving services (transportation and utilities).

In comparison to the US data mentioned in Fig. 4, Broughton et al. (2018) came up with the following proportional distribution of gig workers in the United Kingdom: professional/creative/high-skilled work (36%), office/short online tasks/admin (25%), taxi/transport (24%), physical low-skilled work (12%), physical skilled work (3%).

In percent

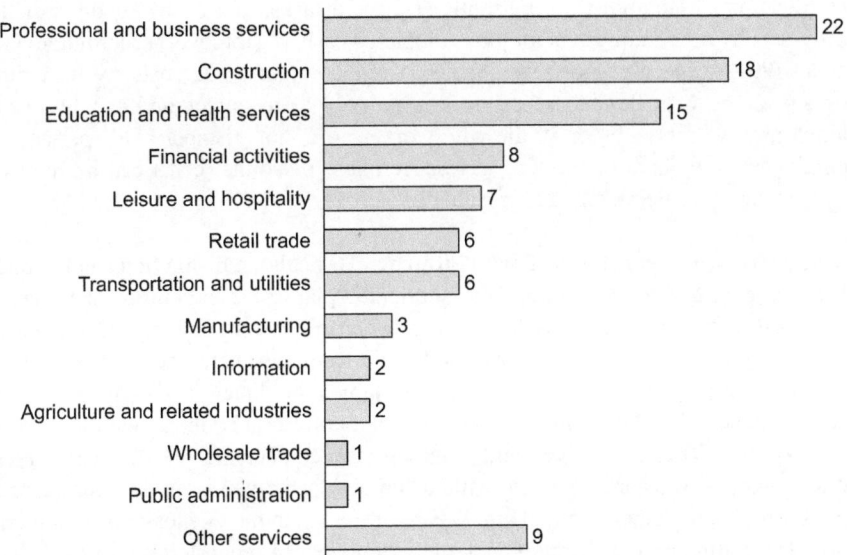

Fig. 4 Distribution of employed workers with alternative work arrangements (independent contractors and on-call workers) by industry sectors in the USA, 2017 (own computations based on the data published by the U.S. Bureau of Labor Statistics 2018, Table 8)

4   Appreciation and Criticism of the Platform-Enabled Gig Economy

4.1   Positive Aspects and Opportunities: Value Creation and Beneficiaries

The platform-enabled gig economy "has the capacity to change the nature of work organization and to provide strategic value to workers, job providers, and intermediary platform owners" (Gol et al. 2019).

Value Creation for Providers For the providers, the intermediary platforms offer a much broader access to potential clients than would be possible exclusively through the respective personal network and thus increase the chances of being awarded a contract. In the case of digitized location-independent work, the geographical scope is also expanded because it avoids barriers such as any necessary work permits and travel costs. Obviously, the gig economy offers more flexibility than a traditional employment relationship, even for those who, as self-employed people, do not want to take care of their own business development or have difficulties with it for whatever reason.

Value Creation for Requesters The mediation platforms offer requesters access to a larger number of suitable potential contractors and thus reduce their search costs. Additionally, they are offered, depending on the platform and their curative activities, a pre-qualification of relevant providers to a certain degree. This can be realized by conducting interviews as part of the registration process, by additional clarification of suitability for currently requested tasks, and by evaluations of the providers by other requesters for jobs completed earlier. Moreover, according to Gol et al. (2019), the gig economy enables a reduction in labor costs by providing organizations with flexible access to a large pool of resources and usually cheap temporary workers. Even if the gig workers are not cheaper than permanent employees, the share of fixed or at least remnant personnel costs can be reduced by making them flexible and terminable on short notice.

Value Creation for Intermediary Platforms Basically, a distinction can be made between peer-to-peer and commercially oriented platforms. In contrast, the former, so-called commons platforms, mediate between requesters and providers free of charge and also allow external parties to benefit from their network, for example, by making the provider profiles publicly available, the latter is clearly aiming at economic benefits. An example of a commons platform is Umbrex, with its derivative Veritux. There, members and externals can contact the registered providers directly and also award contracts without involving the platform. The commercial platforms, on the other hand, claim a share of the value they generate as remuneration. Depending on the billing model, the willingness of requesters and providers to pay means that the value created by the platforms for these players can also be quantified. Platforms have been found to be more efficient than their non-platform competitors, like traditional consulting companies or recruitment agencies; they generate roughly the same revenue with significantly fewer employees because they access resources outside the company and build a business without actually owning nearly as many assets as comparable non-platform companies (Cusumano et al. 2019).

4.2   Disadvantages and Risks

Basically, (profit-oriented) platforms tend to shift most of the costs, risks, and responsibilities to the other parties. They usually offer only a virtual service such as an app or a website. They hence can grow exponentially without having to bear proportionally increasing labor costs or production resources (Schmidt 2017). Research commissioned by the European Union (Duch-Brown 2017) and the International Labour Organization (Berg et al. 2018) provides evidence of unfair practices by online platforms towards business users. The European Commission (2018, pp. 9, 32–33), which pursues the goal of "a fair, trusting and innovation-driven ecosystem around online platforms [. . .], in which business traders have the necessary safeguards to prevent harm from unfair trading practices, general lack of redress, and regulatory fragmentation [. . .]" to fully exploit the potential of the online platform economy, has adopted findings of de Bas et al. (2017) and developed them further, by addressing the key problems driven by "imbalanced bargaining power" and the "dependency of businesses on online platforms". These research results were reflected with own ethnographic experiences, and, on that basis, critical propositions on digital gig economy platforms were developed.

Lack of Transparency Only a minority of digital matchmaking platforms follow a fully open and transparent approach about their terms and conditions; the platforms tend to fog up the asymmetric terms and conditions.

Delisting and Suspension of Accounts There is a clear imbalance of (market) power between digital matchmaking platforms and platform workers. In case of conflict, the platforms tend to fully exploit their power over platform workers.

Search and Ranking The quality of matching, which should be the core competency, varies significantly between digital matchmaking platforms. Search costs are partially externalized to the crowd of platform workers. Digital matchmaking platforms tend to use rankings and feedback not as objective information towards the client but as a means of pressure on platform workers.

Discrimination and Favoring of Own Services Digital matchmaking platforms tend to follow aggressively a "grow-fast imperative" to get on the safe side of a probable future market consolidation (so-called winner takes it all phenomenon) at the cost of the individual platform worker. In order to maintain or expand their market position accordingly, platforms typically offer contracts with strict anti-circumvention clauses that do not allow the platform worker to work for a (potential) client organization or company group to that the platform worker was introduced by the platform without involving the platform, usually for a period of 18–36 months. Platform workers are usually subject to such a ban on circumvention even in cases when they—for various possible reasons—forward their own project requests to platforms. Furthermore, digital matchmaking platforms tend to make use of their workers' expertise and working power free of charge, for example, for the preparation of pitch presentations in situations where the platforms compete against traditional consultancies and need more substantial content rather than candidate profiles or when it comes to press inquiries to the platform, in order to impose opportunity and transaction costs towards the platform workers but do not allow them to mention the names or brands of their own legal entities.

Lack of Access to Data and Breaches of Data Security When it comes to feedback, the digital matchmaking platforms are hardly concerned about personal and professional development. Consequently, the data behind worker ratings are frequently not made transparent to the platform worker (Rahman 2020), which was pointed out in the fictitious release for ECareer and EHire in the introduction to this chapter. Some platforms do not push the clients for (qualitative) feedback or discuss that with the platform worker for purposes of professional development. Digital matchmaking platforms have less interest in securing important organizational data for the platform worker and take personal data protection rights less seriously than demanded from their platform workers. For instance, the data stored in the log in area of platforms that display historical data like applications to the user are not always complete. In addition, they let platform workers access to the personal profiles or résumés of other platform workers, for example, when forwarding proposal documents.

Pricing Digital matchmaking platforms prefer to refrain from business opportunities to enforce asymmetric commissions with platform workers. Moreover, they intentionally intensify price competition as part of their business model. This means lowering earning possibilities for highly qualified platform workers and increasing the price pressure for the traditional consulting industry.

Termination Risk, Especially on Short Notice and Occurring Opportunity Cost Platforms strive for the entrepreneurial risks to be borne as far as possible by the platform workers. At the same time, the opposing opportunities are claimed for the platform. The platforms insist on the adherence to given promises of availability. On the other hand, a project or a task can usually be withdrawn without compensation from the platform worker by the platform or client at short notice. Platform workers have to bear the opportunity costs for any other, not accepted projects themselves.

Lack of Effective Redress Digital matchmaking platforms deliberately prohibit effective internal redress mechanisms to protect their own interest and shift the business risks towards platform workers. Reasonable out-of-court external redress mechanisms hardly exist. Digital matchmaking platforms intentionally take advantage of the limited use of judicial remedies on the side of the platform worker.

5   The Platform-Enabled Gig Economy in 2030

Possible scenarios for the future development of the platform-enabled gig economy up to 2030 are challenging to make. This is partly due to the still fuzzy database on its current state and the very open question of future state regulation of the sector. Therefore, in the following part, we only describe trends that are already visible or are, in our opinion, very likely to occur in the future.

Likely Consolidation of the Platform Landscape Even though the term "gig economy" appeared for the first time in 2009, the concept of labor-intermediating Internet platforms is actually older. Its emergence reaches back to the so-called dot-com boom at the end of the 1990s. As evidence one only has to look at Guru, the first platform for the intermediation of management consulting services (independent knowledge work) launched in the USA in 1998. As Fig. 5 shows, the absolute increase in such platforms was strongest from 2014 to 2016, from 21 to 37 platforms. According to Haslam et al. (2018) as well as Mazareanu (2020), it is not surprising

Number of platforms

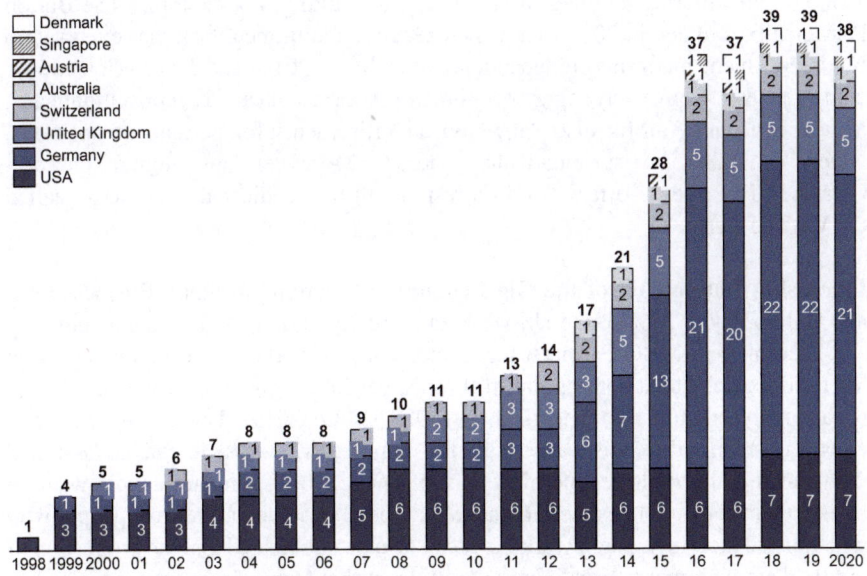

Fig. 5 Numerical development of platforms for the intermediation of management consulting services, 1998–2020 (own research)

that these platforms were established in the largest markets for consulting services in terms of total revenue, that is, the USA, the United Kingdom, Australia, and the German-speaking countries Germany, Austria, and Switzerland.

Platforms typically scale up their business by expanding rapidly into other countries. This growth is largely due to the fact that there are hardly any market-entry barriers for such platforms and that they can be brought to market quickly and easily as me-too solutions. It is very questionable whether all these platforms will be successful in the long run. The first consolidations of the platform landscape have already taken place. The platforms Elance and oDesk, founded in 1999 and 2003, respectively, merged in 2013 to form Upwork. In 2017, only 2 years after its foundation, the platform projectchamps was integrated into the more recently established platform consultingheads (founded in 2016). Furthermore, the platform KLAITON, founded in 2015, was acquired by the Haufe Group and renamed Haufe Advisory in 2018. In 2019, the Hillgate platform, established in 2014, joined the Business Talent Group and became its European branch. The platform Zentaur, founded in 2015, was put up for sale in 2019 and finally shut down in the spring of 2020. Significant consolidation of the platform landscape can be expected in the long term.

Convergence of the Operations of the Digital Labor Platforms and Those of Traditional Recruitment Agencies This convergence could be one of the steps towards the consolidation mentioned above. It involves both sides, that is, on the one hand traditional recruitment agencies are expanding their business to include digital mediation platforms, and on the other hand, the digital platforms of the gig economy are entering the field of classic HR consulting. For example, The Barton Partnership, founded in 2007 as a niche executive recruitment firm, has even set up two recruitment platforms: Independent Consulting (2014) and HourlyConsulting. com (2018). Conversely, gig economy platforms such as consultingheads, Movemeon, and TalMix also show job advertisements for permanent positions, which can also be systematically filtered. Moreover, the digital platform COMATCH even offers a correspondingly dedicated service called COMATCHperm.

Increasing Importance of the Gig Economy According to Smart Business Labs and Gallup, about 36% of the US workers currently participate in the gig economy and according to MBO Partners, the number of US workers who participate or at least did participate at some point in their career in the gig economy, even if only occasionally, should be up to 52% by 2023 (Mitic 2019). Due to the currently emerging economic crisis caused by the Sars-CoV-2 virus, it can be assumed that—analogous to the economic crisis of 2008/2009—companies will want to reduce their personnel costs or at least make these variable and release people who will then try their luck as gig workers. It can also be anticipated that the proportion of gig workers who make their living entirely from this form of work will increase.

Increasing Control and Regulation of the Gig Economy for the Benefit of Gig Workers Analogous to the Protection of Permanent Employees in Labor Law As already described, gig work is associated with disadvantages and risks, especially for the providers. In order to reduce these, it is very likely that more appropriate measures will be taken in the future. These could be regulatory interventions on the part of the state responsible. For example, "California's new measure requiring the state's gig workforce to be treated as conventional employees is only the latest sign of the limits of this approach" (Irwin 2019). Another possible development towards avoiding the negative aspects of the gig economy could be the promotion of more peer-to-peer oriented platforms with elements of decentralized platform governance. This is because such platforms are less prone to the concentration of power, which can then be misused (Gol et al. 2019).

Key Insights Regarding the Platform-Enabled Gig Economy in 2030

- The Great Recession, which followed the global banking and economic crisis from 2007 onwards has led to a strong dissemination of the platform-enabled gig economy. High youth unemployment has forced young people to look for jobs outside of the traditional labor market. Also, on the client side, the economic crisis with the concurrent budget cuts led to an increase in demand for gig work as a cheaper alternative, which comes with variable rather than fixed personnel costs.

- This chapter develops a typology for the platform-enabled gig economy, including all types of gig work reaching from location-independent microtasking towards location-bound and interaction-intensive knowledge work. Leaders should be very aware of these different types of gig works as they include different tasks to accomplish, different kinds of workers, and therefore have to be managed with a situational leadership approach to achieve sustainable results.

- Besides the advantages of the gig economy by creating strategic value to workers, job providers, and intermediary platform owners, there are also some already visible disadvantages with which we have to deal in a growing gig economy. The most important among them is that profit-oriented platforms tend to shift most of the costs, risks, and responsibilities to the other parties. They very often have a lack of transparency in their terms and conditions, and there is a clear imbalance of (market) power between digital matchmaking platforms and platform workers. This may lead to platforms tending to exploit their power over platform workers in case of conflict, and they can intentionally take advantage of the limited use of judicial remedies on the side of the platform workers.

- In order to reduce the disadvantages of the gig economy, more appropriate measures will likely be taken by 2030. These could be, for instance, regulatory interventions on the part of the responsible governing bodies.

(continued)

Another possible development towards avoiding the negative aspects of the gig economy could be promoting more peer-to-peer-oriented platforms with elements of decentralized platform governance. Such platforms are less prone to the concentration of power, which can then be misused.

References

Baldwin, C. Y., & Woodard, C. J. (2008). *The architecture of platforms: A unified view*. Working Paper. Harvard Business School. Accessed March 31, 2020, from https://www.hbs.edu/faculty/Publication%20Files/09-034_149607b7-2b95-4316-b4b6-1df66dd34e83.pdf

Berg, J., Furrer, M., Harmon, E., Rani, U., & Silberman, M. S. (2018). *Digital labour platforms and the future of work: Towards decent work in the online world*. Geneva, Switzerland: International Labour Organization. Accessed September 04, 2020, from https://www.ilo.org/wcmsp5/groups/public/%2D%2D-dgreports/%2D%2D-dcomm/%2D%2D-publ/documents/publication/wcms_645337.pdf

Boudreau, K. J., & Hagiu, A. (2009). Platform rules: Multi-sided platforms as regulators. In A. Gawer (Ed.), *Platforms, markets and innovation* (pp. 163–191). Cheltenham, UK: Edward Elgar.

Broughton, A., Gloster R., Marvell, R., Green, M., Langley, J., & Martin, A. (2018). *The experiences of individuals in the gig economy*. Report. HM Government, UK. Accessed April 24, 2020, from https://assets.publishing.service.gov.uk/government/uploads/system/uploads/attachment_data/file/679987/171107_The_experiences_of_those_in_the_gig_economy.pdf

Brown, T. (2009). The gig economy. Blog post. *The Daily Beast*. Accessed April 02, 2020, from https://www.thedailybeast.com/the-gig-economy

Cable News Network. (2009). *American morning: Obama to issue veto threat on bailout; Clinton shows broad knowledge in confirmation hearing; fugitive pilot caught; lawmakers debate on remaining balance of bailout; Osama bin Laden releases videotape calls for holy war*. Transcript of the newscast of 14 January 2009. Accessed April 02, 2020, from http://edition.cnn.com/TRANSCRIPTS/0901/14/ltm.01.html

Condagnone, C., Abadie, F., & Biagi, F. 2016. *The future of work in the "sharing economy": Market efficiency and equitable opportunities or unfair precarisation?* JRC Science for Policy Report. Institute for Prospective Technological Studies. Seville, Spain: European Commission, Joint Research Centre.

Cusumano, M. E., Gawer, A., & Yoffie, D. B. (2019). How digital platforms have become double-edged swords. *MIT Sloan Management Review, 60*(4), 1–7.

de Bas, P., et al. (2017). *Business-to-business relations in the online platform environment*. Final Report. European Commission, Brussels, Belgium: Directorate-General for Internal Market, Industry, Entrepreneurship and SMEs.

de Groen, W. P., Kilhoffer, Z., Lenaerts, K., & Mandl, I. (2018). *Employment and working conditions of selected types of platform work*. Report. European Foundation for the Improvement of Living and Working Conditions (Eurofound). Luxembourg: Publications Office of the European Union.

de Reuver, M., Sørensen, C., & Basole, R. C. (2018). The digital platform: A research agenda. *Journal of Information Technology, 33*(2), 124–135.

Duch-Brown, N. (2017*). Platforms to business relations in online platform ecosystems*. JRC Technical Reports, JRC Digital Economy Working Paper 2017-07. Seville, Spain: European Commission, Joint Research Centre.

Edelman Intelligence. (2019). *Freelancing in America: 2019*. Presentation. Accessed April 03, 2020, from https://www.slideshare.net/upwork/freelancing-in-america-2019/1

Edwards, N. (2018). The gig economy: The good, the bad and the future. Blog post. *People First*, MHR International. Accessed April 02, 2020, from https://people-first.com/blog/the-gig-economy-the-good-the-bad-and-the-future/

European Commission. (2018). *Impact assessment accompanying the document 'proposal for a regulation of the European Parliament and of the council of promoting fairness and transparency for business users of online intermediation services'*. Commission staff working document. Brussels, Belgium: European Commission.

Friedman, G. (2014). Workers without employers: Shadow corporations and the rise of the gig economy. *Review of Keynesian Economics, 2*(2), 171–188.

Gadiraju, U., Demartini, G., Kawase, R., & Dietze, S. (2015). Human beyond the machine: Challenges and opportunities of microtask crowdsourcing. *IEEE Intelligent Systems, 30*(4), 81–85.

Gandini, A. (2019). Labour process theory and the gig economy. *Human Relations, 72*(6), 1039–1056.

Gol, E. S., Stein, M.-K., & Avital, M. (2019). Crowdwork platform governance toward organizational value creation. *Journal of Strategic Information Systems, 28*(2), 175–195.

Graham, M., Lehdonvirta, V., Wood, A., Barnard, H., Hjorth, I., & Simon, D. P. (2017). *The risks and rewards of online gig work at the global margins*. Report. University of Oxford, Oxford, UK: Oxford Internet Institute.

Haslam, S., Bodenstein, R., & Abdel-Jaber, T. (2018). *Towards the consulting readiness index*. The International Council of Management Consulting Institutes. Accessed April 28, 2020, from https://www.cmc-global.org/sites/default/files/public/consulting_readiness_index_nov_2018_v8.1.pdf

Heeks, R. (2017). *Decent work and the digital gig economy: A developing country perspective on employment impacts and standards in online outsourcing, crowdwork etc*. Working Paper No. 71. University of Manchester, Manchester, UK: Centre for Development Informatics.

Horton, J. J. (2010). Online labor markets. In A. Saberi (Ed.), *Internet and network economics* (pp. 515–522). Berlin, Germany: Springer.

Howcroft, D., & Bergvall-Kåreborn, B. (2019). A typology of crowdwork platforms. *Work, Employment and Society, 33*(1), 21–28.

Huws, U., Spencer, N. H., Syrdal, D. S., & Holts, K. (2017). *Work in the European gig economy: Research results from the UK, Sweden, Germany, Austria, the Netherlands, Switzerland and Italy*. Report. Foundation for European Progressive Studies, Uni Europa and Hertfordshire Business School. Accessed April 17, 2020, from https://uhra.herts.ac.uk/bitstream/handle/2299/19922/Huws_U._Spencer_N.H._Syrdal_D.S._Holt_K._2017_.pdf?sequence=2

Irwin, N. (2019). Maybe we're not all going to be gig economy workers after all. *The New York Times*. Accessed April 29, 2020, from https://www.nytimes.com/2019/09/15/upshot/gig-economy-limits-labor-market-uber-california.html

Lehdonvirta, V., Barnard, H., Graham M., & Hjorth, I. (2014, September 25–26). *Online labour markets: Levelling the playing field for international service markets?* In Paper presented at IPP2014: Crowdsourcing for politics and policy, University of Oxford, Oxford, UK: Oxford Internet Institute.

Lepanjuuri, K., Wishart, R., & Cornick, P. (2018). *The characteristics of those in the gig economy*. Report. Department for Business, Energy & Industrial Strategy, UK. Accessed April 24, 2020, from https://assets.publishing.service.gov.uk/government/uploads/system/uploads/attachment_data/file/687553/The_characteristics_of_those_in_the_gig_economy.pdf

Manyika, J., Lund, S., Bughin, J., Robinson, K., Mischke, J., & Mahajan, D. (2016). *Independent work: Choice, necessity, and the gig economy*. Report. McKinsey Global Institute. New York, NY: McKinsey & Company.

Mazareanu, E. (2020). Size of the global management consulting market in 2019, by country. *Statista*. Accessed April 28, 2020, from https://www.statista.com/statistics/1065188/management-consulting-market-size-country/#statisticContainer

Meijerink, J., & Keegan, A. E. (2019). Conceptualizing human resource management in the gig economy: Toward a platform ecosystem perspective. *Journal of Managerial Psychology, 34*(4), 214–232.

Melián-González, S. (2019). *The impact of digital technology on work.* SSRN's eLibrary. Accessed April 16, 2020, from https://papers.ssrn.com/sol3/papers.cfm?abstract_id=3353258

Mitic, I. (2019). Gig economy statistics: The new normal in the workplace. *Fortunly.* Accessed April 28, 2020, from https://fortunly.com/statistics/gig-economy-statistics#gref

Pongratz, H. J. (2018). Of crowds and talents: Discursive constructions of global online labour. *New Technology, Work and Employment, 33*(1), 58–73.

Rahman, H. (2020, July 02–04). *Invisible cages: How opaque control tactics influence worker behavior.* In Presented paper at the 36th EGOS Colloquium, Digitalization and artificial intelligence: Reshaping professional service firms, professions, and expert work (sub-theme 08), Hamburg, Germany (virtual conference).

Rinehart, W., & Gitis, B. (2015). Independent contractors and the emerging gig economy. Research Post. *American Action Forum.* Accessed April 02, 2020, from https://www.americanactionforum.org/research/independent-contractors-and-the-emerging-gig-economy/

Risak, M. (2020, January 14). *Personal phone call with Thomas K. Hamann.*

Rochet, J.-C., & Tirole, J. (2003). Platform competition in two-sided markets. *Journal of the European Economic Association, 1*(4), 990–1029.

Schmidt, F. A. (2017). *Digital labour markets in the platform economy: Mapping the political challenges of crowd work and gig work.* Report. Friedrich-Ebert-Stiftung. Bonn, Germany: Division for Economic and Social Policy.

U.S. Bureau of Labor Statistics. (2018). Contingent and alternative employment arrangements. *News Release.* Accessed April 20, 2020, from https://www.bls.gov/news.release/pdf/conemp.pdf

Walsh, B., Maiers, C., Nally, G., Boggs, J., & Praxis Program Team. (2014). Crowdsourcing individual interpretations: Between microtasking and macrotasking. *Literary and Linguistic Computing, 29*(3), 379–386.

Yildirmaz, A., Goldar, M., & Klein, S. (2020). *Illuminating the shadow workforce: Insights into the gig workforce in businesses.* Report. ADP Research Institute, Roseland, NJ: ADP.

Thomas K. Hamann is the Executive Director of the top-management consultancy T. K. Hamann. Thomas is a licentiatus oeconomiae (lic. oec. HSG) and holds a doctoral degree from the University of St. Gallen, Switzerland. In addition to his advisory services for various companies, Thomas conducts scientific research and lectures at various business schools. He focuses on strategic management, including business war-gaming, sales and marketing, leadership and organization, and operational issues. Before founding his own consulting firm, he worked for various top-tier consultancies as well as in the Department of Strategy and Corporate Development at Porsche.

Stefan Güldenberg is a pioneer and leading expert on the future of work, digital strategies, sustainable leadership, and knowledge management. He is a university professor, platform founder, strategy consultant, executive coach, and knowledge entrepreneur. He studied Business Mathematics, Philosophy, and English at the University of Ulm, then received his doctorate and habilitation at the Vienna University of Economics and Business. Stefan has 25 years of experience in research, knowledge transfer, and practice. He conducts research on and supports the development of strategy and transformation processes. Stays abroad led him, among others, to Harvard University, the Massachusetts Institute of Technology (MIT), and the National University of Singapore. He is the current Vice President Practice of the European Academy of Management (EURAM) and President of the New Club of Paris, a think tank and agenda-setter for the knowledge economy.

Working in 2030: Heaven or Hell?

Why Regulation, Standards, and Workers' Representation Will Still Matter

Martin Gruber-Risak

> Although there is a general impression, which is fostered by official academic and journalistic opinion, that all of this is happening because of the rise of scientific technology and development of machinery, this process of degradation of work is not really dependent upon technology at all (H. Braverman, Labour and Monopoly Capital—*The Degradation of Work in the Twentieth Century* (1974), 1998, p. 319).

Although the quote above refers to technical developments during the course of what we now consider the second and the third industrial revolution in the nineteenth and twentieth centuries, it also applies to the fourth industrial revolution that is unfolding now and that again fundamentally changes the way we organize work. And again, it is not clear which direction these developments will take. Therefore, this chapter starts out with two scenarios of how working might look in 2030. From the viewpoint of those delivering the work, their working and living conditions can change for the better or the worse now. For the sake of this argument, the scenarios will be called "Heaven 2030" and "Hell 2030," although I choose not to exaggerate too much but try to stay rather realistic.

Heaven 2030	Hell 2030
In the coming decade, digital automation will displace many manufacturing jobs worldwide but, at the same time, will generate many more—and not just new ones: better ones, too. By 2030, artificial intelligence will most likely	As in 2030, workers can work from home and freely choose and manage their working hours as well as their course of work. They now operate autonomously as hyper-flexible one-person-cost units. Because they are self-

(continued)

The author indebted to Hanna Palmanshofer for discussing and drafting the Heaven and Hell 2030 scenarios as well as to Juan Chacaltana and Maria Prieto (ILO) whose valuable inputs were included in subchapters 6–8.

M. Gruber-Risak (✉)
Department of Labour Law and Law of Social Security, Vienna University, Vienna, Austria
e-mail: martin.gruber-risak@univie.ac.at

© Springer Nature Switzerland AG 2021
S. Güldenberg et al. (eds.), *Managing Work in the Digital Economy*, Future of Business and Finance, https://doi.org/10.1007/978-3-030-65173-2_7

replace *tasks*, not jobs, and robots will, for the most part, work collaboratively with humans. Workers will depart from having to do "one single task every day, all day" to more strategic roles that require more critical thinking. Robots instead will perform those standardized, repetitive, mechanized tasks—those monotonous and dehumanizing tasks that pursuant to Karl Marx lead to labor alienation. At the same time, the unlikely-to-be-automated jobs will gain in importance. These are, on the one hand, occupations that require human interaction and critical, empathetic thinking, like a social worker or a school teacher. On the other hand, these are jobs that resist standardization as a whole and, therefore, cannot be easily automated, like professional cleaning. While cleaning *tasks* can surely be automated—and incidentally lift some weight off the shoulders of a cleaner—the cleaning process itself requires strategic thinking and a comprehensive understanding of the process. Thus, jobs that for a long time have been underpaid and underestimated, as well as taken for granted, will be recognized as essential and consequently will be respected and valued in society. This will result in better wages and a higher social status.

But the automation of work just paints a part of the general picture. Overall, jobs in 2030 will be more autonomous, self-determined, flexible, and creative. Because of the stay-at-home policies worldwide during the coronavirus pandemic, companies discovered that remote working is not only possible but also a plausible alternative way of organizing work that benefits both the employer and the employee. Flexible time management leads to more efficiency that results in greater productivity. With that comes more revenue, which ultimately leads to fewer working hours for better wages for employees and greater profits for employers who can, at the same time, easily assume more social responsibility.

determined and not subject to orders concerning their work-related behavior, they do not need protective labor and employment legislation anymore. Everybody is their own boss and responsible only for themselves. Self-employment means being self-dependent, choosing your work equipment, working place, and working hours, as well as your insurance policies. Therefore, companies will successfully rid themselves of labor-law provisions and shift both responsibility and risk to workers. Unemployment benefits are hard to come by because it is widely believed that every cent spent on an unemployed person reduces the incentive to work and encourages a lifestyle of social parasitism.

And finally, not depending on society to help you out is what defines your freedom. Paid sick leave? No need, because you're free to insure yourself (or not). Moreover, if you can work from home, you might as well work from your bed. Mandatory occupational accident risk insurance? You choose your work equipment and workplace, which is why you are responsible for work-related accidents yourself.

Because of the automation of labor, millions of unskilled manual workers will lose their jobs. Today's lower-income households will slide directly into poverty, with no reliable safety net to catch the fall. Masses of unemployed workers with no means lead to a severe loss of purchasing power and demand. This is followed by a decrease in productivity and an increase of prices, which ends in reducing the purchasing power even further, leading to a vicious cycle that will eventually be followed by a new great depression and an increase in inequality.

1   The Starting Point: Two Views on Flexibility

All developments in the world of work since the 1980s and 1990s, from both employers and employees' perspective, are targeted toward increased flexibility. This was made possible by deregulation and widening the spaces in which both parties maneuver. Whether they both benefit from this and to what extent is a yet unanswered question. The outcome though will be the result of a struggle as both parties to the employment relationship have different perspectives on what this increased flexibility might mean for them.

For workers, flexibility means increased autonomy, i.e., to decide where, when, how much, and what work to do as well as how to organize it. This is not actually a new aim but one that is as old as the critical debates about capitalism and its effect on the individual. This is well mirrored in one of the best-known quotes of Karl Marx in *The German Ideology* (1845/1846): "For as soon as the distribution of labour comes into being, each man has a particular, exclusive sphere of activity, which is forced upon him and from which he cannot escape. He is a hunter, a fisherman, a herdsman, or a critical critic, and must remain so if he does not want to lose his means of livelihood; while in communist society, where nobody has one exclusive sphere of activity but each can become accomplished in any branch he wishes, society regulates the general production and thus makes it possible for me to do one thing today and another tomorrow, to hunt in the morning, fish in the afternoon, rear cattle in the evening, criticize after dinner, just as I have in mind, without ever becoming hunter, fisherman, herdsman or critic. This fixation of social activity, this consolidation of what we ourselves produce into an objective power above us, growing out of our control, thwarting our expectations, bringing to naught our calculations, is one of the chief factors in historical development up till now." In this view, technical progress is organized in an empowering way, making it possible for all individuals to lead an autonomous life and enjoy a maximum amount of freedom. The vision, therefore, is to spread the benefits of a change in the way work is organized as widely and as evenly as possible.

This is not that different from the vision J. M. Keynes (1930) lays out in his famous essay "Economic Possibilities for our Grandchildren" on what working and living might look in 2030 due to technological change: "I draw the conclusion that, assuming no important wars and no important increase in population, the economic problem may be solved, or be at least within sight of solution, within a hundred years. This means that the economic problem is not—if we look into the future—the permanent problem of the human race. Why, you may ask, is this so startling? It is startling because—if, instead of looking into the future, we look into the past—we find that the economic problem, the struggle for subsistence, always has been hitherto the primary, most pressing problem of the human race—not only of the human race, but of the whole of the biological kingdom from the beginnings of life in its most primitive forms. Thus we have been expressly evolved by nature—with all our impulses and deepest instincts—for the purpose of solving the economic problem. If the economic problem is solved, mankind will be deprived of its traditional purpose. Will this be a benefit? If one believes at all in the real values of life, the prospect at least opens up the possibility of benefit."

But increased autonomy for all is not an inevitable consequence of technological progress though, as employers often—more or less explicit—have another view on flexibility. For them, this is less about increased employee autonomy but about adjusting working hours, as well as the course of work, or even the number of workers to business needs and to avoid unproductive times. The aim is to "cut the slack" and to lower the costs of labor. The fruits of technological change that help to organize work more efficiently, therefore, shall not be distributed that evenly but mostly left with the employer. Following this approach, increased flexibility may also mean less security for workers, more competition between them, and a race to the bottom concerning wages and working conditions.

2   Is Everything Really that New?

If we look at the possible future of work and the two scenarios above, one often finds oneself asking what is actually new and what are just old issues over again—of course, painted in bright colors and worded in a fancy new language. In a situation like this, it very much helps to read some of the classics like Harry Braverman and his seminal book *Labour and Monopoly Capital* (1974) about the effects the first two industrial revolutions had on who controls the labor process. Building on Marx, Braverman, in his harsh critique, especially on the Taylorist mode of production, argues that the use of monopoly power over knowledge to control each step of the labor process and its mode of execution led to power shifts within the workplace. And this had negative effects on the quality of work, especially on the autonomy of the employees, the degradation of work in the twentieth century as Braverman calls it in the subtitle of the book. But, and here comes the positive twist, this is not the automatic effect of the technological development but of what people made of it. Braverman condenses this idea in a speech that is included in an annex to the 25th-anniversary edition of the book and the quote at the beginning of this chapter is taken from this. Pointedly, it argues that neither heaven nor hell is the automatic result of technological changes but that the direction the future of work will take will be the result of decisions people make at different levels, whether in the workplaces, in parliaments and administration in the different national states, on the EU level and globally. And not everything has to be invented from scratch. We can build on what generations before us have developed to deal with the challenges that the first waves of industrialization presented us with.

3   Enter Labour Law and Collective Bargaining

One of the answers found then was the regulation of work and the development of collective bargaining based on the finding that individual contracts only will not lead to satisfactory results for the many and will only benefit the few. Therefore, to use the language in the title of this chapter, the approach was to look at the possible hell and try to divert it as much toward heaven as possible. This is very much the approach labor law has: It deals with what is called the "labor problem"—the inherent imperfections and vulnerabilities in employment relationships, i.e., the potential that work can be hell and how we might make it a little bit more like heaven on earth by way of regulation and institutions.

In a market-based economy, we, of course, have to ask for the justification of such regulatory intervention. The mainstream understanding of our economic model in Europe is that we usually trust the market to organize the relationships of its participants by way of a contract to reach outcomes that benefit us all. But when it comes to organizing work, we have realized that the market approach does not function that well because of at least two factors: the subordination and the dependency of the worker.

- *Subordination*, meaning that those workers have, in a way, sold their freedom to a certain extent—usually for a certain number of hours of the day they have subjected themselves to orders of their employers. They can, therefore, tell them what to do during that time. This way of exerting authority over another person not only restricts the autonomy of the workers but also leads to democratic deficits.
- The second factor, *dependency*, is usually understood as an economic dependency, which means the dependency on the income from the work to sustain oneself due to the lack of other sources of income. This leads to unequal bargaining powers and often to low levels of pay and other unfair working conditions. Some have an even broader understanding of the notion of dependency, also taking into account the importance of work for fulfilling social and psychological needs making employees even more vulnerable and dependent on their employment relationships.

This is nothing new, and in the past, we have found arrangements and compromises that made work, if not heaven, at least bearable to some extent: unions and collective bargaining, codetermination at the workplace and company level, and—last but not least—protective labor laws regulating among other issues minimum wages, working time restrictions, antidiscrimination legislation, and protection against dismissal.

If we now look at the changes in the labor markets—or, in other words, at the future of work—we have to ask ourselves if these strategies of the past are still fit for purpose in the future. In a way, they still are because the mode of production has not changed so much that the two factors, subordination and dependency, do not play a role anymore. Regardless of all narratives about disruption and business models that allegedly do not fit into existing regulations, they are still prevalent but—and this is the change—may look differently now.

But let's ask ourselves briefly what is actually happening. Globalization, technological developments, demographic change, and climate change, as well as the change of personal values like individualization, all alter the way we are working today, and they will do so in the future.

4   And Again: Flexibility

There seems to be a need for increased flexibility by both employers and employees. It seems that nobody wants a classic "nine to five" office job anymore. Everybody is looking for a flexible work schedule but for different and often conflicting reasons: a better work-life-balance and reconciliation of work and family life on the one hand and, on the other, a reduction of idle times and costs for extra work. Before this background, we see the emergence of new forms of employment across Europe and also globally. On the one hand side, these new forms have transformed the traditional one-to-one relationship between employer and employee, and on the other, they are characterized by unconventional work patterns and places of work or by the irregular provision of work. To name but a few; employee or job sharing, ICT-based mobile work, voucher-based work and platform work (Eurofound, New forms of employment, 2015a). These examples give a good impression of the present dynamics of the labour markets and the contractual parties' as well as policymakers' creativity to fulfill the need for the increased flexibility of both employers and employees. And usually, they only work because of the availability of new technologies like smartphones, cloud technology, and big data.

This leads us to the technical side of the developments: Here, the concept of the fourth industrial revolution and the digital transformation of work comes in. Like the revolutions that preceded it, the so-called "Fourth Industrial Revolution" has the potential to raise global income levels and improve the quality of life for populations around the world. Technology has made new products and services possible that increase the efficiency and pleasure of our personal lives. Following this line of argument, technological innovation may lead to a supply-side miracle, with long-term gains in efficiency and productivity. Transportation and communication costs will drop, logistics and global supply chains will become more effective, and the cost of trade will diminish. All of this will open new markets and drive economic growth. This sounds like a globalized consumers' heaven.

But at the same time, this digital revolution—and this is where the hell perspective comes in—could yield greater inequality and lead to the degradation of the quality of work. This may be particularly true for the potential of technology to disrupt labor markets. As automation substitutes labor across the entire economy, the net displacement of workers by machines might exacerbate the gap between the returns to capital and the returns to labor. On the other hand, it is also possible that the displacement of workers by technology will, on the whole, result in a net increase in safe and rewarding jobs.

The influential green paper *"Arbeiten 4.0"* (Working 4.0) by the German Ministry of Labour and Social Affairs, published in 2015, names the following possible areas of conflict: labor market effects, digital platforms, big data, industry 4.0, flexible working—beyond a culture of employee presence—and finally changes in the company organization. Here, all the topics that are touched upon are where existing regulations may not be fit for purpose anymore. It has to be stated that—at least in Europe—instead of an abrupt, disruptive change, a rather linear continuation of the megatrend away from the formal employment relationship toward atypical employment and beyond into the realms of self-employment can be detected (Risak 2017; Eurofound 2015a). The current developments can be clustered under three headers that stress the flexible and even liquid form of organizing work in the twenty-first century. Central to all of them is that the use of new technologies is blurring the boundaries between the traditional employment contract and self-employment:

- "Working beyond working time"
- "Working beyond the internal workplace"
- "Working beyond two-party relationships" (Risak 2017)

Interestingly, in some fields (especially working time), the changes were driven by new legislation and policy decisions like the extension of the daily and weekly maximum working hours in Austria in 2018 or the increased possibilities to opt-out of the maximum weekly working hours (48 on average according to the EU Working Time Directive 2003/88/EC) over the last decade in the member states of the European Union (Eurofound 2015b). In others (especially mobile working and home office), new forms of work organization are becoming more prevalent due to practices in some companies and lately due to externalities like the COVID-19 pandemic (Deloitte 2020). They will then lead to the adaption of existing legislation. And other forms of work, especially platform work, are often not regulated yet (European Commission 2019).

5   Where Do We Go from Here?

And this brings us back to the title of this chapter: Working in 2030: Heaven or Hell? The direction developments will take also depend very much on how we will adapt existing legislation and labor market institutions like unions, collective bargaining, and company-level employee representation to a changing environment. All these institutions are the product of learning how to deal with technological progress during the (first and second) industrial revolution and the societal changes resulting from it if left unchanneled. Not dealing with the abovementioned "labor problem" not only led to enormous inequality and social conflict but also to the First World War. It is, therefore, no surprise that after this war that the Versailles Peace Treaty of 1919/1920 also includes the foundation of the International Labour Organisation (ILO) based on the finding that "universal and lasting peace can only be established if it is based upon social justice." The rest of the preamble addresses issues that are as pressing now as they were 100 years ago:

"And whereas conditions of labour exist involving such injustice, hardship and privation to large numbers of people as to produce unrest so great that the peace and harmony of the world are imperiled; and an improvement of those conditions is urgently required; as, for example, by the regulation of the hours of work, including the establishment of a maximum working day and week, the regulation of the labour supply, the prevention of unemployment, the provision of an adequate living wage, the protection of the worker against sickness, disease and injury arising out of his employment, the protection of children, young persons and women, provision for old age and injury, protection of the interests of workers when employed in countries other than their own, recognition of the principle of equal remuneration for work of equal value, recognition of the principle of freedom of association, the organization of vocational and technical education and other measures."

The question is again how to direct the future of work in 2030 toward heaven and not, as one might be tempted to say, back toward hell. One of the main challenges is the scope of application of labor law and collective bargaining that now culminates in the question: employed or self-employed? The answer is essential as, in the past, only persons working in subordination were seen needing protection and therefore covered by labor laws and collective agreements. However, new ways of organizing work have led to the conclusion that there is a growing number of self-employed workers that are in a similar situation as employees and therefore in need of protection. It is, therefore, essential to adapt the personal scope of labor laws and to include vulnerable self-employed as well (Risak and Dullinger 2018).

Just like 100 years ago, the question of flexibility has to be dealt with. Then, it was about the limitation of work hours and the introduction of the 8-hour working day. Now, it is also about safeguarding rest periods in times when employees can be reached 24/7 due to modern information and communication technology (ICT). In order that flexibility works not only in favor of employers but also to the benefit of employees, a real right to disconnect is now essential to protect not only the health but also the social life of workers.

At the core of this discussion is also about how governments and social partners will have to deal with labor market disruptions by adapting collective representation, institutions, and—last but not least—social protection that is often very much based on the concept of the standard employment relationship. The answers to the question are still open and very much depends on both sides of the employment relationship as well as the governments and parliaments what direction the future of work will take. It is important to work together toward the goal and that this time it will not be a process of degradation of work in the twenty-first century but one of increased autonomy, better job quality, and more self-fulfillment inside and outside work. The potential to move in this direction, toward heaven, is there, but this will not come without a struggle.

6   The Role of Social Dialogue and the ILO Towards a Heavenly Path

Like 100 years ago, the ILO can play a significant role in making the transition into the new way of working, one that takes into account all the stakeholders, promoting social dialogue between governments as well as between worker and employer representatives on an international level. It has increased importance as innovative ways of organizing work make use of the virtual sphere and therefore do not stop at physical borders—ways to regulate work therefore have to follow this development and aim toward universal application to avoid a race to the bottom with regard to labor conditions.

Social dialogue, as promoted by the ILO, is first and foremost a fundamental principle of democracy, and it is at the heart of the work of this international organization. It embodies the right of representative groups to express their views on public policies affecting their interests and to have these views taken into serious account in the formulation and implementation of policies. Social dialogue includes all types of negotiation, consultation, or simply exchanging information between, or among, representatives of governments, employers, and workers, on issues of common interest. In the past, this has led to better policies by drawing on the knowledge and experience of the social partners, and it provides a forum where the trade-off between competing interests can be negotiated and resolved in the overall national interest. Social dialogue also induces support for the proposed measures and hence preempts future opposition and conflict that would otherwise reduce their effectiveness.

One of the issues of social dialogue is how proper representation of all members of society can be achieved. This has been discussed throughout the ILO's more than 100 years of existence. Each time new structures were created in the labor market, the issue of freedom of association of those new structures was debated. The rapid developments in the beginning of the twenty-first century took these debates to the extreme. For example, it soon became evident that *a wave of change in the way we live and work* was ongoing, provoked by the fourth industrial revolution due to artificial intelligence and digitalization. And this also led to new ways of organizing work in the gray zone between dependent employment and self-employment. It is yet not sure who represents this group and if existing labor regulations apply to them.

However, it wasn't until after the COVID-19 crisis that it became evident that *the wave had become a tsunami*. The crisis not only challenged health systems but also how we work. This tsunami of change gave a final push to the ongoing shift in the way we valued and organized work, both paid and unpaid, and thus called for a change in how the different actors in society are represented. This was translated into a shift from shareholder to stakeholder engagement, where all actors in society became the protagonist. It became evident that social dialogue was the way out from a deep depression/recession, resulting from the lockdowns in 2020 and 2021. And in my view, it will also be the avenue of choice to face the challenges of making work in 2030 more like heaven and less like hell. But again, this is not an automatism but the result of struggles between the different interest groups. Proper representation of all stakeholders at all levels of regulation (company and industry level, national and international) as well as participatory processes safeguarding the voice and influence of all relevant actors remain of vital relevance to make use of the advances in technology to benefit all: not only employers but also workers and society as a whole.

7   In 2030, Social Dialogue and Representative Participation Will Be as Relevant as Ever

It is assumed that debates, followed by initiatives and programs, including in the ILO, address the issue of proper representation for all in the name of social justice (ILO 2019a, b). For such social dialogue to take place, the following must exist in 2030:

- Strong, independent workers' and employers' organizations with the technical capacity and access to relevant information to participate in social dialogue
- Political will and commitment to engage in social dialogue on the part of all the parties
- Respect for the fundamental rights of freedom of association and collective bargaining
- Appropriate institutional support

Social dialogue has also changed. In order to facilitate social dialogue, industrial relations, collective bargaining, and the conclusion of collective agreements, many countries have:

- Adapted legal, institutional, and other frameworks that enable the parties to engage effectively. Many institutions have also strengthened their ability to function and influence the dialogue by improving their technical capacity, structure, and effectiveness.
- Encouraged collective bargaining in emergency situations to mitigate negative effects on workers. For example, in a health emergency, collective bargaining can establish any cuts in working hours, safety at work, etc.
- Governments facilitate forums for social dialogue that include different groups in society, such as youth, older workers, and disabled workers, including youth organizations and others that represent civil society in social dialogue.
- Informal workers (including domestic workers) and unpaid workers (including care workers), as well as some platform workers, are organized by occupation in order to encourage long-term association.
- Autonomous social dialogue between workers and employers and their respective organizations is also encouraged and supported.
- Resources are made available to strengthen the capacity of social partners.
- Include all workers in the economy, from those just starting out to those approaching retirement in unions or employers' organizations. Young people

are particularly encouraged to join, and membership can be transferred to the many jobs that they may do during their working life.
• Communication to members of unions is facilitated digitally. Information campaigns target schools, students, and young academics, while others have opened up membership to the self-employed and students. Trade unions have also developed new forms of digital support and services and online communities.

By 2030, many countries have made a considerable effort to include all members of society in social dialogue for the development and maintenance of decent work for all as a reaction to putting in place suitable structures and institutions for a "better normal" post-COVID-19. The dialogue has supported the development of better employment outcomes and attempts to address the polarization of jobs. In 2030, there could be, however, other countries that are still struggling with the organization of social dialogue. The ILO supports creating an enabling environment for social dialogue in all its member states as a lifelong active society supported through social dialogue facilitates the transitions of people between school, jobs, training, care, and eventually retirement. An approach to lifelong social dialogue is conducive to meet the many challenges of today's and tomorrow's world of work (cf. Chacaltana and Prieto 2019).

8   Implications for Managers, Employers, Trade Unions, and Governments

It has become evident that the direction the future of work will take is not yet clear. As the Global Commission of the Future of Work of the ILO (2019a, p. 44) pointed out, technical advances can free workers from arduous labor as well as from dirt, drudgery, danger, and deprivation. They can also reduce work-related stress and potential injuries. But on the other hand, the recent technological changes may also reduce worker control and autonomy, as well as the richness of work content, resulting in a potential deskilling and decline in worker satisfaction. Thus, realizing the potential of technology in the future of work depends on fundamental choices about work design and, in the end, deciding on whom the new way of work should benefit in the end: the employer, the employees, or society as a whole? Or, in other words, will it result in heaven 2030 or hell 2030?

Which direction working in 2030 will take should be negotiated in a manner that allows the representation of all relevant interests and thereby balancing them evenly. We should never forget what we have learned from the past, i.e., that "universal and lasting peace can only be established if it is based upon social justice." In this endeavor, employers and managers, as well as trade unions and governments, play an essential role in the implementation of a "renewed social contract" that works for all. Thus, they should not overstate their individual interests but also take into account those of the other side and of society in general. This way, the developments can be directed toward the vision of "heaven 2030" or, in other words, toward more rewarding and autonomous work that does not lack security and social protection.

This especially means avoiding the "flexibility trap" resulting from the narrative promoted especially by the business models of the platform (gig) economy: Flexibility and worker autonomy have to come at the price of giving up protection. This was not true in the past as the European, especially the Scandinavian, social model showed. And it should also be remembered that there is nothing new or even innovative about precarious working conditions. To avoid losing the benefits gained, the fruits of increased productivity due to technical change have to be spread evenly between everybody concerned. It can lead to fewer working hours for better wages for employees and greater profits for employers who can, at the same time, assume social responsibility more easily. Social dialogue and collective bargaining at all levels, as well as state intervention by way of legislation, have proved to be an adequate tool to achieve this in the past and are still able to do so in 2030 and beyond. They still matter.

References

Braverman, H. (1974, 1998). *Labour and monopoly capital – The degradation of work in the twentieth century.* New York: NYU Press.

Chacaltana, J., & Prieto, M. (2019). Evolution and future of youth employment policies: Global debates and their implications for Latin America. In F. Bertranou & A. Marinakis (Eds.), *Reflections on work, perspectives from the Southern Cone of Latin America on the occasion of the ILO Centenary* (pp. 109–116). Santiago: ILO.

Deloitte. (2020). *Flexible working studies 2020.* Vienna: Deloitte.

Eurofound. (2015a). *New forms of employment.* Luxembourg: Publications Office of the European Union.

Eurofound. (2015b). *Opting out of the European Working time directive.* Luxembourg: Publications Office of the European Union.

European Commission. (2019). *Study to gather evidence on the working conditions of platform workers.* Luxembourg: Publications Office of the European Union.

ILO. (2019a). *Work for a brighter future - Global commission on the future of work.* Geneva: International Labour Office.

ILO. (2019b, June 21). *ILO Centenary Declaration for the future of work,* adopted by the Conference 108th Session, Geneva.

Keynes, J. M. (1930, 1963). Economic possibilities for our grandchildren. In *Essays in persuasion.* New York: W.W. Norton & Co. (pp. 358–373).

Marx, K. (1846, 1964). *The German ideology.* Moscow: Progress Publishers.

Risak, M. (2017). Arbeiten 4.0. *Journal für Arbeitsrecht und Sozialrecht, 1/1,* 12–42.

Risak, M., & Dullinger, T. (2018). *The concept of worker in EU law: Status quo and potential for change.* Brussels: ETUI.

Martin Gruber-Risak is an Associate Professor at the Department of Labour Law and Law of Social Security at the University of Vienna (Austria). He was the chairman of Senate II of the Austrian Equal Treatment Commission (2016–2020), an associate with the international law firm CMS Reich-Rohrwig Hainz, Professor of Labour Law and Civil Law at the University of Passau (Germany), and a Marie Curie Fellow at the University of Otago (New Zealand). Martin is the co-editor of the HSI Report on European Labour and Social Security Law and a member of the scientific advisory board of the Austrian journal "The Law of Work." He is also the Austrian national expert at the European Centre of Expertise ("ECE") in the field of labor law, employment, and labor market policies that advises the European Commission.

Values Versus Technology? Why We Need to Consider a New Foundation for Work

Thomas K. Hamann

Freiburg im Breisgau, Germany, October 8, 2030
  Hans Doering's Day

7:00 a.m. The alarm clock rings; Hans stretches and gives his wife Johanna a kiss. They both get up. While his wife prepares breakfast, Hans takes a shower and is already looking forward to the self-grown coffee, which Johanna roasts gold brown for her own family and the other people in the neighborhood. Last year, the board of trustees of the local MakerSpace, a workshop with all kinds of machines that are jointly used and financially supported by everyone in the district, decided to purchase a drum roaster at Johanna's suggestion—roasting and blending her own coffee creations were a long-cherished childhood dream of the former call center employee.

7:45 a.m. After breakfast, Hans drives to the gardens maintained by the MakerSpace. He takes care of the coffee plants, which thrive in the ultramodern greenhouses even in the local, nontropical climate. Then, he harvests a small pumpkin and lamb's lettuce for lunch.

9.15 a.m. Hans returns home and picks up Max, his twelve-year-old son, to walk with him to the MakerSpace. The two of them want—under expert guidance—to produce a lampshade from kraftplex, an innovative wooden metallike sheet, with a laser cutter. Max is supposed to help and learn how to do it—after all, he was the one who smashed the old lampshade while playing football. Together with his mother, Johanna, Max had created the design with Adobe Illustrator after breakfast and saved it as a vector graphic file.

T. K. Hamann (✉)
T. K. Hamann Gesellschaft mbH, Munich, Germany
e-mail: thomas.hamann@tkhamann.com

© Springer Nature Switzerland AG 2021
S. Güldenberg et al. (eds.), *Managing Work in the Digital Economy*, Future of Business and Finance, https://doi.org/10.1007/978-3-030-65173-2_8

12.10 p.m. Hans and his son Max carefully pack the manufactured lampshade into a transport box and make their way home, where they want to have lunch together with Johanna and Ina, the Doerings' youngest child.

1.50 p.m. After lunch, Hans looks after Ina and helps her with her homework. Then, he takes about one and a half hours to go through and answer emails.

3.30 p.m. Hans closes the door to his home studio and devotes himself to preparing a lecture until dinner. A group of interested parties had invited him to report on his experiences and satisfaction with the alternative form of work organization he is pursuing and to discuss these with them. The event will take place two days later in a coworking space in Stuttgart.

7.25 p.m. Hans looks at the clock in disbelief; while working on his presentation, the time has just flown by. He was completely at one with himself, and now, after a long period of great concentration, he is happy about what he has achieved today. He now prepares dinner with his two children.

8.05 p.m. Before three-year-old Ina falls asleep, Hans reads her a bedtime story. Afterward, he plays with his son Max with the model crane, which Hans made himself as a birthday present in the MakerSpace.

9.30 p.m. Now, Max has gone to bed, too. Hans and his wife Johanna spend the rest of the evening reading before they also go to sleep.

10.30 p.m. Hans turns off his bedside lamp. He briefly thinks about spending the next day at the publishing house, where he still works two days a week in his original profession as an editor. He then falls into a deep, restful sleep.

1 Key Drivers of Change in Our World of Work

The changes in the world of work during our time are attributed to two key drivers: First, to a change in the values prevailing in society as younger generations gradually replace their predecessors and, second, to the spread of digital technologies (Klös et al. 2016). Unfortunately, as will be explained below, these two key drivers are causing the way in which work is organized to drift further apart from people's expectations concerning their work. This means that the jobs and positions on offer are less and less in line with people's actual demands on their (working) lives—especially for those born between 1997 and 2012 (Generation Z), who will make up a significant proportion of the working population in 2030 (about 40%). To overcome this widening gap, alternative approaches to work organization must be considered.

1.1   Changes in Values and the Associated Work Ethic Prevailing in Society

Currently, there is a widespread discussion about an ongoing change in values and attitudes, especially with relevance to work, and its effects on social and economic development—especially regarding the organization of work. This assumes that, due to the influence of current typical characteristics, large parts of a generation adopt similar values and attitudes and stick to them for the rest of their lives. If these values of a generation differ from those of the preceding generation(s), a corresponding change in values that prevail in society occurs when the members of the younger generation increasingly replace those of the preceding generation(s) due to demographic developments. In demography, this is referred to as a generation effect.

In 2030, the world's working-age population will be constituted by members of the various generations roughly according to the proportions shown in Fig. 1. Generations Y, also called Millennials, and Z will make up by far the largest part of the working population, with about 40% each. This raises the question of in what way and to what extent do the values espoused by these two generations differ from those of preceding generations.

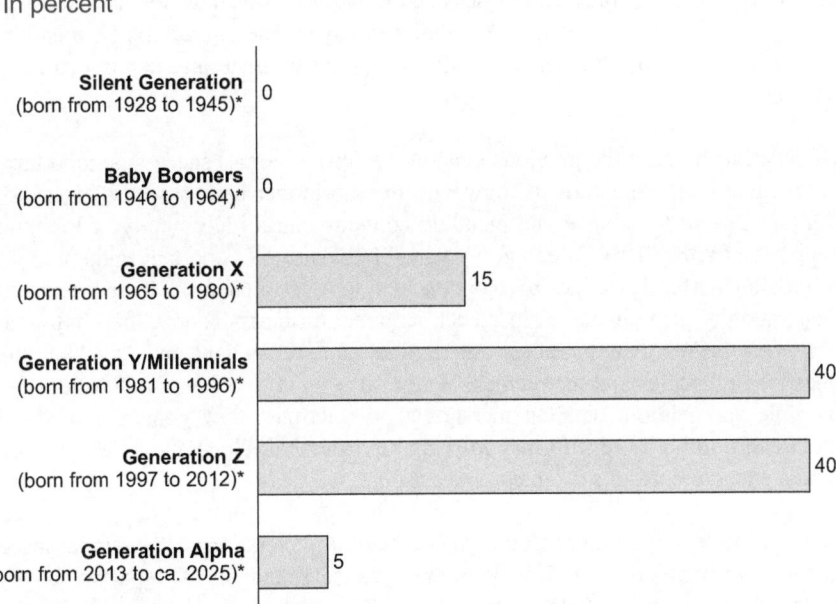

* The definition of generations varies by a few years of birth, depending on the study or source

Fig. 1 Projected proportions of the various generations in the worldwide working-age population, 2030 (own representation based on the United Nations and Cushman & Wakefield as cited in Cushman & Wakefield 2020, p. 7)

Of course, not all members of a generation share exactly the same values (intra-generational variance). Nevertheless, generations can be generally characterized on the basis of the values and attitudes predominantly advocated by their members (inter-generational difference)—in this article based on the following sources: Kranenberg (2014), Mörstedt (2017), Heller (2018), Maas (2019), Shell Deutschland Holding (2019), Eswein (2020), and ibau (2020).

Baby Boomers This generation will not have a large share of the working population in 2030. However, it can be questioned whether in the year 2030 there will really be no Baby Boomer still working as indicated by the database on which Fig. 1 is drawn. It is quite conceivable that some members of this generation will still be professionally active in 2030, e.g., due to higher pensionable age or part-time employment. For this reason and in order to be able to follow the change in values over several generations more clearly, the Baby Boomers will also be described in more detail here. This generation is fundamentally motivated by performance, success, and prosperity. The values of (self-)discipline, efficiency, and determination are important to Baby Boomers. That is why they attach the highest priority to their career and are characterized by a high commitment—the term "workaholic", coined by Wayne Edward Oates (1971), has been seen as typical for this generation. Other important values for the Baby Boomers are obedience, probity, and a sense of order. Accordingly, they prefer clear hierarchies and a structured way of working. Given the strong values of conscientiousness and reliability as well as fidelity and loyalty, Baby Boomers are typically loyal to their employer. The characteristics mentioned so far allow the Baby Boomers to satisfy their desire for material and job security and prosperity.

Generation X Like the previous generation, (professional) success is important to the members of Generation X; however, this no longer enjoys such high priority. They also want to achieve and maintain contentment, a high quality of life, and a happy family life. Therefore, a good work-life balance is important to them in their professional life. They like to separate their professional from their private life. Generation X also pursues values such as freedom, independence, and individualism. This makes their members autonomous and self-reliant, and it makes them question authorities and hierarchies. Hence, they want to work as independently as possible and without detailed managerial instructions; they generally prefer flat hierarchies and a more informal working environment. Generation Xers are pragmatic, adaptable, results-oriented, and creative.

Generation Y/Millennials Compared to previous generations, professional success and advancement are much less important for the Millennials. They strive above all for contentment and friendship. In doing so, they adhere to a certain idealism and seek sustainability and meaningfulness. Generation Y is skeptical about the self-exploitation of the older generations and pays attention to a balance between professional and private life. They, therefore, demand sufficient free time and freedom for their private lives, which they integrate flexibly into their professional activities (work-life blending); they also expect flexible working hours, working from home or free choice of work location, and longer periods of time off (sabbaticals). They have high expectations and demands; they want to pursue meaningful activities. Furthermore, Millennials want to take on responsibility from the very beginning; that is why they attach great importance to flat and flexible hierarchies. Recognition is particularly important to them, and they do not want to have to wait long for it (instant gratification). Millennials expect decent remuneration. Due to their flexibility, they are open to change and have a pronounced willingness to learn. This facilitates the pursuit of specialist careers and interesting project work, which they prefer over management positions. They want a caring work environment and certainly want to be supported in their development.

Generation Z This generation can currently only be characterized with some reservations. The youngest members of this generation are only about 8 years old today and have not yet completed their formative socialization; even for the older members of Generation Z, socialization may still remain in force due to their relatively young age of about 23 years. Thus, the values and attitudes they promote may be subject to future changes. Notwithstanding this, an outlook is given here as to the direction that Generation Z is expected to take. The primary motivators of this generation are material prosperity and a cohesive family structure. A central value is security, especially regarding (permanent) employment and (long-term) subsistence, to which Generation Z sets high standards. Nonetheless, leading a meaningful life is also of immense importance for their members, especially within their private life. Consequently, they regard work as only a part—and not the most important—of their lives. In combination with more conservative and traditional values, this leads to a refusal to accept blurred boundaries between professional and private life—they want to avoid encroachment and reject work-life blending. Instead, the members of Generation Z are looking for fixed working hours (nine-to-five jobs) and clear structures. Rather than leadership responsibility, they prefer to take on well-defined tasks within a collaborative network and a collegial working atmosphere. Generation Z is less loyal to their employers due to an overall lower career orientation compared to the Baby Boomers and Generation Xers. Generation Z pursues their personal goals with enthusiasm and creativity.

Generation Alpha Although, as shown in Fig. 1, the first members of this generation will have entered the workforce by 2030 at the age of 17 or 18 years, this generation clearly will still play a minor role in 2030. Besides, it is still too early to describe the values of Generation Alpha—given that their socialization phase is not yet complete and some members of this generation have not even been born yet.

Figure 2 summarizes the motives, values, characteristics, and demands placed on work-life by the generations relevant here.

	Baby Boomers	Generation X	Generation Y	Generation Z
Funda-mental motives	• Performance capability • Success • Prosperity/wealth	• Contentment/satisfaction • Success • Family	• Contentment/satisfaction • Friendship	• Prosperity/wealth • Family
Prevalent values	• (Self-)discipline/prowess • Determination • Obedience/probity • Sense of order • Conscientiousness/reliability • Fidelity/Loyalty • (Material/job) security/safety	• Freedom/independence • Individualism • Responsibility	• Idealism • Sustainability • Meaningfulness • Flexibility • Appreciation • Friendship/team spirit • Optimism	• (Material/job) security/safety • Meaningfulness • Enthusiasm • Conservativism
Charac-teristics	• Career-oriented (work has top priority) • Loyal to the employer	• Striving for high quality of life (more important than professional fulfilment) • Independent/autonomous • Questioning authorities and hierarchies • Pragmatic/adaptable • Results-oriented • Resilient • Creative	• Caring to balance work and private life • Cherishing high hopes • Self-aware • Desiring to take responsibility right from the start • Impatient • Open to changes • Willing to learn	• Wishing to develop and realize their potential freely (privately rather than professionally) • Acting as lone wolves • Shattered expectation of self-efficacy • Creative
Demands on work	• High commitment ("workaholism") • Distinct hierarchies • Structured working style	• Good work-life balance • Separation of professional and private life • High level of autonomy/low guidance • Flat hierarchies • Informal working environment	• Abundant time and space for private life • Work-life blending • Meaningful activities • Flat/flexible hierarchies • Good pay and benefits • Specialist careers and project work more important than management positions • Nurturing work environment • Advancement opportunities	• High material standard and security • Strict separation of professional and private life • Extensive recreational time • Solid demarcations and clear structures • No or low (long-term) commitment to companies • Collegial working atmosphere

Fig. 2 Fundamental motives, values, characteristics, and demands on work: Generational comparison (own representation)

1.2   The Spread of Digital Technologies

Digital technologies make it possible to increasingly become flexible in regard to working time and place of work. Communication and coordination with other people or entire groups no longer have to be conducted solely by telephone but also via Internet telephony or, above all, web meetings or video conferences. Using augmented reality glasses with integrated cameras, specialists can view a car like an onsite mechanic and give instructions from a distance, as well as supplement these with corresponding illustrations via superimpositions in the field of vision. Files and data stored in the cloud can be accessed anytime and from anywhere with an Internet connection. Moreover, the fields of application and the quality of artificial intelligence (AI) continue to increase. Thus, workflows can be automated up to entire process chains. These developments have implications both for the types of work that people will do in the future and for the design and organization of that work.

1.2.1   Implications for the Types of Work

Behavioral scientists distinguish between algorithmic and heuristic tasks (Pink 2006): In an algorithmic task, one follows a series of fixed instructions on a predetermined path to a result, i.e., there is an algorithm to solve it. On the contrary, there is no algorithm for solving a heuristic task, so that one has to try out different possibilities and thus find not only a new solution but also the path to it. The work of a cashier at the supermarket checkout is mostly algorithmic; pretty much the same activity is repeated continuously in a certain way. The creation of an advertising campaign, on the other hand, is predominantly heuristic; it is a matter of coming up with something new. With the digitalization and automation of processes, jobs are being replaced by computers. So, James Manyika and Kevin Sneader (2018) from the management consultancy McKinsey & Company estimate that a total of about 30% of all activities in 60% of all professions can be automated. Based on this, they conclude that in the period from 2016 to 2030, around 15% of the global workforce, i.e., approximately 400 million workers, could be displaced by automation. Conversely, however, new jobs will also be created to a considerable extent. This development will cause a massive shift in the relationship between algorithmic and heuristic (and less structured) tasks performed by humans in favor of the latter. Routine activities can be outsourced or automated, whereas this is generally not possible for artistic, empathy-demanding, or other non-routine work (Pink 2006).

1.2.2   Impact on the Organization of Work

The variants of digitization in the world of work can be divided into four different categories: First, the self-regulating potential of technical systems; second, the cross-linking of technical systems, information/data pools, and acting people (human-machine interaction); third, technical assistance systems; and fourth, simulations based on virtual realities (Kuhlmann and Schuhmann 2015 as cited in Väth 2016). Among these categories, it is probably the interaction between man and machine that affects the work areas of most people to the greatest extent, e.g., in the form of cloud working, real-time communication and reporting, and digital leadership (Pink 2018;

see also Chaps. 2 and 10 in this book). This increasingly leads to a blurring of professional and private affairs, i.e., both working time and social contacts with colleagues are no longer clearly separated from private life (work-life blending); for instance, work is done from home after finishing time, or leisure activities are enjoyed with colleagues (Kordouni 2017). Some also speak in this context of the dissolution of work boundaries. As can be seen in part from the previous examples and according to the Professor Emeritus of Sociology Günter Voß (1998), this dissolution of work boundaries, often referred to as flexibilization, is—unlike in the pre-industrial era—taking place today not only in terms of time and place but also with respect to various other dimensions:

- Work equipment and technology:
  De-standardization of the applied technologies and devices used.
- Social organization:
  Workload compression, the breakup of the operational work and control structures through group work, project organization in flexible teams, decentralization, thinning out of hierarchies under keywords such as intrapreneurship, and profit- or cost-centered strategies.
- Work content:
  See the above section "Implications for the Types of Work".
- Professional qualifications:
  Rapid deterioration of expertise and thus pressure for lifelong learning, a shift in the importance of specialist knowledge to so-called interdisciplinary or methodological qualifications such as social and communication skills, self-management, media literacy, creativity and enthusiasm, ego strength, ability to cope with stress, etc.
- Meaning and motivation:
  A growing variance of attitudes and orientations in organizations, changing or even differentiated corporate cultures, strengthening of self-motivation and self-dependent endowment of work with meaning by employees—evoked through modern approaches to human resource management and cooperative leadership philosophies.

Some of the developments mentioned above are seen—with quite positive connotations—as subjectivation of work. This means that individual actions and interpretations of the people bound in the work process have a subjective meaning and the individuals put more subjectivity into the work or, vice versa, work demands more and more subjectivity from the individuals (Kleemann et al. 1999). Following the psychologist and author of relevant textbooks Markus Väth (2016), this subjectivation can, however, be not only a valorization of work but also a danger—if it no longer means a centering and self-assurance of one's own person but an overstimulation and dissolution of the subject and work becomes inappropriately overloaded with existential significance for one's own life. The notion of man as the center of his working world, on which subjectivation is based, presupposes the person as a true subject, i.e., an acting, autonomous being. However, such an assumption is unrealistic; this will become clear at the latest when job reduction programs or target agreements come about. Usually, these are not agreements, but rather targets which the employee is expected to accept and fulfill—codetermination and scope for action are something else (Väth 2016). According to him, the reasons why the dark sides of subjectivation come into play are as follows: First, subjectivation requires trust on the part of the manager—something that many managers struggle with. After all, trust means accepting a certain loss of control. Second, there are certainly people who prefer to strictly adhere to predefined procedures and who explicitly want to be controlled. Subjectivation would be inappropriate in this case, as it would be too much of a challenge. Third, subjectivation is a possible stress factor. Autonomy and improvisation must also be mastered. Leaving well-trodden paths often means fighting one's way through the undergrowth again and requires one to be able to fill the vacuum of leadership on one's own (see also Chap. 9 in this book). The change in work organization outlined above brings along certain side effects such as an excessive flood of information and emails, deadline pressure, permanent stress, and sometimes also a certain helplessness in handling or dealing with new media. According to the BKK Dachverband (2019), the association of company health insurance funds in Germany, this change in the world of work poses new challenges with regard to the mental health and ability to work of employees. It is no coincidence that work-related mental stress and, ultimately, illnesses like burnout syndrome have massively increased and will—under the current circumstances—presumably continue to increase in the future:

> Studies on the impact of the digital transformation on employees have noted an increase in psychological stress at the workplace. A research report commissioned by the German Federal Ministry of Labour and Social Affairs (2016) states that 65% of the 7109 respondents perceive a compression of their workload. 78% see the need to continuously develop themselves further. According to another report, more than 40% of 3000 employees indicate that digitization has made it necessary for them to complete tasks faster and to perform several tasks simultaneously (Knieps and Pfaff 2017). Every fifth person feels overloaded or burnt out. Furthermore, Böhm et al. (2016) revealed in a survey of 8019 Internet-using professionals that digitization entails an increasing complexity of work content, growing amounts of information, more communication noise (e.g. constant email traffic) and higher technological requirements. The authors find significant links between digitization on the one hand and emotional exhaustion and conflicts between work and family on the other. Müller-Thur et al. (2018) list psychological stress resulting from fast and abrupt task combinations, multi-tasking, and work interruptions based on an evaluation of 41 studies. Lechleiter et al. (2018) found out that mental stress is increasing. (Sonntag 2019, pp. 242–243; text translated from German into English and abbreviated by the author)

This clearly signals that the current direction in which the organization of work is developing as a result of the spread and use of digital technologies neither is good for the current generations nor does it fit in with the values attributed to the Generation Z. This raises the question of alternative ways of meaningfully organizing work.

2   Toward a New Foundation for Work

2.1   The Incompatibility of the Effects of Spreading Digital Technologies with Changing Values and Work Ethic

The two key drivers of change in our world of work mean that the resulting organization of work and the related working methods and structures will become less and less compatible with people's needs.

The spread of digital technologies, because of their potential for automating (mainly algorithmic) activities, is leading to an increase in the proportion of heuristic and, thus, intellectually more demanding work. Simultaneously, the organization of the remaining or upcoming heuristic work is getting increasingly unbounded, which leads to work-related mental problems and diseases. It is scientifically proven that work that is perceived as meaningful fundamentally fosters job satisfaction and mental health. The two professors of psychology Edward L. Deci and Richard M. Ryan (1985) jointly developed the so-called Self-Determination Theory (SDT). "SDT [...] begins with a notion of universal human needs. It argues that we have three innate psychological needs—competence, autonomy, and relatedness. When those needs are satisfied, we're motivated, productive, and happy. When they're thwarted, our motivation, productivity, and happiness plummet" (Ryan and Deci 2000 as cited in Pink 2018, p. 72)—and these are also the preconditions for meaningfulness and a meaningful life (Martela et al. 2018). However, the nature of the activities and a flexible organization of work do not seem to be sufficient for this purpose. Despite, or perhaps because of, the increasing flexibilization of work, a survey conducted by the global analytic and advice firm Gallup (2017, pp. 4–5) in 155 countries revealed the following: "Worldwide, the percentage of adults who work full time for an employer and are engaged at work—they are highly involved in and enthusiastic about their work and workplace—is just 15%. [...] It implies an incredible amount of wasted potential, given that business units in the top quartile of our global employee engagement database are 17% more productive and 21% more profitable than those in the bottom quartile." It is therefore reasonable to assume that other factors, such as the ultimate purpose of the work, may be decisive. If work is not meaningful or—in other words—not what "someone [...] really, really wants to do" (Bergmann 2019, p. 726), then the flexibilization of work organization serves at most to sweeten work that is actually unpleasant (e.g., Bergmann 2019).

Due to the second key driver, changes in values and the associated work ethics, more and more people, especially among younger generations, are looking for just a sense of meaning and also reject the very flexible, unbounded work organization, e.g., excessive work-life blending. The current and—if the current situation is extrapolated—the work on offer will increasingly incur rejection.

According to Gallup (2017, p. 5), there are many potential reasons why so few people are engaged in their work, but reluctance to change is a common problem in this context: "In particular, organizations and institutions have often been slow to adapt to the rapid changes produced by the spread of information technology, the globalization of markets for products and labor, the rise of the gig economy, and younger workers' unique expectations." Therefore, the question clearly arises as to which alternatives are better suited to the needs of future generations—and perhaps even of humanity in general. Such a choice is often referred to by the term New Work. Drawing on this concept as a basis, the following outlines the direction that the constitution of the world of work should take in order to become more viable, sustainable, and future-ready.

2.2   Developing a New Way of Living and Working

To begin with, it is important to realize that New Work does not only mean "a tabletop soccer and funny seating furniture" (Trautmann 2019)—it is about more than just this kind of sugar coating on the world of work as we know and experience it so far; it is about a fundamental change. The concept of New Work, originally coined by the professor of philosophy Frithjof Bergmann (2019) as early as the late 1970s/early 1980s, is based on three different elements that deviate quite considerably from a pure flexibilization of work:

- Doing "more meaningful and more fulfilling work, and beyond this even earn serious money with that 'pursuit' or 'calling'," i.e., taking up "work that makes use of people's best talents, work that corresponds to their full and deep desires, that they believe in, that they experience as a pursuit or a calling" (Bergmann 2019, pp. 12, 16–17).
- Reducing the dependency on jobs which would mean far-reaching confinement or even dismantlement of what Bergmann (2019) calls Job System.
- Ensuring the provision of (material and basic) supplies that allows one to pursue one's calling by drawing on state-of-the-art technology (Hi-Tech-Self-Providing, HTSP), i.e., developing "an array of tools, devices, materials and machines that would enable a small group of people to *make* 60 percent or 90 percent of everything they need" and making them available in a kind of workshop (Bergmann 2019, p. 34).

New Work is based on the individual. The individual human being should not sell one's labor to do something that someone else, namely, the employer, wants but should pursue what the individual "really, really" wants to do (calling). This necessitates making oneself as independent as possible from the material compulsion of having to earn money for one's living and from the jobs that are nowadays needed to do so. On the one hand, this can be achieved by seriously asking oneself how one desires to live and, to a large extent, by renouncing material temptations. On the other hand, this can be also mean further reducing one's need for money by self-producing as much as possible based on technology. This goes beyond the mere cultivation of an allotment for some fruit and vegetables. The vision is rather to organize into local groups and set up workshops analogous to the MakerSpaces in the start-up sector, which one can visit and where one will produce about 80% of the things necessary for life under the guidance of experienced coaches in the future. This is made possible by technological progress and simplified product design.

When it comes to shaping the future world of work, it is not only the individual with their needs that must be considered, but also additional aspects must be addressed. No one will seriously deny that we can achieve more by joining forces with others than if we were on our own. Therefore, we should clarify how we want to organize work on an inter-individual level. Moreover, the entire economic activity is embedded in a sociopolitical system that defines the relevant general conditions. Although Bergmann's concept of New Work demonizes today's Job System and vehemently calls for its abolition or at least a drastic reduction, he leaves the more detailed questions of an alternative organization of work—apart from individual aspects—largely unanswered, especially on the inter-individual level (e.g., Väth 2016).

Figure 3 summarizes what it takes to transform into a new way of living and working—a transformation that younger and coming generations will call for. In the following sections, the specific aspects of these three levels will be discussed in more detail.

2.2.1 General Sociopolitical Conditions

In many cases and at different times, it was projected that technological progress and the associated increase in productivity or automation would lead to less demand for labor. For example, in 1930, John Maynard Keynes predicted that by 2030, workers would only need to work about 15 hours per week. More recently, Jack Ma, the founder of the Chinese Internet platform Alibaba, asserted that by the year 2050, workers will work 3 or 4 days a week, 4 hours a day (e.g., Balakrishnan and Gernon 2017; Chen 2019). In our current employment system, the imperative of economic growth is considered a vital (political) goal to avoid unemployment or inactivity (e.g., Antal 2014). If younger generations now increasingly renounce the pursuit of excessive material wealth—beyond basic provision—and this manifests itself in a decline in demand for goods and services, this will not, however, lead in our current economic system to a situation in which everyone works less, but rather to some people working as before or even more, while the number of unemployed or precariously employed people rises considerably, i.e., they will become crowded out of the labor market. This would further increase the gap in the unequal distribution of income and wealth. It is precisely this circumstance that, according to Piketty (2014), leads to a threat to the economic basis of society and ultimately to democracy. In order to alleviate the outlined pressure for economic growth, a basis should indeed be laid on which a high degree of self-sufficiency is possible and promoted. For those who are not able to provide for themselves and hence cannot cover their basic needs, for example, due to age or health reasons, the granting of an unconditional basic income could be considered. Since technological progress means that people are not fully occupied by the provision of basic supplies, they have the freedom to pursue activities which—although fulfilling social and societal functions or promoting cultural diversity—have been reduced in recent years, partly due to economic pressure, e.g., cultural activities such as classical music performances or

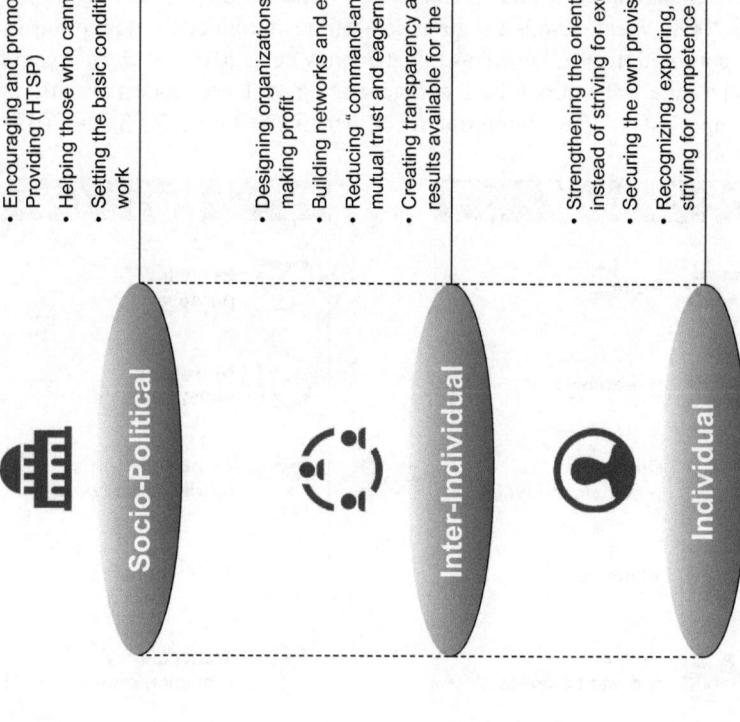

Socio-Political

- Forsaking economic growth as a political goal
- Encouraging and promoting technological progress and Hi-Tech-Self-Providing (HTSP)
- Helping those who cannot provide their basic supplies themselves
- Setting the basic conditions for new forms of inter-individual organization of work

Inter-Individual

- Designing organizations to serve a higher purpose instead of primarily making profit
- Building networks and ecosystems to coordinate the joint work of people
- Reducing "command-and-control" structures and strengthening a culture of mutual trust and eagerness to experiment
- Creating transparency and (possibly state-subsidized) making of work results available for the benefit of the general public

Individual

- Strengthening the orientation towards meaning and social contributions instead of striving for excessive material wealth
- Securing the own provision of basic supplies by means of HTSP
- Recognizing, exploring, and following one's own personal inclination and striving for competence and true mastery in this field

Fig. 3 The development toward a new way of living and working on the various relevant levels (own representation)

theater productions. Under New Work, these activities can be carried out by those who have the corresponding calling with less financial pressure.

2.2.2 Inter-individual Organization of Work

How can work be organized without the Job System or possibly even outside or independently of companies? The guidelines shown in Fig. 4 provide some orientation in regard to this aspect. These can be used not only as a basis for changing the management style within a single organization but also as guidelines for shaping the landscape of organizations throughout the economy.

From Profit to Benefit or Purpose Typically, the work is organized by companies or organizations that either earn money and maximize shareholder value (for profit) or do good (nonprofit) (Pink 2018). As has already been explained, the importance of meaningful work—in contrast to the pure pursuit of profit—is on the increase. Indeed, this strict distinction between either for-profit or nonprofit organizations has been increasingly diluted for some time. For instance, the United Kingdom introduced the community interest company (CIC) in 2005 (O'Rourke n.d.). "A CIC is a special type of limited company which exists to benefit the community rather than private shareholders" and no charity (Government Digital Service n.d.). Moreover, in 2008, Vermont was the first US state to introduce the low-profit limited liability corporation, also known as L3C (Cooney et al. 2014). Such an organization "operate[s] like a for-profit business generating at least modest profits, but its primary aim [is] to offer significant social benefits" (Moore 2008). In 2019, L3C

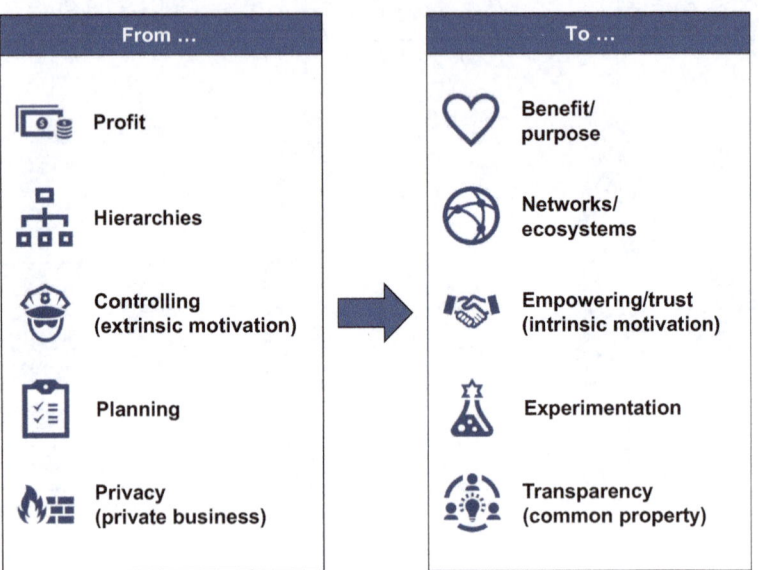

Fig. 4 Shifts in mindset for the transformation of organizations (own representation based on Sachs and Kundu 2015, Vora 2015)

was approved in 11 US states, and it is expected that more states will be added in 2020 and 2021 (Verde 2019). Furthermore, there is also the so-called benefit corporation in the USA, which is approved in even more US states (Feldmann 2020). The social impact of benefit corporations is typically voluntarily assessed by certifiers like B Lab; such a certification is a helpful but not sufficient element to achieve the legal status of a benefit corporation (Rawhouser et al. 2015). B Lab (n.d.) claims on its website that the B Economy is a global movement. Other countries, such as Denmark, also have such types of companies (Pink 2018). Overall, this approach is expanding as the so-called fourth sector (see the websites www. fourthsector.net and www.fourthsector.org). There is much more behind this than adding a sentence on a (pseudo) purpose to a company's vision or mission statement. Foundations can also be a suitable vehicle for New Work (Bergmann 2019). Organizations of this kind have a long tradition. Thus, early in their history, unions developed; such groupings were geared to a specific, often not purely economic, purpose, e.g., mutual support, charity, or pastoral care (Gierke 1868). As early as 1799, Robert Owen (1817) tried to improve the working and living conditions in his cotton spinning mill in Scotland. As already mentioned, cooperatives often pursue not only economic but also social purposes:

> A cooperative is a business driven by purpose and values, not just profit, to create a better world through cooperation (R+V Allgemeine Versicherung 2020).
>
> The purpose of cooperatives is to provide solutions to social problems and challenges. These include solutions for improving climate protection, energy, mobility, housing, health/care, food/agriculture, skilled crafts and trade, services, digitization/infrastructure, work, education, as well as culture/leisure and finance (R+V Allgemeine Versicherung 2020; text translated from German into English by the author).

From Hierarchies to Networks or Ecosystems Together with the German Friedrich-Alexander-Universität Erlangen-Nürnberg (FAU) and the Fraunhofer Institute for Integrated Circuits IIS, the Indian Institute of Management Bangalore (2020) recently ran a web-based seminar titled "Innovation Ecosystems between Academia, Industry and Society". In the description, they explained that "[i]n today's fast-moving business world, innovation and value creation tend to happen in new organizational forms beyond single corporations or simple markets. Innovation ecosystems with several interest groups are such a form of organizing". The boundaries between individual organizations are thus blurring—a trend that is not limited to innovation. Instead, the work in networks or ecosystems is organized on a need basis, i.e., similar to the initiatives of the open-source movement, people can contribute if they have something to add. It remains to be seen whether this aspect of the dissolution of boundaries of work will please Generation Z, which again increasingly seeks clear structures. But clear structures may not necessarily mean traditional structures and can also be realized in networks and ecosystems. What is required here and how exactly this can be implemented should be the subject of further research. A strong commitment and loyalty to the employer, which can also mean preserving orderly structures, are the least concern of this generation. Since the Generation Zers rather do not strive for leadership positions and prefer a collegial working atmosphere on equal terms, the further erosion of the classical "command-and-control" hierarchy is likely to progress in line with their ideas. In this respect, the future will probably look more like Sahana Chattopadhyay (2019) describes the shift from forced to natural hierarchies in an online article:

> Natural hierarchy emerges in an organizational setting when individuals are free to collaborate and contribute as per their capability, experience, and passion. This is not driven from the top but is an organically emergent process within a community of diverse, differently-talented, and passionate individuals. This kind of hierarchy doesn't operate from positional power or through control. It's an ever-evolving process, dynamically shifting and unfolding, including everyone in its emergence. In an inclusive community, people are free to be who they are meant to be in their wholeness and authenticity. In such situations, hierarchy is contextual, need-based, and voluntarily taken up and let go of when the context shifts.

From Controlling to Empowering and Trust This development is linked to the shift from control-centered to "natural" hierarchical structures discussed in the previous paragraph. According to SDT, one of the basic psychological needs is autonomy. Acting autonomously requires a longer leash for the actors involved, which in turn means allowing them more scope for action and placing the confidence in them not to exploit it. According to some studies in behavioral science, autonomous motivation leads to greater conceptual understanding, better persistence, higher productivity, less burnout, and a higher level of psychological well-being (Baard et al. 2004, Deci and Ryan 2008). In this context, autonomy must not be confused with complete independence—even if Generation Zers like to act as lone wolves. Instead, autonomy means numerous degrees of freedom with regard to one's decisions and actions. However, there is no way around fruitful cooperation with others. To ensure such cooperation, the lone wolves must find their own way to exploit these degrees of freedom while living and working in happy interdependence with others. Nevertheless, according to SDT, there is a deep need for people to be connected with others (relatedness). Networks and ecosystems, in particular, with their looser character compared to companies, can make this possible. Along with greater autonomy, the transition from a "carrot-and-stick" incentive system based on extrinsic motivation to an intrinsic drive is also important (Pink 2018). This will be discussed in one of the following sections. Not only must the working structures be designed in such a way that the acting individuals are given more autonomy, but also organizations must free themselves from the control mechanisms to which they are subject as an entity. Organizations, especially those oriented to the capital market, are forced by our current economic system to meet the expectations (short term, often linked to quarterly or even monthly targets) of financial players. Here, too, greater trust is needed to enable the pursuit of long-term strategies that may not appear to maximize profits in the short run—as is often the case with family-owned businesses that are much more independent of the capital market. This is about a reciprocal relationship of trust—on the one hand, on the part of the decision-makers vis-à-vis those who evaluate them directly and indirectly, such as supervisory bodies and powerful actors on the capital market, and, on the other hand, on the part of the latter vis-à-vis the corporate leaders that they do not abuse their power, but really pursue the long-term corporate and common good. The Russian saying "Доверять, но проверять [dowjerjaj, no prowjerjaj]", which translated means "trust but check", is most certainly also true in this context. But how should control and sanction mechanisms be designed? These mechanisms have to consider workers' true intentions and how their decisions can drastically affect the future of a company or organization without limiting their creativity and scope to act as they see fit. The question about the motivation and incentives to have such trust is, therefore, not yet fully clear. Perhaps networks and ecosystems will not pursue long-planned strategies, but will rather emerge as a response to specific circumstances.

From Planning to Experimentation It has already been mentioned here that most traditional organizations are based on "command-and-control" hierarchies and more or less long-term planning. Nate Fink (2015) of Microsoft Yammer excellently summarized a widely held position in his talk at the William and Phyllis Mack Institute for Innovation Management at the Wharton School of the University of Pennsylvania:

> Most old style organizations are very command-and-control, built on planning and hierar-chy. That worked really well when organizations needed to design for efficiency and planning and predictability. In today's world, things are changing too quickly and there's important information that's locked up in silos around the organization that we need to unlock. We need to connect people within the organization as easily as they can connect with their peers and colleagues outside of the company so information can travel, new ideas can be exchanged and creativity can flourish.

This leads to a rather short-term orientation to the spontaneous conditions. Through this and by working in looser structures or groupings, a culture of experi-mentation is promoted. In a world that is increasingly affected by volatility, uncer-tainty, complexity, and ambiguity (VUCA), this is absolutely essential. This is more important for heuristic activities, which will become more important since innovation and new ideas are in the foreground and not efficiency as in the processing of algorithmic tasks. The latter can be performed more and more by computers. Frithjof Bergmann (2019) also attaches great importance to experimen-tation in the sense of trying out different activities in his New Work concept, since this makes it easier to find out what one "really, really" wants.

From Privacy to Transparency Fast-paced innovation in the form of collabora-tion and knowledge sharing is at the heart of open source (Sijbrandij 2018)—"the most powerful new business models of the twenty-first century" (Pink 2018, p. 21). Efficiency in solving heuristic challenges lies in not having to try out all the possibilities for oneself, but in being able to take advantage of the already tried and tested paths of others that have already proven to be erroneous or successful. A culture of experimentation is virtually dependent on the sharing of information and work results and, thus, on extensive transparency. The already outlined abatement of the excessive profit orientation of organizations and individuals will certainly help in this regard. Nevertheless, an open-source business model can also be operated profitably (Sijbrandij 2018). Moreover, leadership in nonhierarchical settings works much better if there is no secrecy but open and honest communication. Furthermore, openness within organizations, networks, or ecosystems is crucial in that strategically relevant data and information are not withheld due to particular interests, but shared without reservation.

2.2.3 Work and the Individual

To a large extent, the occupational sphere determines the quality of a person's life. Basically, it should not be difficult to get people to work, because the human organism is made for this very purpose: The human neural system works best when it is challenged and directed toward a specific task; most people feel most comfortable with themselves when they have mastered a problem well (Csikszentmihalyi 2003). Moreover, according to Professor Emeritus of Psychology Mihaly Csikszentmihalyi (2003)—and on this Frithjof Bergmann (2019) agrees with him—most jobs are not created for people, but to get the most out of them. This is a criticism related to the current Job System. Employees are squeezed like a lemon by their employers due to the latter's striving for maximum efficiency. An environment that attracts enthusiastic people who are eager to work must first and foremost provide the conditions that meet their drive, i.e., their motivation, to work.

In the future, more and more individuals could be able to secure their provision of basic supplies—largely through HTSP—with a reasonable amount of their time. People will be able to use the rest of their time to pursue an occupation which they "really, really" want to do and which is therefore meaningful to them. The pleasure experienced is a great motivator; it does not necessarily require material incentives or even the threat of negative consequences to overcome a reluctance to work. Rather, one works because one enjoys it—in other words, it is a matter of intrinsic motivation.

Basically, as Pink (2018) notes, scientists distinguish three drives for behavior:

- Biological drive, i.e., thirst, hunger, and sexual desire.
- Rewards and punishment, i.e., external forces based on (material) incentives or punishments.
- Intrinsic rewards, i.e., the joy of the task being its own reward.

"As humans formed more complex societies, bumping against strangers and needing to cooperate in order to get things done, an 'operating system' based purely on the biological drive was inadequate"—on the contrary, one must restrain this urge, as one cannot simply steal food from others or engage in sexual misconduct with others (Pink 2018, p. 18). Therefore, a social operating system has been developed that regards a person as more than the sum of their biological needs. To keep these under control, extrinsic incentives and punishments have been developed. This incentive system has so far worked quite well in the business world for algorithmic tasks, but not for heuristic and creative activities: "Intrinsic motivation is conducive to creativity; controlling extrinsic motivation is detrimental to creativity" (Amabile 1996 as cited in Pink 2018, p. 30). Accordingly, the younger and coming generations will increasingly turn away from a system based on extrinsic motivation toward one based on intrinsic motivation.

One might think that the approach that allows people to do the work they "really, really" want to do may lead to dilettantism and the erosion of professional quality standards. But the opposite seems much more likely. Self-determined work and autonomy promote engagement. Following the SDT, one of the innate psychological needs is competence, which is quite related to "mastery—the desire to get better and better at something that matters" (Pink, 2018, p. 111). So, under the conditions outlined here, people will be highly committed to perform well. This striving for achievement is also connected with people's search for meaningfulness—or as Carol S. Dweck (1999, p. 41), a professor of psychology, puts it: "Effort is one of the things that gives meaning to life. Effort means you care about something, that something is important to you and you are willing to work for it. It would be an impoverished existence if you were not willing to value things and commit yourself to working toward them."

3   A Possible Scenario for the Year 2030

Fundamental changes in the principles by which societies organize themselves or parts of them do not usually change very quickly. It can therefore be assumed that the new way of working and living described above will by no means be fully developed in 2030. The Job System as we know it today will certainly not have been completely abolished by 2030. But the shifts in mindset discussed here and summarized in Fig. 4 will take place and will be implemented in the best possible way utilizing suitable measures—as the prevailing conditions in today's companies and organizations allow. In addition, the relevant developments that are already effective today, such as the increase in the number of social businesses and for-purpose organizations, will continue and most likely gain momentum. More profound changes, such as the elements of Frithjof Bergmann's New Work concept described above, will be taken up and exemplified by a small avant-garde, to which the fictional character Hans Doering in the introductory section of this chapter would belong. Individuals and smaller communities will use the well-equipped and already publicly accessible (prototype) workshops such as the MakerSpace in Garching b. München, Germany, which is connected to the Technical University of Munich (TUM), and the FabLab of the Friedrich-Alexander-Universität Erlangen-Nürnberg (FAU), in order to produce certain products such as furniture or smaller objects, e.g., business card cases—following the idea of Hi-Tech-Self-Providing. The media will increasingly report about such early adopters, so that their experiences will be made public and discussed by a broader number of people. Until the year 2030, the currently young Generation Z will continue to mature and clearly articulate their needs and engage in the sociopolitical discourse.

By 2030, the destination of the journey toward a new foundation for work will not yet have been reached, but a noticeable departure in this direction may have happened.

Key Insights for the Path Toward a New Foundation of Work in 2030

- The changes in today's working world are related to two key drivers: First, to a change in the values prevailing in society as younger generations gradually replace their predecessors and, second, to the spread of digital technologies. These two key drivers make the actual organization of work, and people's needs drift further and further apart.
- On the one hand, the prevailing values change from generation to generation. In 2030, the people born between 1981 and 1996 (Generation Y/Millennials) and those born between 1997 and 2012 (Generation Z) will make up about 80% of the working population. Compared to previous generations, professional success and advancement are much less important for these generations. They are skeptical about the self-exploitation of preceding generations. Consequently, Generation Yers and Zers seek to pursue meaningful work and lead a meaningful life in general. Adequate (material) security is important to them. Nonetheless, they want to have enough time for their private lives. Rather than leadership responsibility, Millennials prefer to take on well-defined tasks within a collaborative network and a collegial working atmosphere. At the same time, Generation Z is particularly supposed to strive for a clear separation of professional and private life as well as clear structures.
- The increasing proliferation of digital technologies has implications both for the types of work that people will do in the future and for the design and organization of that work. First, simple activities that follow a clear scheme can be automated, so that humans are faced with an increasing proportion of more demanding and unstructured nonroutine tasks. The successful execution of the latter requires—at least in companies of today's type—leadership roles to be exerted. Second, it comes to a blurring of the boundaries between professional and private concerns (work-life blending). These are both developments that tendentially do not meet the expectations of the Generations Y and Z. Moreover, the negative consequences of the spread of digital technologies, such as increased work-related mental stress and illness, can already be observed today. Simply going on in this way is, therefore, not a sustainable option.
- An alternative way to organize work in our society is often referred to by the term New Work that was largely coined by Frithjof Bergmann, a professor of philosophy. The concept of New Work is based on three different elements that deviate quite considerably from a pure flexibilization of work:
  - Taking up work that makes use of people's best talents and that corresponds to their full and deep desires that they experience as a calling.
  - Reducing the dependency on the current Job System.

(continued)

- Ensuring the provision of basic supplies that allows one to pursue one's calling by drawing on state-of-the-art technology (Hi-Tech-Self-Providing).
- When it comes to shaping the future world of work, aspects on three levels must be addressed: the sociopolitical environment, the inter-individual organization of work, and the individual with their needs:
  - Regarding the sociopolitical conditions, the imperative of economic growth as a (political) goal needs to be questioned in order to avoid increasing unemployment and a further widening of the gap in the unequal distribution of income and wealth.
  - On the inter-individual level, shifts in the mindset regarding what and how organizations operate are necessary—from profit to purpose/benefit, from hierarchies to networks/ecosystems, from controlling to empowering/trust, from (long-range) planning to experimentation, and from privacy to transparency.
  - In 2030, a small avant-garde of individuals could be able to secure their provision of basic supplies—largely through Hi-Tech-Self-Providing—with a reasonable amount of their time. This allows these people to pursue their respective calling as work. In doing so, they become less extrinsically driven by (material) incentives but rather more intrinsically motivated.

References

Amabile, T. M. (1996). *Creativity in context*. Boulder, CO: Westview Press.

Antal, M. (2014). Green goals and full employment: Are they compatible? *Ecological Economics, 107*, 276–286.

B Lab. (n.d.). The *B Economy: A global movement*. Berwyn, PA: B Lab. Accessed August 11, 2020, from https://bcorporation.net/b-economy

Baard, P. P., Deci, E. L., & Ryan, R. M. (2004). Intrinsic need satisfaction: A motivational basis of performance and well-being in two work settings. *Journal of Applied Social Psychology, 34* (10), 2045–2068.

Balakrishnan, A., & Gernon, D. (2017). *Alibaba's Jack Ma says in 30 years people will only work 4 hours a day*. Englewood Cliffs, NJ: CNBC. Accessed August 08, 2020, from https://www.cnbc.com/2017/06/21/alibabas-jack-ma-says-in-30-years-people-will-only-work-4-hours-a-day.html

Bergmann, F. (2019). *New work, new culture: Work we want and a culture that strengthens us*. Winchester, UK: Zero Books.

BKK Dachverband. (2019). *BKK Gesundheitsreport 2019: Psychische Gesundheit und Arbeit [BKK health report 2019: Mental health and work]*. Accessed August 10, 2020, from https://www.bkk-dachverband.de/publikationen/bkk-gesundheitsreport.html

Böhm, S. A., Bourovoi, K., Brzykcy, A., Kreissner, L. M., & Breier, C. (2016). *Auswirkungen der Digitalisierung auf die Gesundheit von Berufstätigen: Eine bevölkerungsrepräsentative Studie in der Bundesrepublik Deutschland [The impact of digitization on the health of working people:*

A population representative study in the Federal Republic of Germany]. Work report. St. Gallen, Switzerland: University of St. Gallen.

Chattopadhyay, S. (2019). *Re-imaging organizations as ecosystems: Exploring the paradigm shifts necessary to move toward a living systems view of organizations*. Online article. San Francisco, CA. Accessed August 12, 2020, from https://medium.com/age-of-emergence/re-imagining-organizations-as-ecosystems-79414488f2f0

Chen, L. Y. (2019). Forget long work hours, Alibaba's Jack Ma feels 4 hours a day, 3 days a week work culture could be the norm soon. Online article. Gurugram, India: *The Economic Times*. Accessed September 24, 2020, from https://economictimes.indiatimes.com/news/international/business/jack-ma-says-12-hour-work-week-could-be-the-norm/articleshow/70887993.cms?from=mdr

Cooney, K., Koushyar, J., Lee, M., & Murray, H. (2014). *Benefit corporation and L3C adoption: A survey*. Stanford, CA: Stanford Social Innovation Review. Accessed August 09, 2020, from https://ssir.org/articles/entry/benefit_corporation_and_l3c_adoption_a_survey

Csikszentmihalyi, M. (2003). *Good business, leadership, flow, and the making of meanings*. New York, NY: Viking.

Cushman & Wakefield. (2020). *Demographic shifts: The world in 2030*. Report. Chicago, IL: Cushman & Wakefield.

Deci, E. L., & Ryan, R. M. (1985). *Intrinsic motivation and self-determination in human behavior*. New York, NY: Plenum.

Deci, E. L., & Ryan, R. M. (2008). Facilitating optimal motivation and psychological well-being across life's domains. *Canadian Psychology, 49*(1), 14–23.

Dweck, C. S. (1999). *Self-theories: Their role in motivation, personality, and development*. Philadelphia, PA: Psychology Press.

Eswein, A.-L. (2020). *Wertewandel auf dem Arbeitsmarkt der Generation Z [Changing values in the labor market of Generation Z]*. Accessed August 10, 2020, from https://www.it-daily.net/it-management/projekt-portfolio-management/23946-wertewandel-auf-dem-arbeitsmarkt-der-generation-z

Federal Ministry of Labour and Social Affairs. (2016). *Digitalisierung am Arbeitsplatz [digitization at the workplace]*. Research report no. 468. Berlin, Germany.

Feldmann, S. (2020). *What is an L3C (low-profit limited liability company): An entity for entrepreneurs who value purpose and profits*. Alphen aan den Rijn, the Netherlands: Wolters Kluwer. Accessed August 09, 2020, from https://ct.wolterskluwer.com/resource-center/articles/what-is-l3c-low-profit-limited-liability-company

Fink, N. (2015). *To create a culture of innovation, learn to celebrate failure. Video file and its transcription*. Philadelphia, PA: The William and Phyllis Mack Institute for Innovation Management, The Wharton School, The University of Pennsylvania. Accessed August 12, 2020, from https://mackinstitute.wharton.upenn.edu/2015/to-create-a-culture-of-innovation-learn-to-celebrate-failure/

Gallup. (2017). *State of the global workplace*. Report. New York, NY: Gallup Press.

Gierke, O. (1868). *Das deutsche Genossenschaftsrecht [German cooperative law]*. Berlin, Germany: Weidmannsche Buchhandlung.

Government Digital Service. (n.d.). *Setting up a social enterprise*. Accessed August 11, 2020, from https://www.gov.uk/set-up-a-social-enterprise

Heller, K. (2018). *Wertewandel in der Arbeitswelt [Changing values in the world of work]*. Blog post. Schwanewede, Germany: Neudenkerei. Accessed July 22, 2020, from https://neudenkerei.de/arbeitgebermarketing/wertewandel-in-der-arbeitswelt/

ibau. (2020). *Der Wertewandel der Generation X, Y und Z: Ein Überblick [The change in values of Generation X, Y, and Z: An overview]*. Accessed July 22, 2020, from https://www.ibau.de/akademie/wissenswertes/generation-x-y-z/

Indian Institute of Management Bangalore. (2020). *Webinar session on innovation ecosystems between academia, industry and society, 12 August 2020*. Social media post. Accessed August

12, 2020, from https://www.linkedin.com/posts/iim-bangalore-executive-education_in-the-contemporary-fast-paced-business-environment-activity-6697523048083521536-1Bnr

Kleemann, F., Matuschek, I., & Voß, G. G. (1999). *Zur Subjektivierung von Arbeit [On the subjectification of labor]. Paper*. Berlin, Germany: Wissenschaftszentrum Berlin für Sozialforschung. Accessed July 29, 2020, from https://bibliothek.wzb.eu/pdf/1999/p99-512.pdf

Klös, H.-P., Rump, J., & Zibrowius, M. (2016). *Die neue Generation: Werte, Arbeitseinstellungen und unternehmerische Anforderungen [The new generation: Values, work attitudes and business requirements]. Discussion paper no. 29*. Munich, Germany: Roman Herzog Institut.

Knieps, F., & Pfaff, H. (Eds.). (2017). *Digitale Arbeit – digitale Gesundheit: BKK Gesundheitsreport 2017 [Digital work – digital health: BKK health report 2017]*. Berlin, Germany: Medizinisch Wissenschaftliche Verlagsgesellschaft.

Kordouni, J. (2017). *Wie Work-Life-Blending die Work-Life-Balance ablöst [How work-life blending replaces work-life balance]*. Kiel, Germany: askDANTE, *Blog für Digitalisierung und Arbeiten 4.0 [Blog for digitization and work 4.0]*. Accessed July 29, 2020, from https://www.askdante.com/de/blog/work-lifeblending/#:~:text=Unter%20Work%2DLife%2DBlending%20versteht,Freizeit%20mit%20den%20Kollegen%20verbracht

Kranenberg, E. (2014). *Work-values differences within Generation Y: Recommendations for HR management in the hospitality industry*. Master thesis. Enschede, the Netherlands: University of Twente.

Kuhlmann, M., & Schumann, M. (2015). Digitalisierung fordert Demokratisierung der Arbeitswelt heraus [Digitization challenges democratization of the world of work]. In R. Hoffmann & C. Bogedan (Eds.), *Arbeit der Zukunft: Möglichkeiten nutzen – Grenzen setzen [Work of the future: Using opportunities—setting limits]* (pp. 122–140). Frankfurt am Main, Germany: Campus.

Lechleiter, P., Purbs, A., & Sonntag, K. (2018). *HR- und Gesundheitsmanagement in der Arbeit 4.0: Bedarfe in deutschen und internationalen Unternehmen – eine quantitative Online-Studie [HR and health management in work 4.0: Needs in German and international companies—a quantitative online study]*. Report. Heidelberg, Germany: University of Heidelberg, Industrial and Organizational Psychology. Accessed August 10, 2020, from https://gesundearbeit-mega.de/sites/gesundearbeit-mega.de/files/u8/bedarfe_hr-_und_gesundheitsmanagement_arbeit_4.0_langfassung.pdf

Maas, R. (2019). *Generation Z für Personaler und Führungskräfte: Ergebnisse der Generation-Thinking-Studie [Generation Z for human resource managers and executives: Results of the generation thinking study]*. Munich, Germany: Hanser.

Manyika, J., & Sneader, K. (2018). *AI, automation, and the future of work: Ten things to solve for*. New York, NY: McKinsey Global Institute. Accessed July 28, 2020, from https://www.mckinsey.com/featured-insights/future-of-work/ai-automation-and-the-future-of-work-ten-things-to-solve-for

Martela, F., Ryan, R. M., & Steger, M. F. (2018). Meaningfulness as satisfaction of autonomy, competence, relatedness, and beneficence: Comparing the four satisfactions and positive affect as predictors of meaning in life. *Journal of Happiness Studies, 19*(5), 1261–1282.

Moore, J. (2008). *Vermont governor expected to sign bill on charity-business hybrid*. Washington, DC: The Chronicle of Philanthropy. Accessed August 09, 2020, from https://www.philanthropy.com/article/Vermont-Governor-Expected-to/194299

Mörstedt, A.-B. (2017). *Erwartungen der Generation Z an die Unternehmen [Expectations of the Generation Z on companies]*. Presentation. Göttingen, Germany: PFH Private University of Applied Sciences. Accessed August 10, 2020, from https://www.pfh.de/fileadmin/Content/PDF/forschungspapiere/vortrag-generation-z-moerstedt-ihk-goettingen.pdf

Müller-Thur, K., Angerer, P., Körner, U., & Dragano, N. (2018). Arbeit mit digitalen Technologien, psychosoziale Belastungen und potenzielle gesundheitliche Konsequenzen [Work with digital technologies, psychosocial stress, and potential health consequences]. *ASU Arbeitsmedizin | Sozialmedizin | Umweltmedizin, 53*(6), 388–391.

O'Rourke, A. (n.d.). *What is an L3C?* Eugene, OR: Palo Alto Software. Accessed August 09, 2020, from https://articles.bplans.com/what-is-an-l3c/

Oates, W. E. (1971). *Confessions of a workaholic: The facts about work addiction.* Nashville, TN: Abingdon Press.

Owen, R. (1817). *The manufacturing system: With hints for the improvement of those parts of it which are most injurious to health and morals.* London, UK: Longman, Hurst, Rees, Orme, and Brown.

Piketty, T. (2014). *Capital in the twenty-first century.* Boston, MA: Harvard University Press.

Pink, D. H. (2006). *A whole new mind: Why right-brainers will rule the future.* New York, NY: Riverhead Books.

Pink, D. H. (2018). *Drive: The surprising truth about what motivates us.* Edinburgh, UK: Canongate.

R+V Allgemeine Versicherung. (2020). *MakerCamp Genossenschaften: Genossenschaften einfach erklärt [Cooperatives explained simply].* Accessed September 03, 2020, from https://www.makercamp-geno.de/genossenschaften-einfach-erklaert/

Rawhouser, H., Cummings, M., & Crane, A. (2015). Benefit corporation legislation and the emergence of a social hybrid category. *California Management Review, 57*(3), 13–35.

Ryan, R. M., & Deci, E. L. (2000). Self-determination theory and the facilitation of intrinsic motivation, social development, and well-being. *American Psychologist, 55*(1), 68–78.

Sachs, A., & Kundu, A. (2015). *The unfinished business of organizational transformation.* Chicago, IL: ThoughtWorks. Accessed August 11, 2020, from https://www.thoughtworks.com/insights/blog/unfinished-business-organizational-transformation

Shell Deutschland Holding (Ed.). (2019). *18. Shell Jugendstudie: Jugend 2019 – Eine generation meldet sich zu Wort [18th Shell youth study: Youth 2019—A generation speaks up].* Weinheim, Germany: Beltz.

Sijbrandij, S. (2018). *How open source became the default business model for software.* Jersey City, NJ: Forbes Media. Accessed August 12, 2020, from https://www.forbes.com/sites/forbestechcouncil/2018/07/16/how-open-source-became-the-default-business-model-for-software/

Sonntag, K. (2019). Organisations- und Personalentwicklung in einer sich wandelnden Welt. In F. Knieps & H. Pfaff (Eds.), *BKK Gesundheitsreport 2019: Psychische Gesundheit und Arbeit [BKK health report: Mental health and work]* (pp. 239–247). Berlin, Germany: Medizinisch Wissenschaftliche Verlagsgesellschaft.

Trautmann, M. (2019). *On the way to New Work: 10 Learnings von einer Reise, die erst begonnen hat [On the way to New Work: 10 lessons from a journey that has just begun].* Video file. Accessed August 07, 2020, from https://www.youtube.com/watch?v=WOhsJ9aUIeg

Väth, M. (2016). *Arbeit – Die schönste Nebensache der Welt: Wie New Work unsere Arbeitswelt revolutioniert [Work—The most beautiful minor matter in the world: How New Work is revolutionizing our working world].* Offenbach, Germany: Gabal.

Verde. (2019). *Why we believe in being an L3C company.* Blog post. Chicago, IL: Verde. Accessed August 09, 2020, from https://www.verde.expert/why-we-believe-in-being-an-l3c-company/#:~:text=L3Cs%20are%20written%20into%20your,%2C%20Utah%2C%20Vermont%2C%20Wyoming

Vora, T. (2015). *Mindset shifts for organizational transformation.* Blog post. Ahmedabad, Gujarat, India: QAspire. Accessed August 11, 2020, from http://qaspire.com/2015/11/23/mindset-shifts-for-organizational-transformation/

Voß, G. G. (1998). Die Entgrenzung von Arbeit und Arbeitskraft: Eine subjektorientierte Interpretation des Wandels der Arbeit [The dissolution of the boundaries of work and workforce: A subject-oriented interpretation of the change of work]. *Mitteilungen aus der Arbeitsmarkt- und Berufsforschung, 31*(3), 473–487.

Thomas K. Hamann is the Executive Director of the top-management consultancy T. K. Hamann. Thomas is a licentiatus oeconomiae (lic. oec. HSG) and holds a doctoral degree from the University of St. Gallen, Switzerland. In addition to his advisory services for various companies, Thomas conducts scientific research and lectures at various business schools. He focuses on strategic management, including business war-gaming, sales and marketing, leadership and organization, and operational issues. Before founding his own consulting firm, he worked for various top-tier consultancies as well as in the Department of Strategy and Corporate Development at Porsche.

Part III

Leadership in 2030

The New Role of Leaders and Leadership in 2030

Stefan Güldenberg

The theme of this year's Earth Day, celebrated in May 1st, is united action:

The ILO, formerly known as the International Labour Organization, has adapted its name and announces its first body of expert leaders:

The United Nations broadcast the news about the newly elected leaders of what is now called the International Leadership Organization. Due to the sixth global crises within the twenty-first century, the demand for global solutions required the selection of a body of 17 experts, one of each of the UN 17 Sustainability Goals (SDGs). They are all experts, knowledge entrepreneurs, pioneers, and visionaries. They have access to the accumulated knowledge of humanity through their personal network within the scientific community. These SDG Leaders are well known and enjoy an excellent reputation among the global population. Their word carries weight, as before, only religious authorities, such as the Pope, had. No national or regional leader can afford to ignore them.

What is happening right now is what many have dreamed of seeing one day: global action to cocreate a sustainable future for future generations. Exactly the opposite was happening during the COVID-19 crises around 10 years ago. It all started with the collective blame game against China. Then, we saw a fight between nations around being the first to get a vaccine. Similar national and populist behavioral patterns occurred while solving the climate, refugee, or economic crises, all of which really required joint global action instead.

It took a while until the UN recognized that they had to give their SDGs not only nice images and quantitative targets but also a personal face, unlike the European Union whose EU commissioners made classical political appointees by endlessly debating the need for balancing of gender and national backgrounds and by nominating politicians of whom the individual member states wanted to get rid of by offering them a second career away from home.

S. Güldenberg (✉)
Institute for Entrepreneurship, University of Liechtenstein, Vaduz, Liechtenstein
e-mail: stefan.gueldenberg@uni.li

© Springer Nature Switzerland AG 2021
S. Güldenberg et al. (eds.), *Managing Work in the Digital Economy*, Future of Business and Finance, https://doi.org/10.1007/978-3-030-65173-2_9

Here, the UN via the ILO chose a different approach, establishing a genuinely global leadership committee of worldwide expert leaders, based on their knowledge, values, and reputation in order to push forward the implementation of the 17 SDGs on a global scale and giving them a personal face as well as a worldwide voice. In order to make long-term change possible and to develop the necessary global and transformational expertise, these leaders get a maximum of 10 years tenure, but with the possibility to resign within the first six months if they see that the challenge is too great for them or the team is not working as expected. There is also a quality check about the outcomes every two years by the UN General Assembly.

As the General Secretary in her speech mentioned, "Today we don't just need a set of international labour standards but also a set of international leadership standards. Globalization has enabled us to see the collective ship we are all in: the magnificent planet earth. All the major problems of the world are global, and they cannot be solved without international cooperation. In its absence, issues such as technological advancements could also pose a threat to our future. Such thought-provoking ideas planted a seed of the new ILO, the International Leadership Organization, which has led to this day and this speech. We once again redefined what it means to be human. An ambitious, free, and insatiable explorer. We are the result of the generation that gave science its deserved credibility after centuries of denial and conflict. That generation showed us what it knew then and what it wanted to change for everyone's sake. Science was showing us that the truth is not harsh; rather, it is consoling and promising when understood correctly.

It seems like we have come a long way, but this is just a minute fraction of time when compared to the beginning of our existence. There is no longer any need for borders; we learned that a long time ago through the unification similar to that of the European Union, or simply every nation before the establishment of states. These experiences helped us accomplish this on a global scale. We have eradicated world hunger using technology. This only became possible after minimizing waste and distributing resources fairly. We knew from the beginning that a disaster such as hunger was only an error in the system and not inherently impossible to solve. We humans trusted our innermost instinct, the exploration instinct, to lead us. We are born explorers, and if we die knowing we didn't understand everything, that is okay. We pass on the information, as others have done before us. It is fulfilling to know that our predecessor's dream became ours, and ours will become the next generation's. Aren't we today well equipped to realize a humanitarian world that once existed only in the skies of our ancient philosophers' imagination?" (speech slightly adapted from the winner essay of the Drucker Challenge Essay Award, Managers/Entrepreneurs Category, Safavi (2020, p. 1).

1   Management vs. Leadership

Control is not leadership; management is not leadership; leadership is leadership. If you seek to lead, invest at least 50% of your time leading yourself Invest at least 20% leading those with authority over you and 15% leading your peers. If you don't understand that you work

Table 1 Differences between managers and leaders in 2030 (inspired by Bennis (1989) with own additions)

Manager	Leader
The manager administers	The leader innovates
The manager is a copy	The leader is an original
The manager maintains	The leader develops
The manager focuses on systems and structure	The leader focuses on people
The manager relies on control	The leader inspires trust
The manager has a short-range view	The leader has a long-range perspective
The manager asks how and when	The leader asks what and why
Managers have their eyes on the bottom line	Leaders have their eyes on the horizon
The manager imitates	The leader originates
The manager accepts the status quo	The leader challenges it
The manager is the classic good soldier	The leader is a cocreating team
The manager does things right	The leader does the right thing
Manager is a job	Leader is a role
Managers have people who work for them	Leaders have people who follow them
Managers focus on best practices	Leaders focus on next practices
By 2030, the job of a manager will to a large degree be automated by AI solutions	*The role of a leader cannot be fully automated by AI solutions*

for your mislabeled 'subordinates,' then you know nothing of leadership. You know only tyranny. (Dee W. Hock, Founder and CEO Emeritus, Visa International)

In 2030, the old dichotomy between management and leadership will appear to us in a completely and radically new light (see also Table 1). Management is basically routine work. Therefore, it can be treated like accounting or management control automated and done by machines. In contrast, leadership is, to a high degree, nonroutine, creative, and people-interactive work. In fact, leadership in our new understanding is about cocreating the future. As already mentioned by Peter F. Drucker, you cannot predict the future in an unstable environment. You can only create it. But you cannot do that by definition alone. Due to your personal cognitive limitations, this has to be a process of cocreation.

In 2030, there was also a remarkable change in the measurement of successful leadership. It was no longer measured like in the 2020s by the amount of artificial power someone possesses or the wealth that someone could accumulate in their life but rather by the scale of the movement one had started and led to bring about a global change:

- In the early 2000s, a teenager, Malala Yousafzai, insisted on going to school and her right to education. Not even a murder attempt by the Taliban could dampen her spirit. She survived and not only went to school but also encouraged education in the world for children and girls in particular.
- Similarly and controversially, another teenager, Greta Thunberg, stopped going to school and insisted on saving the earth from overheating. In 1 year, she had

started a global movement that inspired teenagers from almost all nationalities to proactively claim their future.
- Last, but not least, a third teenager, Felix Finkbeiner, had started an action plan to plant 1 billion trees all around the world. The movement he started eventually turned into the "Stop talking, Start planting" campaign.

Despite the fact that individual human beings can make a huge difference in 2030, it is not the individual human being but the whole movement, the leadership team, who will be the new hero. Every leader will depend heavily on their personal network, the knowledge workers, and experts they know and work with, be it inside or outside the specific organizations. Together with them, they will cocreate the future. This work is inherently creative and requires high capacities of empathy and sensemaking. It will therefore be much harder to replace it by machines than autocratic and bureaucratic management, which is much more routine and rule-based (see also Chap. 10 Güldenberg and Langhof in this book):

In the following chapter, we will describe the five most profound challenges and changes of leadership in 2030.

2   Five Major Leadership Challenges in 2030

- **Leading Into the Unknown**

In the past, the main task of leadership was optimization, which is managing growth and efficiency. In a relatively stable world, you can manage the known and extrapolate it into the future. To build an extension to a house, you don't need to tear it down and build a new one. This is no longer possible in a VUCA world, which consists of four elements: volatility, uncertainty, complexity, and ambiguity (Achi and Berger 2015; Bennett and Lemoine 2014). In such a world, optimization is not enough and can be dangerous or even deadly, because you may optimize for the wrong circumstances. In such a world, profitable growth is replaced by long-term survival, financial optimization is replaced by holistic resilience, and extrinsic motivation is replaced by intrinsic motivation and meaningful work.

- **Leading the Knowledgeable**

In the past, the best expert in one task would sooner or later in their career end up in a leadership position. The leader was the best expert, and knowledge meant power. In a knowledge economy, this is no longer true. Experts are no longer willing to step into leadership roles because they risk losing their expertise while being busy in leading other people. This has led to a separation between professional and management careers, making leaders heavily dependent on their experts to fulfill their primary responsibility: to be effective and make the right decision.

- **Leading Four Generations**

For the first time in history, leaders will have to lead four generations at the same time (see also chapter People@Work): Baby Boomers, Generation X, Generation Y, and Generation Z, all with very different values, motives, and expectations in regard to their work-life and leadership. In addition, leadership itself will consist of these four generations, which have to work smoothly together to fulfill their leadership responsibilities. This requires a deep understanding of the underlying needs and demands of each of these generations. It will also replace the old principle of seniority: Taking over a leadership position is no longer based on your age but on your empathy and your ability to create a productive human community of four generations.

- **Leading Diversity**

In the past, leaders were responsible mainly toward their shareholders. Today and in the future, this responsibility will shift toward a more diverse set of groups, the stakeholders. Leaders are no longer responsible only toward their owners and financers but toward their employees, customers, suppliers, and society at large. Therefore, besides the four generations, leaders have to deal successfully with diverse and often contradictory expectations. In a more and more globalized and polarized world, it is vital to bring people with very different skills, cultural backgrounds, mindsets, values, capabilities, and nationalities together in a productive way. This requires an open mindset and the capability of deep listening. Diversity also plays a major role in digital transformation and digital leadership (see next chapter Güldenberg and Langhof).

- **Leading Transformation**

In the past, when something fundamental changed in the environment, leaders were often replaced by someone else, more fitting in the new situation. A leader well known for being good at managing a crisis was replaced in better times by someone who had a reputation for being good at driving growth only to be replaced again during the next crises. Today, this model has come to an end, as the average term for leaders has dramatically decreased from well over 10 years some decades ago to just about 5 years nowadays. Professional reorientation in top management becomes the rule, not the exception. This goes in line with the regular occurrence of a new global crisis every 5 years. In contrast, the tenure of CEOs in successful companies is, on average, 15 years (Ignatius 2019). Leading the next significant transformations, therefore, should become the task of every future leader. This requires a new set of leadership capabilities, and change management in 2030 will become an essential part of every leadership curriculum.

3   The New Leadership Priorities in 2030

In the past, the leader was typically considered as the strong autocratic person, most likely male in front of the organization or a group of people. He led by power, the power of his position, his age, his wealth, or his charisma. Still, some success stories of successful leaders in our times follow this kind of pattern when you look at the examples of Steve Jobs, Elon Musk, Jeff Bezos, and Jack Welch. But will these strong leaders be accepted in the future?

In our view, the leader of the future has to work on five dimensions which are vital in order to get the attention of their followers:

3.1   From Leading Others Toward Leading Yourself

* *New Delhi, India, in the 1930s:*
  A worried mother embarks on a long and arduous journey. She wants to meet the famous moral teacher Mahatma Gandhi. She has high hopes of meeting the spiritual leader. Her sugar-obsessed son should definitely change his bad eating habits and eat fewer sweets. When she finally met Gandhi, she received a sobering answer. Gandhi is said to have told her, "Unfortunately, I cannot talk to him now. Please bring your son back in a few weeks. I will talk to him then." Although the mother was naturally disappointed and sad, she came back to Gandhi a few weeks later. This time, Gandhi took the time to talk to her son, and indeed, the conversation was successful. The son even agreed to refrain from excessive consumption of sweets in the future. The mother, who was deeply impressed by Gandhi's compassion and wisdom, expressed her gratitude to him. One thing she wanted to know, why had Gandhi not wanted to speak to her son at the first meeting? Gandhi replied, "Well, two weeks ago, I ate a lot of sugar myself. I first had to go this way myself to explain to him that he should not eat sugar" (based on Edwards 2017*).*

Leadership always begins with self-leadership: According to Dee Hock (1999), only those who can lead themselves will be capable of leading others effectively. This is particularly true for knowledge workers, who do not like to be managed by orders and rules. Drucker (1999) says that, in general, leadership styles can be acquired. However, this also means that leading knowledge workers needs to be learned intensively and systematically through evidence-based theory, personal reflection, and practical experience. Leadership styles and especially self-leadership are not innate, although there may be people of varying talent out there. The first thing about leadership styles is the optimal execution of one's tasks (Senge 1990, 2003).

Each great transformation in organizations therefore begins with the recognition and the transformation of one's mental models. This is indeed a factor that makes the implementation of change in an organization so difficult (Göpel 2016; Schneidewind 2018). We have a fatal tendency to first try and make others change their behavior without realizing that we need to begin by changing our mindset and behavior. If we want to create trust, if we're going to succeed, then we must start with ourselves. Self-leadership will become the most important capability in a digital economy because you have to manage processes of unlearning your old mindsets and learning new leadership skills (Klammer and Güldenberg 2019).

Most change processes are doomed to fail right from the beginning because of the notion that one can bring about a change in the organization without any changes in one's thinking. Particularly harmful is the notion that this change can be implemented without any change in the mindset and personality of the leaders themselves. An example of this would be the belief that change can be brought about merely by investing in new digital technologies or by roping in external consultants who advise on how to drive one's employees to change. Change programs that are rolled out in organizations are usually not able to address the critical question: Do the current management executives, their competences, and their style of leadership fit the vision of the organization in the future?

Individual change and individual learning, especially on the management side, is a prerequisite in order to achieve organizational change and learning. Although an increasing number of leaders are taking this personal aspect into account, the implementation of this insight in the prevailing leadership practice is still quite far from reality.

The perceived threats to one's position, the cultural prejudices, and the barriers which prevent the awareness and acceptance of one's shortcomings are still prevalent among today's leaders. With that in mind, it would be just to say that we have a leadership crisis in today's times, and we can see it everywhere in the form of the dwindling trust of employees in their leaders. On the other hand, more and more leaders have realized their personal responsibility to learn and ask the right questions. For instance, a member of the board recently confessed to his colleagues that every day he strives hard to remain human while he executes his duties as a leader.

3.2   From One-Size-Fits-All Toward Situational Leadership (Improvisation Is the New Leadership Paradigm)

Hawthorne, North America, in the 2030s: A biotech supplier based in North America was in a deep crisis. Great uncertainty spread throughout the workforce. So, the two managing directors came up with an unusual, almost foolhardy plan, perhaps their last chance for the biotech supplier in the crisis:

They shut down all online communication, approached every single employee personally, and developed individual plans with and for each employee. These individual plans included the personal needs and goals of each employee. "Our main task was to listen above all else," said the Managing Director, who had made it his duty to have lunch with a different employee every day. The plan was daring and extraordinary since for more than 10 years digital and virtual had been the standard approach. But in the end, it surprisingly worked. The productivity of the employees increased considerably, which has been not the case during the last 10 years. The profits of the company also increased in the medium term.

As one of the two leaders noted, "Giving personal attention and listening makes the difference. Whether it is a general feeling of uncertainty, fear, increasing complexity, or the unreliability of modern technology; digitalization brings with it countless challenges. Given the dramatic changes brought about by digitization, it is important that we listen and respond to the concerns of our employees" (based on Christ 2014).

Knowledge workers are different, and they require different leadership styles and answers. The future leader has to improvise and act situationally. What works in one situation does not fit at all to another situation. Think, for example, on the kind of innovation you want to reach: Should it be radical or incremental? Both would require utterly different leadership approaches in terms of effectiveness and efficiency.

This is especially true in times of crisis. At the beginning of the 2020s, we are now experiencing the fourth major crisis (terrorist attacks, financial, migrants, pandemic), and there is no reason to assume that this mode of permanent crises will change until 2030. On the contrary, the next crises are just waiting around the corner, and there are a couple of candidates for it: climate, economic conflict, social riots, inequality, fundamentalism and populism, blackouts, and most probably some yet unknown ones as well.

Situational leadership cannot prepare for everything coming, but one thing is certain: It has to react fast and effectively to deal with such crisis situation and to protect lives and jobs. This can only be done by changing our previous success paths, those concentrated on the optimization of costs and maximization of profits rather than toward building more resilience into our political and economic systems and therefore increases its chances for survival. In short, situational leadership replaces short-minded by long-term thinking and one way by multiple ways. In the end, nothing is without alternatives.

3.3 From Shareholder Toward Stakeholder Leadership

"The purpose of a company is to engage all its stakeholders in shared and sustained value creation. In creating such value, a company serves not only its shareholders but all its stakeholders—employees, customers, suppliers, local communities, and society at large. The best way to understand and harmonize the divergent interests of all stakeholders is through a shared commitment to policies and decisions that strengthen the long-term prosperity of a company.

A company is more than an economic unit generating wealth. It fulfills human and societal aspirations as part of the broader social system. Performance must be measured not only on the return to shareholders but also on how it achieves its environmental, social, and good governance objectives. Executive remuneration should reflect stakeholder responsibility.

A company that has a multinational scope of activities not only serves all those stakeholders who are directly engaged, but acts itself as a stakeholder—together with governments and civil society—of our global future. Corporate global citizenship requires a company to harness its core competencies, its entrepreneurship, skills and relevant resources in collaborative efforts with other companies and stakeholders to improve the state of the world" WEF (2020).

Knowledge workers are looking for purpose and meaning in their work. The future leader has to give meaningful answers for that search of purpose. It is no longer enough to incentivize extrinsically and run the company by pure numbers, which are completely meaningless. At the height of Shareholder Value Management in the late 1990s, more and more employees felt disconnected and disengaged (De Vulpian 2005). They saw no fit between their personal objectives, what they wanted to achieve in their lives, and the company objectives. The result was disengagement and a dramatic loss of commitment. If one cannot fulfill her or his personal objectives within an organization, one is concentrating more and more on activities outside of the organization leading to a disadvantage of what is being achieved within the organization and an enormous waste of human energy. That is the main disadvantage of Shareholder Value Management.

Stakeholder management provides that meaning and creates this shared value (Porter and Kramer 2011; Porter et al. 2012) which thereby focuses human energy. In order to be successful, it requires a shift in leaders' measures, time horizon, and priorities. Whereas Shareholder Management seemed to be comfortable and easy, it entails a tragedy in itself once stated by William Edwards Deming and very visible through several incidents during the last years: *"Management by numerical goal is an attempt to manage without knowledge of what to do, and in fact usually management by fear. If management sets only quantitative targets and makes people's jobs depend on meeting them, they will likely meet the targets—even if they have to destroy the enterprise to do it"* (Deming 1982, p. 76).

Therefore, in turbulent times, it is even in the best interest of shareholders if a company changes toward Stakeholder Leadership: *"As we approach a period of significant capital reallocation, companies have a responsibility—and an economic imperative—to give shareholders a clear picture of their preparedness. And in the future, greater transparency on questions of sustainability will be a persistently important component of every company's ability to attract capital. It will help investors assess which companies are serving their stakeholders effectively, reshaping the flow of capital accordingly. But the goal cannot be transparency for transparency's sake. Disclosure should be a means to achieving a more sustainable and inclusive capitalism. Companies must be deliberate and committed to embracing purpose and serving all stakeholders—your shareholders, customers, employees, and the communities where you operate. In doing so, your company will enjoy greater long-term prosperity, as will investors, workers, and society as a whole"* (*Larry Fink Chairman and CEO Blackrock, 2020*).

3.4 From Autocratic Toward Servant Leadership

Knowledge workers are independent as they know what to do best. They don't require directives, but they expect attention, appreciation, and respect. This is best shown by the expectations of one of the leading orchestras worldwide, the Vienna

Philharmonic. Asked what they expect from the management board they stated, that they should visit their performances because that shows their respect and appreciation of their work, but they should never tell them if they performed well because that is not their business at all. Such performance evaluation should be left to the professionals in the field of music, like colleagues or music critics. Now, transfer this experience to other businesses like the design department of a car manufacturer or the management of a research institution.

In these environments, future leaders should see themselves more like gardeners: They help their knowledge workers grow, but they should never drive them to growth. Future leaders wouldn't be able to do so as they no longer possess the necessary expert knowledge, which could lead to wrong management decisions with very adverse side effects on the motivation and commitment of their experts. This could ultimately lead to the destruction of the whole company.

Servant leadership as a modern leadership philosophy was coined by the American management consultant Robert Greenleaf (1970), Greenleaf et al. (2002), who, in turn, was inspired by Hermann Hesse's (1956) novel *Journey to the East*. In his original essay, Greenleaf (1970) describes servant leadership as follows:

> The servant-leader is servant first. . . It begins with the natural feeling that one wants to serve, to serve first. Then conscious choice brings one to aspire to lead. That person is sharply different from one who is leader first, perhaps because of the need to assuage an unusual power drive or to acquire material possessions (Greenleaf 1970).

The central notion of servant leadership involves a strict focus on the followers' interests and needs (Langhof and Güldenberg 2020b; Liden et al. 2014). Hence, servant leadership stands in contrast to other leadership styles (such as authoritarian leadership), where the *followers serve* their organization or their leader (Langhof et al. 2020).

In the modern literature of servant leadership, one can identify three main principles of servant leadership: uncompromising service, selflessness, and the willingness to help other people to grow (see also Table 2).

3.5 From Egocentric Toward Shared (Global) Leadership

> No institution can possibly survive if it needs geniuses or supermen to manage it. It must be organized in such a way as to be able to get along under a leadership composed of average human beings. No institution can endure if it is under one-man rule. Industrial dictatorship like any other dictatorship threatens the survival of the institution in the event—an inevitable event—of the dictators death (Peter Drucker 1946, p. 26).

When asked in advance of the World Economic Forum in Davos, where the founder Klaus Schwab sees the greatest challenge for leadership today, his answer was simple and powerful at the same time: egoism, which he wrote in big letters on a piece of paper. His famous interviewer Richard Quest from CNN seemed to be surprised and asked him for an explanation. Klaus Schwab replied:

Table 2 Are you a servant leader? (source: Langhof and Güldenberg 2020a)

Questions you can ask yourself	Description
Are you asking the right questions?	*"reflecting the leader's competency in solving work problems and understanding the organization's goals"* (Liden et al. 2015, p. 255)
Are you empowering others?	*"assessing the degree to which the leader entrusts followers with responsibility, autonomy, and decision-making influence"* (Liden et al. 2015, p. 255)
Are you helping subordinates grow and succeed?	*"capturing the extent to which the leader helps followers reach their full potential and succeed in their careers"* (Liden et al. 2015, p. 255)
Are you putting subordinates first?	*"assessing the degree to which the leader prioritizes meeting the needs of followers before tending to his or her own needs"* (Liden et al. 2015, p. 255)
Are you caring?	*"the degree to which the leader cares about followers' personal problems and well-being"* (Liden et al. 2015, p. 255)
Are you creating value for your community?	*"the leader's involvement in helping the community surrounding the organization as well as encouraging followers to be active in the community"* (Liden et al. 2015, p. 255)
Are you behaving ethically?	*"being honest, trustworthy, and serving as a model of integrity"* (Liden et al. 2015, p. 255)

> What we are seeing in the world is a king of increased egoism; it is a polarization of views. When you can't cope with change, you feel overwhelmed and you look for a simple solution, he said (Reid 2016).

Simple answers, simple solutions, simple rules, and simple leadership all suffer from the same problem: They are fast and wrong because they do not take into account the complexity that is out there and necessary to master it successfully: The greater the variety of a leadership system, the more it can master the variety of its environment, also known as Ashby's law; it is one of the key insights of cybernetics, the scientific study of control, and communication in the animal and the machine (Wiener 1948).

So, it is not a coincidence that collaboration is the key element of knowledge work. In order to achieve it, leadership has to be shared. Gibb already (1954, p. 884) mentioned that shared:

> Leadership is a group quality... a set of functions which must be carried out by the group. This concept of 'distributed leadership' is an important one. If there are leadership functions which must be performed in any group, and if these functions may be 'focused' or 'distributed', then leaders will be identifiable both in terms of the frequency and in terms of the multiplicity or patterns of functions performed.

Von Krogh et al. (2012) defines shared leadership as a dichotomy between centralized and distributed leadership:

Fig. 1 The five required leadership styles of 2030

In centralized leadership, leaders are selected according to predefined criteria of what constitutes effective leadership in knowledge creation. For example, (...) leaders would be chosen on the basis of their ability to formulate a strategic direction in the organization (...). In a distributed model, leadership needs to be 'stretched' over situations and individuals who are leaders and followers (...), and is therefore characterized by concerted activities rather than aggregated individual activities. Distributed leadership seeks to diffuse personal growth and development among participants so that they may take on leadership and followership in a peer structure (...). Developing these skills is not simply a question of instruction and the teaching of rule-based behavior (...). Rather, the practice of care, helping behavior, mentoring, guidance, and teaching-by-doing between peers will develop individuals' distributed leadership skills (...). Because they are removed from specific situations and processes of local knowledge creation, central, upper-echelon leaders cannot substitute for peers in diffusing these skills among participants.

Shared leadership is the anchor and focal point of the other four leadership styles (see also Fig. 1). Executed correctly, they lead to shared leadership. Without shared leadership, the joint cocreation of the future is not possible. If successfully established, it can be used to create a long-lasting strategic competitive advantage for the organization and a high potential for attracting talents.

4   The New Roles Leaders Have to Enact in 2030

Today, executives are increasingly realizing that fundamental change cannot be managed from the top. This fundamental change is, however, necessary to successfully transform organizations from the industrial age into the digital age. We can, therefore, see successful organizations in today's world gaining competitive advantage by changing their entire leadership system. Less individualistic and more collective, i.e., development of new knowledge and sharing it, lead to sustained growth.

The consequences that this development will have for the theory and practice of leadership should not be underestimated. In a digital society, we first need to change the mindset of our leaders, who are until today looked upon as lone heroes at the top, influencing and controlling the whole organization. Top-down instructions, even if they are actually implemented, foster an atmosphere of fear, mistrust, and internal competition, which in turn reduces the willingness to work as a team and learn together. Directives coming from the top are followed but do not help employee retention or identification with the company. Only real identification forms the basis for the courage, the power of imagination, the patience, and the consequence which are required to boost learning processes in the organization.

Precisely for these reasons, leadership in the future has to be distributed to various members and groups of the organization who are collectively responsible for shaping the future of the company:

- Servant leaders are aware of their responsibility toward employees and the organization as a whole and therefore strive to serve both—the employees and the overall goal of the organization. Usually, they are members of the top management team of an organization, who mentor the local line leaders and function as their thinking and sparring partners. These members of the management are also responsible for supporting cultural change by being aware of their influence as role models and conducting themselves accordingly. Moreover, they invest in the learning infrastructure of the organization and simultaneously try to overcome learning barriers.
- Community leaders are people who often have very little authority or no in the organization, e.g., counselors, experts, controllers, or workers. These people link employees and ideas and thus help to detect new opportunities at the right time. They are a source of inspiration and encourage an excellent working atmosphere and commitment.
- Learning leaders, instead of giving all the answers, ask the right questions. In particular, they make the employees and the organization aware of the limitations of the existing models of thought and work on enhancing these models. They are usually specialists with comprehensive basic responsibilities at the bottom of the organization, e.g., business unit heads who implement new product ideas and innovations.

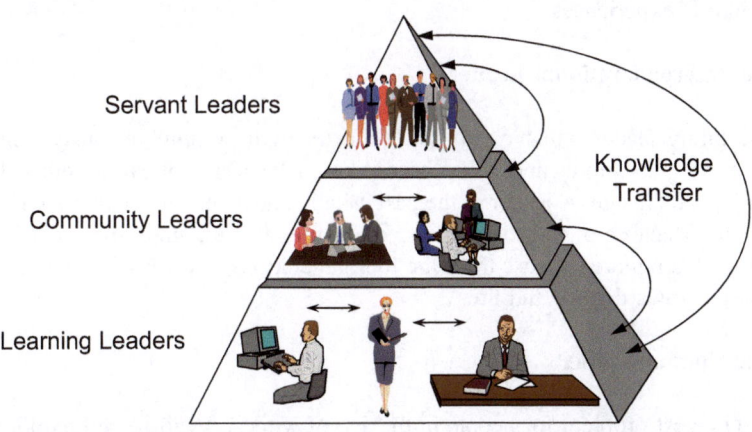

Figure Shared leadership Roles

In future organizations, these leadership roles are essential and interdependent. Alone, none of them are in a position to create an environment that is attractive for knowledge workers, which can encourage learning, and which can contribute to the generation and transfer of new ideas and new knowledge. And all three are to be considered and recognized as leaders, even if not officially. Together, with their different roles, they form shared leadership in our future organizations.

5   Competences a Leader Will Need in 2030: Learning Instead of Knowing

1. The Learning Leader

Lifelong learning and continuous training are necessary for leaders in order to remain effective. However, to keep learning something new and to stay abreast of the latest knowledge in their field of work should also be a personal desire of future leaders. Continuous leadership training should match the requirements of the company and the leader. Besides technical and specialized knowledge, social competence and the ability to communicate effectively and to work in a team are of primary importance to future leaders. The continuous training programs arranged by the company must also include imparting and fostering these soft skills (see also Chap. 14 in this book).

2. The Multicultural Leader

The world is not flat. Therefore, future leaders need to understand cultural differences and appreciate them as entrepreneurial opportunities instead of risks or threats. The time of nationalistic leaders belongs to the past. You cannot learn culture in textbooks and classrooms. You have to experience it. Therefore, future leaders will have to step out of their comfort zone by opening up to learning journeys and new cultural experiences.

3. The Intergenerational Leader

The future leader will have to lead four generations simultaneously. This has never happened before, and never before has it been as critical as today due to technological change. A leader of the past usually had a personal network within his age group. Because of the seniority principle, this worked quite fine. In 2030, that won't work anymore because there are four generations at work with very different approaches toward work and life.

4. The Human Leader

The biggest problem for people in the age of work 4.0 will be self-exploitation. Social ratings, like the Chinese social credit system and social pressure, like growing inequalities, is forcing people into keeping up with technology standards and increasing consumption, even if they don't have the time, means, or qualification to do so, leading to even more significant problems, like personal privacy issues, social burnout, or even illegal behavior. The future leader has to deal with these challenges, meaning that he or she is forced to make decisions that are not purely economically driven but also social and ethical. This will have profound consequences for the education of future leaders.

5. The Wise Leader

The significant impact of the COVID-19 crises at the beginning of the 2020s means that our society will never be the same as it used to be. In such an unpredictable and uncontrollable environment, leadership with practical wisdom to make judgments based on the "common good" is becoming decisive for our own future and destiny (Nonaka and Takeuchi 2011) . In times of pandemics, social inequality, and climate change, it is not only a question of success or failure; it will become, in some cases, even a question of life or death. Wise leadership is based on altruistic behavior, sympathy with people, things, and surroundings "now and here" (Nonaka and Koizumi 2020). It is based on what the Greek philosopher Aristotle called "phronesis," not a technique, but an intellectual virtue, ability to determine and undertake the best action in a specific situation to serve the common good (Nonaka and Toyama 2007).

Key Insights for Leaders and Leadership in 2030
- Knowledge workers will require new leaders in 2030 as old principles of leadership and leadership styles will no longer work for them. In the book, we propose a new 5S model of leadership (self, situational, stakeholder, servant, shared) that will fit much better to the requirements of a new leader in 2030 to make them more effective toward the knowledge worker to make her/him more productive.
- Traditional leadership functions, like performance measurement, incentivizing, or management control, will be increasingly replaced by AI solutions. Modern leaders have to concentrate on the innovative and creative tasks of leadership that cannot be replaced by machines. The main task of modern leadership is to cocreate the future of the organization in an unpredictable and turbulent world.
- New leaders in 2030 have to change their self-perception from the leadership generations of the past. The leader of the future does not know everything better than their followers but is the one creating a movement toward change and is asking the right questions. This requires curiosity and lifelong learning skills from the leader.

(continued)

- New leaders in 2030 have to develop intergenerational and multicultural competences. Never before have they had to work with so many different cultures and generations at the same time.
- As a consequence of this, seniority principles in promotion do not matter anymore. It is not the oldest and most experienced who makes a good leader, but the one who can connect and build a strong personal network.
- Last, but not least, self-leadership will become even more critical than in the past. In a world where attention is a scarce resource, managing focus and attention of oneself and employees is the decisive factor in getting things done.

References

Achi, Z., & Berger, J. G. (2015). Delighting in the possible. *McKinsey Quarterly*, (March), 1–8.

Bennett, N., & Lemoine, G. J. (2014). What VUCA really means for you. *Harvard Business Review, 1*, 27.

Bennis, W. (1989). *On becoming a leader*. London: Business Books.

Christ, G. (2014). Leadership & strategy: Servant leadership in a crisis. *IndustryWeek*. Retrieved from https://www.industryweek.com/leadership/article/21964881/leadership-strategy-servant-leadership-in-a-crisis

De Vulpian, A. (2005). Listening to ordinary people: The process of civilization on the way to a new society. *Reflections, 6*(6/7), 1–19.

Deming, W. E. (1982). *Out of the crisis*. Cambridge: The MIT Press.

Drucker, P. F. (1946). *Concept of the cooperation*. New York: John Day.

Drucker, P. F. (1999). Knowledge-worker productivity: The biggest challenge. *California Management Review, 41*(2), 79–94.

Edwards, J. C. (2017). *Champion leaders pursuing excellence to win essentials for effective leaders*. Bloomington: West Bow Press.

Fink, L. (2020). *A fundamental reshaping of finance*. CEO Letter. Retrieved from https://www.blackrock.com/us/individual/larry-fink-ceo-letter

Gibb, C. A. (1954). Leadership. In G. Lindzey (Ed.), *Handbook of social psychology* (Vol. 2, pp. 877–917). Reading, MA: Addison-Wesley.

Göpel, M. (2016). *The great mindshift: How a new economic paradigm and sustainability transformations go hand in hand*. New York: Springer.

Greenleaf, R. K. (1970). *The servant as leader*. Cambridge, MA: Center for Applied Studies.

Greenleaf, R. K., Spears, L. C., Covey, S. R., & Senge, P. M. (2002). *Servant leadership: A journey into the nature of legitimate power and greatness*. New York: Paulist Press.

Hesse, H. (1956). *The journey to the east*. Stellar Classics.

Hock, D. W. (1999). *Birth of the chaordic age*. San Francisco, CA: Berrett-Koehler.

Ignatius, A. (2019). The truth about CEO tenure. *Harvard Business Review*, (November–December), 92.

Klammer, A., & Güldenberg, S. (2019). Honor the old, welcome the new: An account of unlearning and forgetting in NPD teams. *European Journal of Innovation Management., 23*, 581–603.

Langhof, J. & Güldenberg, S. (2020a). Identifying antecedents of servant leadership: A historical examination of king Frederick the Great's leadership. *Journal of Management History*.

Langhof, J., & Güldenberg, S. (2020b). Servant leadership: A systematic literature review- toward a model of antecedents, outcomes, causes, and effects. *German Journal of Human Resource Management, 34*, 37.

Langhof, J., Renzl, B., & Güldenberg, S. (2020). Arbeiten im Takt der Algorithmen? Mensch bleiben durch dienende Führung. *Zeitschrift OrganisationsEntwicklung, 3*, 12–16.

Liden, R. C., Wayne, S. J., Liao, C., & Meuser, J. D. (2014). Servant leadership and serving culture: Influence on individual and unit performance. *Academy of Management Journal, 57*(5), 1434–1452.

Liden, R. C., Wayne, S. J., Meuser, J. D., Hu, J., Wu, J., & Liao, C. (2015). Servant leadership: Validation of a short form of the SL-28. *The Leadership Quarterly, 26*(2), 254–269.

Nonaka, I & Koizumi, H. (2020, May 5). Urgent proposal for the global society after & during the era of COVID-19: Shift from "egoism" towards "altruism" & "sympathy", Future Center Alliance Japan News Release.

Nonaka, I., & Takeuchi, H. (2011). The wise leader. *Harvard Business Review, 89*, 58–67.

Nonaka, I., & Toyama, H. (2007). Strategic management as distributed practical wisdom (phronesis). *Industrial and Corporate Change, 16*(3), 371–394.

Porter, M. E., & Kramer, M. R. (2011). The big idea: Creating shared value, rethinking capitalism. *Harvard Business Review, 89*(1/2), 62–77.

Porter, M.E.; Hills, G.; Pfitzer, M.; Patscheke, S. & Hawkins, E. (2012). *Measuring shared value: How to unlock value by linking social and business results*. Retrieved from https://www.hbs.edu/faculty/Publication%20Files/Measuring_Shared_Value_57032487-9e5c-46a1-9bd8-90bd7f1f9cef.pdf

Reid, D. (2016, January 18). *Traditional thinking won't work anymore: WEF founder Schwab*. Retrieved from https://www.cnbc.com/2016/01/18/traditional-thinking-wont-work-anymore-wef-founder-schwab.html

Safavi, S. (2020). *The clock wasn't showing 100 seconds to midnight any more*. Winner essay of the Drucker Challenge Essay Award, Managers/Entrepreneurs Category. Retrieved from https://www.druckerchallenge.org/uploads/pics/the_clock_wasn___t_showing_100_seconds_to_mid night_anymore.pdf

Schneidewind, U. (2018). *Die große Transformation: Eine Einführung in die Kunst gesellschaftlichen Wandels*. Frankfurt: Fischer.

Senge, P. M. (1990). *The fifth discipline: The art and practice of the learning organization*. New York: Doubleday/Currency.

Senge, P. M. (2003). Taking personal change seriously: The impact of organizational learning on management practice. *The Academy of Management Executive, 17*(2), 47–50.

von Krogh, G., Nonaka, I., & Rechsteiner, L. (2012). Leadership in organizational knowledge creation: A review and framework. *Journal of Management Studies, 49*, 240–277.

WEF (2020). *Davos Manifesto 2020: The Universal Purpose of a Company in the Fourth Industrial Revolution*. Retrieved from https://www.weforum.org/agenda/2019/12/davos-manifesto-2020-the-universal-purpose-of-a-company-in-the-fourth-industrial-revolution/

Wiener, N. (1948). *Cybernetics: Or control and Communication in the animal and the machine*. Cambridge, MA: MIT Press.

Stefan Güldenberg is a pioneer and leading expert on the future of work, digital strategies, sustainable leadership, and knowledge management. He is a university professor, platform founder, strategy consultant, executive coach, and knowledge entrepreneur. He studied Business Mathematics, Philosophy, and English at the University of Ulm and then received his doctorate and habilitation at Vienna University of Economics and Business. Stefan has 25 years of experience in research, knowledge transfer, and practice. He conducts research on and supports the development of strategy and transformation processes. Stays abroad led him, among others, to Harvard University, the Massachusetts Institute of Technology (MIT), and the National University of Singapore. He is the current Vice President Practice of the European Academy of Management (EURAM) and President of the New Club of Paris, a think tank, and agenda-setter for the knowledge economy.

Digital Leadership and Technology

Stefan Güldenberg and Jan G. Langhof

Future Work News
Singapore, 31.08.2030
Taylor Reloaded: The Organization as the Perfect Machine?
Today at the beginning of the 2030s, we can see the problems that arise from the development of more and more capable and independent algorithms. Here, digital leaders in business are challenged, and it is not clear how things will play out. Adding algorithms to all levels of work will clearly make work streams more efficient, but as machines start making decisions, the criteria for good and bad decisions, as well as loyalty (to the firm, to the stakeholders, to humanity), may lead to unexpected results.

CEOs back in the early years of the Internet economy may have thought their management positions were safe from the rise of the machines. Still, Alibaba founder Jack Ma had already stated in 2017 that he believed that companies could be run by better robotic chief executives than by human beings. Speaking at a China Entrepreneur Club event, Ma explained why he thinks machines will be able to do what humans cannot and how a lack of emotion will help robo-chief executives get things done.

"30 years later, the Time Magazine cover for the best CEO of the year very likely will be a robot. It remembers better than you, it counts faster than you, and it won't be angry with competitors" (Morgan 2017), Ma said at the event, according to the New York Post. A few years later, the Chinese People's Party announced that their future party leader might be an artificial intelligence: "We have learned our own lessons from the political disasters in the past. Look at the United States or what used to be the United Kingdom. Human narcissistic leaders have divided the population and countries. We don't want to have the same happen with China."

S. Güldenberg (✉) · J. G. Langhof
Institute for Entrepreneurship, University of Liechtenstein, Vaduz, Liechtenstein
e-mail: stefan.gueldenberg@uni.li; jan.langhof@uni.li

© Springer Nature Switzerland AG 2021
S. Güldenberg et al. (eds.), *Managing Work in the Digital Economy*, Future of
Business and Finance, https://doi.org/10.1007/978-3-030-65173-2_10

So far, there has been no CEO replaced by a robot, but according to the same researchers, this development might occur within the next ten years. In the meantime, even Western companies like Amazon and Google have started to experiment with what they call robot leadership by introducing more and more artificial intelligence in the monitoring and decision-making process. Jeff Bezos even stated lately that without it, Amazon would have lost its competitive advantage.

At the very opposite end in France, the unions have fought successfully for a new labor law that no leadership function in organizations may be allowed to be exercised or supported by a solely technical solution, including staffing, monitoring, strategy, and firing. This was the result of a three-year fight against Chinese and US companies trying to introduce more and more AI management solutions in many of their French subsidiaries. But this comes at a price: In comparison to China and the United States, France has lost more ground in its already mediocre position in the newest World Competitiveness Index. Many international IT companies try to avoid France as their European headquarters. "We just can not stay competitive with our labor costs in such an environment," the spokesman of a US-based work match-making platform stated.

One current example from the United States shows that this European skepticism when it comes to robot leadership may be well justified: In 2025, Biosensor, a Boston biotech start-up, started to introduce digital leadership solutions first in their staffing and then in new product development. Encouraged by first successes in attracting talent, they even expanded these solutions into personal development and corporate communication, trying to get the messages of their venture capitalists as quickly as possible toward their employees. A couple of years later, they experienced an unprecedented brain drain followed by a loss of trust on the side of their customers and, finally, no more funding on the side of their venture capitalists. So what happened here?

While the recruiting machinery was very successful in getting the best talent in the first place, it was just blindly imposing the financial goals of the venture capitalist through a personal reputation score on these experts which negatively affected their further career path, HR development options, and motivation. The result was a mismatch between the personal ambitions of the experts (doing something good for society) and the venture capitalists' objectives (earning a lot of money from the products and services of the company). Even worse, by letting AI take over corporate communication, the public image of the company shifted dramatically from a very innovative company at the beginning to an artificial money-making machine in the end. All too often, knowledge workers of Biosensor experienced critical questions from their former colleagues and friends about for whom they are working for, how they can accept machines manipulating them, and if they have now become mere cyber soldiers. This lead to many of them leaving the company.

Robot leaders, while optimizing, always tend to become extremists, as one of the developers correctly stated. That was the same thing that some companies already experienced in early 2020 when using AI and machine learning in their recruitment process. By learning from best practices, one may end up recruiting a very homogenous group, typically white male, which the AI thinks are the best you can get based on their CVs. But it is always the programmer in the background which starts giving the machines this false impression, typically a white male, and in the end, the people recruited all tend to look alike.

Elon Musk already warned in 2018 that if not regulated or controlled soon, "we have to be careful not to end up in a new immortal AI dictatorship." (Godlewski 2018) Very comparable to the human-based Enron and Wirecard scandals, robot leadership might get into a similar problem by sometimes going too far in purely optimizing economic outcomes and not reflecting laws or the human dimensions. This might happen because these issues are not usually covered in the education of digital natives.

So while we have to see the advantages of AI over human beings in leadership positions, we shouldn't be naive about their potential and possibilities. As long as we don't want to leave leadership to the programmers and creators of AI alone, we need to balance humanity with the technological opportunities of our time. Maybe the old management guru Peter Drucker might still be right today in saying that for successful management, you always need a two-handed approach: one systematic left hand, which can be in our modern times an AI management solution supporting a leader. But never leave him or her alone with that. It would be best if you always had a much more holistic and creative right hand, and that one has to still be a human leader to ensure that leadership will be not only efficient but also effective.

As a consequence, there is no neither-nor approach between humans and robots. Those companies and also national cultures who appreciate the strength of both and learn how best to integrate them into their political and economic leadership systems will get the most out of it. Neglecting one dimension, be it the human or AI, may reduce future leadership capabilities significantly and may end up in political or economic disaster.

---

1   Digital Transformation

"We stand on the brink of a technological revolution that will fundamentally alter the way we live, work, and relate to one another. In its scale, scope, and complexity, the transformation will be unlike anything humankind has experienced before." (Klaus Schwab, World Economic Forum, 2016)

1.1   What It Is and What It Is Not

In business practice, the terms "digitization" and "digitalization" are often used synonymously. However, while digitization in its original sense only means the conversion of information into a digital format, digitalization involves technology-driven change processes in companies and organizations (Gersch et al. 2020). These changes are driven in particular by the factors "digital data," "automation," "networking," and "digital customer access." New, digital technologies (e.g., artificial intelligence or blockchain) are changing (sometimes massively) traditional industry structures and therefore pose particular challenges for companies that want to remain competitive under these conditions (Riasanow et al. 2019; Vial 2019). Capital is losing its value as an economically scarce resource, and access to knowledge and the careful management of effective knowledge processes are becoming crucial success factors (Güttel et al. 2019). This places special challenges and demands on future digital leaders.

The technological change brought about by digitalization is not a new topic for leadership. It began decades ago: from the advent of the first computers in the 1950s and 1960s, computer-aided design and manufacturing in the 1970s, and the networking of corporate divisions through enterprise resource planning systems from the 1980s onward. However, due to the "Internetization" of companies and industries since the 1990s, the digital transformation is gaining momentum, changing markets, business models, and value chains (Gersch et al. 2020). From 2000 onward, the Internet was affecting not only sourcing and production but also management and marketing. With the rise of smartphones and social media, digital transformation was changing the ways of coordination, communication, and how we sell products and services. In the 2010s, the rise of smartphones and apps was opening up completely new markets and distribution channels. The market was no longer local but global, even for smaller companies. At the beginning of the 2020s, the Covid-19 pandemic hit the whole world, bringing digital transformation into our everyday workplace. Suddenly, the new working space became the Bin mir nicht sicher, ob das so im Englischen gesagt wird, and leadership was no longer a matter of face-to-face meetings but increasingly virtual ones. And here we are approaching the 2030s with artificial intelligence and blockchains taking over more and more power and decision-making responsibilities from human leaders. Many leaders fear not only losing their job but also that the Internet of things will take over the internet created by humans for humans and social media.

1.2 Internet of Things or Internet of Humans?

The Internet, as perhaps most technologies, was invented to serve humanity. People were intended to be able to communicate and exchange information on a global scale. Scholars (e.g., Forman et al. 2005) referred to a "global village" that is moving closer and closer together. Today, however, it is no longer only people but primarily machines that communicate with each other. The numbers speak for themselves. Experts (e.g., Dahlqvist et al. 2019) forecast that the number of devices connected to the Internet will reach 43 billion by 2023 (far more than the world population and far more than people who communicate via the Internet). Many machines already interact with each other, entirely independently, without any human interaction. Even in social media, it is no longer clear if communication or likes were generated by human beings or artificial algorithms, so-called social bots, or in the worst case misused to manipulate elections and to erode democratic structures.

This transformation is tremendously affecting digital leadership and the power of leaders. The philosopher David Skrbina (2015, p. 286) talks about the Internet as an *autonomous system* that was brought into being. In other words, both organizations and people will be integrated into a system dominated by machines. The organizations of the future will depend (more than ever) on the smooth functioning of the network and the infrastructure in which they are embedded. On the one hand, its smooth functioning requires the state to provide the appropriate infrastructure. Here, entrepreneurs and managers themselves can become active by choosing the appropriate location. On the other hand, the leaders themselves are expected to decide in which technical solution to invest. Therefore, they are required to have a good knowledge about the infrastructure and the interconnection of their individual machines. Without this kind of digital literacy, they are lost, and their power is eroded. This is very comparable to many portfolio managers in the financial industry who, at the beginning of the financial crisis of 2007, did not understand in what kind of investment vehicles of the real estate market they had been investing or which one they had been recommending toward their customers. Leaders may feel more and more alienated and at the mercy of algorithms. As in the case of autonomous driving, essential and sometimes even life-threatening decision might be taken by machines and by robot leaders, not by human leaders anymore.

1.3 From Digital Transformation to Robot Leadership?

Я твой слуга ("I am your servant"). Я твой работник ("I am your worker"). We are programmed just to do. Anything you want us to (From the song "The Robots" by the electronic music group Kraftwerk).

The song by the music group *Kraftwerk* was released in the 1970s and addressed the rapid progress in robotics, which, at that time, can indeed be considered revolutionary (see also the chapter on Smart HRM on other *Kraftwerk* songs). The song's leitmotif bears a note of optimism: The robot loyally helps humans and takes heavy work off their hands. The robot does exactly what humans command. The allocation of roles and duties is well defined: Man is the robot's master. The robot, however, remains in the position of a loyal servant or slave.

The notion of "servant" is also reflected in the word's etymology. The term "robot" was first popularized by the Czech writer Karel Capek, who used the term in a theater play (Launius and McCurdy 2007). The play tells the story of a corporation that produces artificial humans ("Robots"), who would eventually revolt against their human masters. In Czech, the word means "serf labor" (in many other Slavic languages, it merely means "labor"). The Czech word, in turn, originates from the Old Church Slavonic word "rabota," which means "serfdom" or "slavery" (Mohammad and Nishida 2018).

The development of robotics back in the 1970s was indeed revolutionary. Companies such as KUKA and ABB made astonishing progress in the area of industrial robotics (Smith 2016). It even seemed as if the loyal servant *robot* would soon be able to relieve us of the heavy physical work completely. In 2030, more than 50 years after the release of Kraftwerk's song, we may observe an astonishing development. Surprisingly, the "Servant-Master" relationship (as hinted at in the song) seems to be reversed. Now, the recipients of commands are humans. Robots are increasingly taking up management positions, which Daniel Weihs described as autosomes, independent thinking machines (Weihs 2018). In the second half of the 2010s, the Japanese company *Hitachi* made headlines by announcing that it would use a robot as a supervisor. The "robot leader" allocates tasks to employees and even alters work instructions based on feedback loops and employees' performance (Ghosh 2017). We are already familiar with very basic forms of "robot leadership" in a very rudimentary form in logistics centers, where workers receive instructions via a system called "pick-by-voice" (Gleissner and Möller 2011). Today, however, we encounter robot "leaders" or "managers" outside of warehouses. The company "Uber," where a computer system manages the drivers, is one prominent example (Gaskell 2018).

What are the effects on humans if robots are increasingly taking on leadership roles? Newspapers report about a person in Belgium who put too much trust in her broken navigation system. Instead of going to Brussels, she drove across Europe, all the way to Croatia. Only in Croatia, 810 miles from her actual destination, is the person said to have noticed her mistake (Matyszczyk 2013).

Now, the question arises: is robot leadership even desirable? And how can we, if at all, integrate human leaders into this kind of autonomous leadership and decision-making process again? What are the key challenges of digital leadership for a typical human being in a digitalized world?

2 Five Very Human Digital Leadership Challenges

1. Working at the Pace of Algorithms (Langhof et al. 2020)?

Andreas is a seemingly ordinary employee, working for a typical medium-sized company in southern Germany. Like all of his colleagues in sales, he is equipped with three devices: the tablet for the road, the PC in the office, and of course his mobile phone. In the thicket of his e-mails, Andreas suddenly receives a reminder message from the company's AI-based management system. He should familiarize himself with the new customer relationship management (CRM) system that was recently rolled out. A new CRM system? "Strange," Andreas thinks to himself. But only last year the in-house AI department set up a new database. The new system could now measure exactly how many customer visits and calls he made per day. From this and the customer feedback received, the system calculates an algorithm rating score (ARS). The ARS was based on a 100-point scale. After the new algorithm was implemented, about 5% of employees got what was considered a top score of 90 or above. When the ARS was first introduced, the company did not explain how it was calculated but based its incentive and personal development policies on it. Andreas and his colleagues found that practice very frustrating, but in the end, they had no choice but to accept it or leave the company.

The story above shows that the digitalization of the working world does not seem to be without consequences. Andreas suffers increasingly from headaches and lack of sleep: "Tiredness and mental exhaustion" that could most likely be burnout and is probably due to stress and multitasking. His family doctor advises him to "Take some time off, no mobile phone, no tablet." Recent research seems to confirm the doctor's assumption. The neuroscientist Manfred Spitzer (2012) even warns against "digital dementia" and a "disease of civilization, cybersickness" (Gabriel and Röhrs (2017), p. 156).

But what exactly are the reasons for Andreas' increasing stress levels and exhaustion? These reasons and stressors will be described in the following challenges.

2. Fear of Missing Out

Like Andreas, his superior Katharina is also increasingly confronted with the challenges of digitalization. While she works on an offer for an important customer, her smartphone is humming. "Another voice message," thinks Katharina. "These are definitely from our an important client." When Katharina later checks her e-mails and opens her browser to do so, the latest headlines of an online newspaper catch her eye. "Let's have a quick read of the news," she thinks to herself. A few seconds become 5 min. "Oh, yes. The offer" comes to her mind again.

Like many of her colleagues, Katharina is plagued by the fear of missing something. As a result, an acronym has become established in literature: "FOMO" ("fear of missing out") (Appel et al. 2019). After Katharina's department has signed the contract with the customers, she decides to take a time-out in a monastery, a place without a smartphone and laptop. Digital detoxification has become a buzz word and refers to the conscious decision not to use digital devices (Welledits et al. 2019). Indeed, temporary stays in monasteries but also long walks in the forest can help to reduce digital stress (Langhof et al. 2020).

The latest research findings suggest that people on technology-free trips interact more attentively and with greater concentration with their surroundings (Cai et al. 2020).

3. Feeling Helpless in the Face of Technology

We, as humans, love to plan and to have control over future events (Rosa 2020). Big data, ERP systems, and reporting tools allow us to quantify the world, plan and "predict" as never before. On the other hand, the complexity of technology also makes our everyday lives more unpredictable and uncontrollable. The German sociologist Hartmut Rosa (2020) illustrates this obscurity and uncontrollability using the example of the car, which suddenly locks itself or makes an emergency stop without any visible reason. These are minor technical errors that the driver used to be able to solve themselves. The increasing complexity of technology, however, makes us dependent on experts (for whom technology is also becoming increasingly opaque). Both leaders and employees will have to get used to the fact that they will mostly be helpless when confronted with many technological challenges. Consequences may include an increasing alienation from work, stress, and feelings of powerlessness and depression.

4. In the "Search for Meaning": In and Outside of Work

For the employees and leaders, it will become increasingly difficult to cope with this uncontrollability, alienation, and frustration. But what if the alienation increases to such an extent that human beings can no longer find any meaning in their work?

Alienation (caused by technology) probably explains practitioners' and researchers' increasing interest in programs and leadership styles that emphasize the search for meaning: e.g., "Servant Leadership" (e.g. Liden et al. 2014; Langhof and Güldenberg 2020), "Spiritual Leadership" (e.g., Gümüsay 2019), "Organisational Spirituality" (e.g., Rocha and Pinheiro 2020; Weinberg and Locander 2014), and "Meaningful Leadership" (Kriger and Seng 2005).

In the United States, the phenomenon of "Workplace Spirituality" has become increasingly important (Rocha and Pinheiro 2020). Advocates of "Workplace Spirituality" are concerned with the question of how an employee's transcendent goals can be incorporated into their work.

In Europe, temporary stays in monasteries are a current trend among managers (Mohr 2007). These retreats are motivated by the idea that the Christian monastic tradition is *fruitful for daily life in the outside world* (Benediktinerabtei Niederaltaich 2020).

In addition, an increasing number of academics are taking up the topic. The Viennese psychologist Raphael Bonelli (2018a, b), a proponent of Viktor Frankl, considers "transcendence" as the ultimate manifestation of meaning (Bonelli 2017a, b, c).

How can we explain this trend? Why do leaders seek comfort behind Catholic monastery walls? A return to ancient traditions and rituals may well serve as an "antipole" to the fast-paced, tumultuous, and technologized world of today. The walls of some monasteries accommodate traditions that are well over 1000 years old. The contrast to today's digital high-tech world could hardly be any greater.

5. The Dangers of Surveillance Capitalism

Only recently, Hanley and Hubbard (2020) published a report on the dangers of the pervasive worker surveillance at Amazon and the solutions that can be used to stop this surveillance and empower workers. The report explains in detail how worker surveillance threatens the mental and physical health of Amazon workers, allows Amazon to discourage workers from unionizing, increases the precariousness of workers who can be fired at any time for deviating from metrics they are not even aware of, and causes other dominant companies to adopt similar practices. Already 5 years earlier, an American parcel delivery company made it into the headlines

(Bruder 2015). The main reason for the attention was their new "telematics system," which monitors and evaluates every single step of their truck drivers' work process. Even minor tasks are monitored, including how they fasten their seat belts or how they open the doors.

In today's technological world, corporations tend to monitor their employees increasingly. Some scholars even warn against "mass surveillance" (Stahl 2016) and "surveillance capitalism" (Andrew and Baker 2019).

Companies and leaders are generally exposed to the principal-agent problem (Eisenhardt 1989). In other words, the follower has a knowledge advantage, and thus, they could act to the disadvantage of the company.

On the one hand, the companies' desire to address this problem and to make processes more transparent is understandable. On the other hand, surveillance technologies bear great dangers. Irrespectively of any freedom rights, an excessive level of monitoring and quantification can also have the opposite effect to the one desired. Monitoring measures may lead to increased stress, which, in turn, harms the employee's performance (Chory et al. 2015).

The digital leader of the future is, therefore, more than ever faced with the responsibility of finding the right balance between control and autonomy.

3 The Task of Leaders in Digital Transformation

Leaders play a crucial role in digital transformation. They are the role models for the other members of the organization. Therefore, the acceptance of the necessary change on the part of the leaders and openness to technical innovations are an essential prerequisite for a successful digital transformation of the whole organization. Digital transformation is not something you can do on a Friday afternoon after the real work is finished. It has to be an integral part of your daily schedule. In addition, digital leaders should concentrate on the following five priorities to master successfully digital transformation:

1. Competence: The Digital-Literate Leader

Even today, leaders largely rely on machines (IT systems, big data, algorithms, etc.) when making decisions. The leaders of the future will be all the more dependent on their "robot colleague." The cooperation between humans and machines, however, can only be effective if decision-makers have a high level of *trust* in their "robot colleagues."

The superior general of the Jesuits, Ignatius of Loyola, is said to have sometimes given his delegates blank sheets of paper bearing his signature (Câmara 2005). During negotiations, they could then issue contracts with his authority. In other words, he placed enormous trust in his employees. On the other hand, however, he required his followers to report to him daily on *what* they were doing and *how* they were working. He could only place so much trust in his employees as he knew them well and knew exactly what they were doing (Kiechle 2019).

This means leaders should only hand over tasks to machines if they understand *how* those machines work (Davenport and Kirby 2016). Today, many decision-makers, however, perceive computers as a "black box" that mysteriously produces results. As a result, technological change requires an entirely new digital leadership expertise, which leaders did not have or require in the past. Future leaders must understand at least the basics of how the new digital solutions work, how they can be used, and, above all, where their limits lie. Digital leaders must become masters of these technological solutions and possibilities, not just wanting to be their servants in order to be effective. Only in this way can the search field of companies be kept broad and diverse, and clear decisions can be made on the relationship between exploitative and explorative development opportunities.

2. Culture: Preventing Social Isolation

The benefits of the new communication technologies (chat programs, messenger apps, video chat programs, etc.) look tremendous. Finally, long trips to conferences, nerve-wracking traffic jams when commuting to work, or on-site visits to customers are no longer an unpleasant necessity. Indeed, we can hope that the trend toward home-based workplaces will lead to fewer cars on the increasingly crowded roads.

However, there is also a downside to working from home (and the digital transformation in general). Digitalization is increasingly driving people into social isolation and loneliness. Even outside a person's home office, this trend is noticeable to the attentive observer.

While in the 1990s people on the commuter train talked to each other, today, we only see people hypnotically staring at their smartphones. Smombie (smartphone zombie) is a popular word among young people. It can be assumed that people's social isolation will increase in the future, even strengthened by the trend toward more and more single households, as can already be seen in many Asian megacities.

The psychologists Deci and Ryan (2008) emphasize how important it is for people to feel socially integrated. According to their theory of "Self-Determination," a person's motivation largely depends on three factors:

(a) The need for social inclusion
(b) The need for autonomy
(c) The need for competence

Both the need for "social inclusion" and the "need for autonomy" are being challenged by increasing digitalization and technologization. Workflows predefined by computer programs restrict the autonomy of many workers.

For digital leaders, the most critical challenge will be to counteract this alienation and social isolation. A corporate culture that promotes empathy, compassion, and interpersonal relationships will become even more important. Therefore, it can be concluded that digital transformation is much more of a cultural than a technological challenge. This includes the design of the working environment (co-working spaces), communication, and learning structures, as well as a collective and shared style of leadership (see Chap. 9). In the future, digital leaders will be required, more than ever, to give people the freedom to flourish in their work (Langhof et al. 2020).

3. **Purpose and Values: Meaningful Leadership**

The Lutheran pastor Wilhelm Busch (known for his resistance during the Nazi period; cf. Stroud 2013, p. 170) writes in one of his books how a high government official bemoaned the purposelessness of his work: "Pastor, just between you and me, I do nothing but sign papers from morning till night. But I know that if all these papers should happen to burn one day, the world would carry on. It really bothers me to have to devote my time and energy to such a senseless job" (Busch 2007, p. 23).

The American anthropologist David Graeber (2018) recently made headlines due to his provocative book title *Bullshit Jobs*. Graeber advocates the shocking view that a large part of today's jobs is essentially meaningless work. Yuval Noah Harari (2016) shares similar concerns, arguing that AI would create a class of "useless" people.

The new technological innovations can only be used effectively if a person has a stable value system, a stable "inner order," and an appropriate priority setting. But how should such an "inner order" look like? Raphael Bonelli (2016) sees the key to "inner order" in Fritz Künkel's distinction between egocentricity and objectivity. Künkel (1936) considers objectivity to be a dedication to suprapersonal goals: goals that transcend the individual's needs. Egocentricity, on the other hand, includes a fear of life and a fear of one's fellow human beings, as well as an exaggerated desire for security (Bonelli 2018a, b). Podolny et al. (2004) show how important it is for leaders to work out the meaning of their activities together with those they are leading. Frankl (1959) emphasizes that meaning is created neither by satisfying needs nor solely through self-realization but must be discovered by the individuals themselves. Meaning is always created through the fulfillment of values. That is why it is so important for digital leadership to ensure that individual and organizational values are in accord with each other during the selection of personnel or technology. To do this, however, one must first know one's organizational values and deal with their content.

For Frankl, creating meaning means both working on the way a human being experiences and expects things and also wanting to contribute something to achieve success together. When employees find meaning in their work and thus a right to exist again, this also helps to reduce the subjective fear of losing their jobs. For digital leaders, it will become even more important to support their followers in their "search for meaning" (Frankl 1959) and to *integrate* this search into their work (Ewest et al. 2016; Frémeaux and Pavageau 2020; Kriger and Seng 2005; Lynn et al. 2020). From a motivational perspective, this means a person's motivation for the work is all the more sustainable and more robust if it is linked to their search for meaning (Afsar et al. 2016).

4. **Digital Ambidexterity: Augmenting Human Beings by Machines**

The Japanese corporation *Nintendo* is a well-known computer game company that has already completed the transition from *analog* to *digital* several decades ago. *Nintendo* was originally founded as a manufacturer of card games in 1889 and is now a leading manufacturer of video games and consoles (Stanton 2019).

Although the company suffered several setbacks in the course of its history, it repeatedly managed to outperform the competition with innovations. In the 1990s, Nintendo was still the leading manufacturer of consoles and games (ahead of SEGA) (Stanton 2019).

In the early 2000s, however, *Sony* (*PlayStation*) and *Microsoft* (*Xbox*) threatened to knock Nintendo out of the race. *SEGA*, their long-standing competitor, had already withdrawn from the console business (Stanton 2019).

In 2006, Nintendo responded to the competition by launching the *Wii* (Inoue and Tsujimoto 2018). Nintendo's *Wii* was fundamentally different from the competitors' consoles, as it required the players to move their whole body. Previous consoles still relied on the use of simple controllers or joysticks.

For Charles O'Reilly III, the American management professor, the key to some organizations' eternal youth lies in their capability of "organizational ambidexterity." Organizational ambidexterity is commonly considered to be the ability of a company to continue its current operations while simultaneously adapting to changing conditions (O'Reilly and Tushman 2008).

This principle of organizational ambidexterity can be easily transferred to the challenges of digital transformation. Therefore, digital ambidexterity could be defined as the capability of an organization to continue its current operations while simultaneously augmenting (and not replacing) its activities by digital technology (Daugherty and Wilson 2018). Augmentation means starting with what humans do today and figuring out how that work could be improved rather than diminished by greater use of machines (Davenport and Kirby 2015).

5. Limiting Robot Leadership: Auftragstaktik 2.0

In the future, machines will increasingly make decisions that were previously made by humans. However, machines are fundamentally different from humans (at least based on the present state of knowledge). Machines neither possess free will nor possess empathy or compassion. Numerous experts criticize the fact that certain technologies are already in use, although many legal issues have not (yet) been addressed (Kingston 2016). But when is it appropriate to allow machines to make decisions? When would it be preferential for people to decide?

In the nineteenth century, the Prussian army developed an approach that proved successful, particularly during the Franco-German war (Shamir 2010). The approach, which is known as "Auftragstaktik" (Visser 2010, p. 342), leaves some leeway to the subordinates for the execution of the command in the context of the overall mission goal (Bloedorn and Muethel 2018; Shamir 2010). Helmuth von Moltke, a Prussian field marshal, argues that the soldier's order should only contain instructions that the soldier cannot initiate out of their own plenitude of power (Bühlmann and Braun 2010, p. 56). According to *von Moltke's* understanding of military command, soldiers have freedom of action within the boundaries of the predefined mission.

Following the model of *Auftragstaktik*, we may imagine robot leadership within firmly defined boundaries. Robot leaders may be authorized to lead and make decisions freely within predefined (and pre-programmed) limits. If the machines reach these limits, digital leadership would automatically be transferred back to a human leader.

Robot and machine ethics is a fascinating and newly emerging discipline within philosophy with the task to define these limits, what an algorithm should and can decide and what it must or cannot (Lin et al. 2011; Moor 2006). Time will show how digital law will translate the insights of this new discipline into concrete guidelines for practical action.

Key Insights for Digital Leadership in 2030

- The digital transformation is not new at all, but it is gaining more and more momentum. Technological changes push leaders to lead more and more via these technologies and interacting with them. This requires a completely new mind and skill set, which leaders in the past didn't have.
- The digital transformation is much more of a leadership and cultural challenge than a technical one. At present, many employees and managers seem to be increasingly frustrated and distressed by technological change. Not only do many employees, especially leaders, fear that they will lose their job but also that the Internet of things will take over the Internet originally created by humans for humans and social media. In short, it is not technology that serves man, but man that surrenders to technological progress. An increase in depression and burnouts is a direct consequence of this development. The challenge for digital leadership will be to reverse this development.
- Digital transformation is much less revolutionary than evolutionary. Digital ambidexterity shows that organizations are not always forced or well advised to disrupt their business model by technological progress in order to continue its current operations. Instead, they should evolutionary augment (and not replace) its activities with digital technology. Augmentation, in this sense, means starting with what humans do today and figuring out how that work could be improved rather than diminished by an increase in the use of digital technology.
- Digital leaders need to understand how these technologies and AI solutions work, how they can use them, and, most importantly, what the limits are or how to limit them proactively. Future leaders need to be masters of these technological solutions and possibilities, not their servants. In the end, it should never be the human being who has to serve the technology. It should always be the technology that has to serve the people (Langhof et al. 2020).

References

Afsar, B., Badir, Y., & Kiani, U. S. (2016). Linking spiritual leadership and employee pro-environmental behavior: The influence of workplace spirituality, intrinsic motivation, and environmental passion. *Journal of Environmental Psychology, 45*, 79–88.

Andrew, J., & Baker, M. (2019). The general data protection regulation in the age of surveillance capitalism. *Journal of Business Ethics*. https://doi.org/10.1007/s10551-019-04239-z.

Appel, M., Krisch, N., Stein, J.-P., & Weber, S. (2019). Smartphone zombies! Pedestrians' distracted walking as a function of their fear of missing out. *Journal of Environmental Psychology, 63*, 130–133.

Benediktinerabtei Niederaltaich. (2020). *Monastic Stay - Kloster auf Zeit*. Retrieved July 27, 2020, from http://www.abtei-niederaltaich.de/accommodation/monastic-stays-kloster-auf-zeit/?L=3

Bloedorn, L. A., & Muethel, M. (2018). When German soldiers disobey for the sake of the troop: Examining pro-organizational misbehavior. *Academy of Management Proceedings, 2018*(1), 13247.

Bonelli, R. M. (2016). *Selber schuld!: Ein Wegweiser aus seelischen Sackgassen*. München: Droemer.

Bonelli, R. M. (2017a). *Der Himmel auf Erden. Psychologie des Glücks. Speech presented at Himmel & Hölle, Heiligenkreuz im Wienerwald*. Retrieved July 30, 2020, from http://www.rpp-media.org/index.php?m=153

Bonelli, R. M. (2017b). Religiosity and psychological resilience in psychiatric patients: An overview. *Journal of Psychology & Clinical Psychiatry, 8*(3), 00487.

Bonelli, R. M. (2017c). An evidence-based review on religiosity in psychiatry. *Journal of Neurology & Stroke, 7*(2), 00231.

Bonelli, R. M. (2018a). *Männlicher Narzissmus Das Drama der Liebe, die um sich selbst kreist*. München: Pantheon.

Bonelli, R. M. (2018b). Selbsttranszendenz und Narzissmus. In *Psychotherapie und Spiritualität. Psychotherapie* (pp. 195–204). Berlin: Springer.

Bruder, J. (2015). These workers have a new demand: Stop watching us. *The Nation*. Retrieved August 9, 2020, from https://www.thenation.com/article/archive/these-workers-have-new-demand-stop-watching-us/

Busch, W. (2007). *Jesus our destiny* (9th ed.). Basel: Brunnen Publishing.

Bühlmann, C., & Braun, P. (2010). Auftragstaktik in Vergangenheit, Gegenwart und Zukunft. Revue de l'Armée suisse der Militärmacht, Beilage zur ASMZ 6/10 und RMS 3/10, 2010 (1), 50–63.

Cai, W., McKenna, B., & Waizenegger, L. (2020). Turning it off: Emotions in digital-free travel. *Journal of Travel Research, 59*(5), 909–927.

Câmara, L. G. (2005). *Remembering Iñigo: Glimpses of the life of Saint Ignatius of Loyola; the memorials of Luis Gonçalves da Câmara* (A. Eaglestone & J. A. Munitiz, Trans.). Herefordshire: Gracewing.

Chory, R. M., Vela, L. E., & Avtgis, T. A. (2015). Organizational surveillance of computer-mediated workplace communication: Employee privacy concerns and responses. *Employee Responsibilities and Rights Journal, 28*(1), 23–43. https://doi.org/10.1007/s10672-015-9267-4.

Dahlqvist, F., Patel, M., Rajko, A., & Shulman, J. (2019). *Growing opportunities in the internet of things*. McKinsey & Company. Retrieved August 27, 2020, from https://www.mckinsey.com/industries/private-equity-and-principal-investors/our-insights/growing-opportunities-in-the-internet-of-things

Daugherty, P. R., & Wilson, H. J. (2018). *Human + machine: Reimagining work in the age of AI*. Boston, MA: Harvard Business Review Press.

Davenport, T. H., & Kirby, J. (2015). Beyond automation. Strategies for remaining gainfully employed in an era of very smart machines. *Harvard Business Review, 93*(6), 58–65.

Davenport, T. H., & Kirby, J. (2016). Just how smart are smart machines? *MIT Sloan Management Review, 57*(3), 21–25.

Deci, E. L., & Ryan, R. M. (2008). Self-determination theory: A macrotheory of human motivation, development, and health. *Canadian Psychology/Psychologie Canadienne, 49*(3), 182–185.

Eisenhardt, K. M. (1989). Agency theory: An assessment and review. *The Academy of Management Review, 14*(1), 57. https://doi.org/10.2307/258191.

Ewest, T. G., Neubert, M. J., & Ngunjiri, F. W. (2016). Faith and work: Christian perspectives on meaning making within organizations. *Academy of Management Proceedings, 2016*(1), 14527. https://doi.org/10.5465/ambpp.2016.14527symposium.

Forman, C., Goldfarb, A., & Greenstein, S. (2005). How did location affect adoption of the commercial internet? Global village vs. urban leadership. *Journal of Urban Economics, 58*(3), 389–420. https://doi.org/10.1016/j.jue.2005.05.004.

Frankl, V. E. (1959). *Man's search for meaning.* Boston, MA: Beacon Press.

Frémeaux, S., & Pavageau, B. (2020). Meaningful leadership: How can leaders contribute to meaningful work? *Journal of Management Inquiry.* https://doi.org/10.1177/1056492619897126.

Gabriel, R., & Röhrs, H.-P. (2017). *Social media: Potenziale, trends, Chancen und Risiken.* Berlin: Springer.

Gaskell, A. (2018). How Uber drivers feel about being managed by machines. *Forbes.* Retrieved July 30, 2020, from https://www.forbes.com/sites/adigaskell/2018/05/08/how-do-uber-drivers-feel-about-being-managed-by-machines/

Gersch, M., Güldenberg, S., Güttel, W. H., Müller-Seitz, G., Renzl, B., & Schulz, A.-C. (2020). Gestaltungsherausforderungen der digitalen Transformation: Pfade erkennen, gestalten oder verlassen? *WiST – Wirtschaftswissenschaftliches Studium, 49*(2–3), 44–48.

Ghosh, P. G. (2017). An artificial intelligence story: The robot boss and data operations. *Dataversity.* Retrieved July 30, 2020, from https://www.dataversity.net/fascinating-artificial-intelligence-story-robot-boss/

Gleissner, H., & Möller, K. (2011). *Case studies in logistics.* Wiesbaden: Gabler Verlag.

Godlewski, N. (2018, April 9). Elon Musk says humans could end up ruled by an immortal AI dictator. In *Newsweek.* Retrieved from https://www.newsweek.com/elon-musk-ai-artificial-intelligence-dictator-immortal-878061

Graeber, D. (2018). *Bullshit jobs: A theory.* New York: Simon & Schuster.

Gümüsay, A. A. (2019). Embracing religions in moral theories of leadership. *Academy of Management Perspectives, 33*(3), 292–306. https://doi.org/10.5465/amp.2017.0130.

Güttel, W. H., Güldenberg, S., Klinger, S., & Renzl, B. (2019). Austrian School of Management: Wissen, Lernen und Unternehmertum. In W. H. Güttel (Ed.), *Erfolgreich in turbulenten Zeiten: Impulse für Leadership, Change Management & Ambidexterity* (pp. 9–26). München: Augsburg.

Hanley, D. A., & Hubbard, S. (2020, September). *Eyes everywhere: Amazon's surveillance infrastructure and revitalizing worker.* Reports & White Papers, Open Markets. Retrieved from https://static1.squarespace.com/static/5e449c8c3ef68d752f3e70dc/t/5f4cffea23958d79eae1ab23/1598881772432/Amazon_Report_Final.pdf

Harari, Y. N. (2016). *Homo Deus: A brief history of tomorrow.* London: Vintage.

Inoue, Y., & Tsujimoto, M. (2018). New market development of platform ecosystems: A case study of the Nintendo Wii. *Technological Forecasting and Social Change, 136,* 235–253. https://doi.org/10.1016/j.techfore.2017.01.017.

Kiechle, S. (2019). *Achtsam und wirksam Führen aus dem Geist der Jesuiten.* München: Herder Verlag.

Kingston, J. K. (2016). Artificial intelligence and legal liability. *Research and Development in Intelligent Systems, XXXIII,* 269–279. https://doi.org/10.1007/978-3-319-47175-4_20.

Kriger, M., & Seng, Y. (2005). Leadership with inner meaning: A contingency theory of leadership based on the worldviews of five religions. *The Leadership Quarterly, 16*(5), 771–806. https://doi.org/10.1016/j.leaqua.2005.07.007.

Künkel, F. (1936). *What it means to grow up: A guide in understanding the development of character.* New York: Scribner.

Langhof, J., & Güldenberg, S. (2020). Servant leadership: A systematic literature review—toward a model of antecedents, outcomes, causes, and effects. *German Journal of Human Resource Management, 34*, 37.

Langhof, J., Renzl, B., & Güldenberg, S. (2020). Arbeiten im Takt der Algorithmen? Mensch bleiben durch dienende Führung. *Zeitschrift OrganisationsEntwicklung, 3*, 12–16.

Launius, R. D., & McCurdy, H. E. (2007). *Robots in space: Technology, evolution, and interplanetary travel.* Baltimore: The Johns Hopkins University Press.

Liden, R. C., Wayne, S. J., Liao, C., & Meuser, J. D. (2014). Servant leadership and serving culture: Influence on individual and unit performance. *Academy of Management Journal, 57*(5), 1434–1452. https://doi.org/10.5465/amj.2013.0034.

Lin, P., Abney, K., & Bekey, G. A. (2011). *Robot ethics: The ethical and social implications of robotics.* Cambridge: MIT Press.

Lynn, M. L., Easter, S., Jessup, R., & Straughn, G. (2020). Harmonizing work: Meaning and meaning making in Christian hymnody. *Academy of Management Proceedings, 2020*(1), 12418. https://doi.org/10.5465/ambpp.2020.12418abstract.

Matyszczyk, C. (2013). GPS sends Belgian woman to Croatia, 810 miles out of her way. *Cnet.* Retrieved July 30, 2020, from https://www.cnet.com/news/gps-sends-belgian-woman-to-croatia-810-miles-out-of-her-way/

Mohammad, Y., & Nishida, T. (2018). *Data mining for social robotics toward autonomously social robots.* Cham: Springer.

Mohr, J. (2007). *Looking for monks and nuns in the new millennium.* Spiegel International. Retrieved July 27, 2020, from https://www.spiegel.de/international/spiegel/monasteries-in-germany-looking-for-monks-and-nuns-in-the-new-millennium-a-460675.html

Moor, J. (2006). The nature, importance, and difficulty of machine ethics. *IEEE Intelligent Systems, 21*(4), 18–21.

Morgan, R. (2017, April 24). Even CEOs will be replaced by robots, Jack Ma predicts. *New York Post.* Retrieved from https://nypost.com/2017/04/24/even-ceos-will-be-replaced-by-robots-jack-ma-predicts/

O'Reilly, C. A., & Tushman, M. L. (2008). Ambidexterity as a dynamic capability: Resolving the innovator's dilemma. *Research in Organizational Behavior, 28*, 185–206. https://doi.org/10.1016/j.riob.2008.06.002.

Podolny, J. M., Khurana, R., & Hill-Popper, M. (2004). Revisiting the meaning of leadership. *Research in Organizational Behavior, 26*, 1–36.

Riasanow, T., Setzke, D., Böhm, M., & Krcmar, H. (2019). Clarifying the notion of digital transformation: A transdisciplinary review of literature. *Journal of Competences Management and Strategy (JCSM), 10*, 5–32.

Rocha, R. G., & Pinheiro, P. G. (2020). Organizational spirituality: Concept and perspectives. *Journal of Business Ethics.* https://doi.org/10.1007/s10551-020-04463-y.

Rosa, H. (2020). *The uncontrollability of the world.* Cambridge, UK: Polity Press. (original edition in German: Rosa, H. (2018) Unverfügbarkeit, Residenz-Verlag).

Shamir, E. (2010). The long and winding road: The US Army managerial approach to command and the adoption of Mission command (Auftragstaktik). *Journal of Strategic Studies, 33*(5), 645–672.

Skrbina, D. (2015). *Metaphysics of technology.* New York: Taylor & Francis.

Smith, G. T. (2016). *Machine tool metrology: An industrial handbook.* Cham: Springer.

Spitzer, M. (2012). *Digitale Demenz Wie wir uns und unsere Kinder um den Verstand bringen.* Munich: Droemer Knaur.

Stahl, T. (2016). Indiscriminate mass surveillance and the public sphere. *Ethics and Information Technology, 18*(1), 33–39. https://doi.org/10.1007/s10676-016-9392-2.

Stanton, R. (2019). *A brief history of video games: From Atari to virtual reality.* London: Robinson.

Stroud, D. G. (2013). Wilhelm Busch: The way of true faith. In D. G. Stroud (Ed.), *Preaching in Hitler's shadow: Sermons of resistance in the third Reich* (pp. 170–176). Grand Rapids: William B. Eerdmans Publishing Company.

Vial, G. (2019). Understanding digital transformation. *Journal of Strategic Information Systems, 28* (2), 118–144.

Visser, M. (2010). Configurations of human resource practices and battlefield performance: A comparison of two armies. *Human Resource Management Review, 20*(4), 340–349. https://doi. org/10.1016/j.hrmr.2010.04.002.

Weihs, D. (2018). Autosomes as managers—A commented case. In K. North, R. Maier, & O. Haas (Eds.), *Knowledge management in digital change. Progress in IS.* Cham: Springer. https://doi. org/10.1007/978-3-319-73546-7_13.

Weinberg, F. J., & Locander, W. B. (2014). Advancing workplace spiritual development: A dyadic mentoring approach. *The Leadership Quarterly, 25*(2), 391–408.

Welledits, V., Schmidkonz, C., & Kraft, P. (2019). *Digital Detox im Arbeitsleben Methoden und Empfehlungen für einen gesunden Einsatz von Technologien.* Wiesbaden: Springer Fachmedien Wiesbaden GmbH.

Stefan Güldenberg is a pioneer and leading expert on the future of work, digital strategies, sustainable leadership, and knowledge management. He is a university professor, platform founder, strategy consultant, executive coach, and knowledge entrepreneur. He studied Business Mathematics, Philosophy, and English at the University of Ulm and then received his doctorate and habilitation at the Vienna University of Economics and Business. Stefan has 25 years of experience in research, knowledge transfer, and practice. He conducts research on and supports the development of strategy and transformation processes. Stays abroad led him, among others, to Harvard University, the Massachusetts Institute of Technology (MIT), and the National University of Singapore. He is the current Vice President Practice of the European Academy of Management (EURAM) and President of the New Club of Paris, a think tank and agenda setter for the knowledge economy.

Jan G. Langhof is a PhD student at the University of Liechtenstein. His research interest focuses on leadership (especially servant leadership), which he examines and explores from various perspectives. His work is often interdisciplinary and draws on management, philosophy, history, and IT. Jan's academic papers have been published in numerous renowned journals, including the *Journal of Management History* and *Tourism Management Perspectives.* Prior to his PhD program, Jan worked in the IT industry across different international locations.

Making Collaboration Work

Daniel Stoller-Schai

It's the 27th of March 2030, and Nadire, a young data analyst, wakes up and spins around on her futon once more before preparing a fresh green tea in the kitchen. Zurich has grown in the last 10 years. At its core, the city has been compacted, and the agglomeration has expanded. Surprisingly, however, the city has not collapsed due to traffic. Since the Corona crisis in 2020, home office, remote work, and digital collaboration have spread virally. It's time for the daily meeting. Every day, the virtual team meets at a different team member's place. Today, it's Nadire's turn. The other team members are represented as holograms and take a seat at Nadire's dining room table.

This chapter focuses on the question, what will collaboration look like in 2030? What will be the role of culture, organization, tools, and people? Technologies are changing the way we work together and what we produce on a massive scale. As physical proximity is no longer necessary for collaboration, dependence on other people also decreases; intelligent assistants, automated routines, and self-learning structures have become our partners in our daily collaborations. This has opened up new opportunities, especially for microenterprises and freelancers. Think about it: The same number of people that were needed to cultivate a field is now enough to operate a satellite-controlled and networked machine park and can often do so on their own. In the field of cognitive work, we will have similar conditions in 2030: One person alone can execute things that used to require an entire open-plan office to do. Many changes will come about as a result of the shifting attitudes among employees, particularly as new digital-savvy generations enter the workforce and bring with them their own notions on communication and collaboration.

However, what is meant by collaboration? Collaboration is defined as the direct and mutually influential active confrontation of two or more people, oriented toward common goals, to solve or master a task or problem. This takes place within a jointly

D. Stoller-Schai (✉)
Collaboration Design GmbH, Bäretswil, Switzerland
e-mail: daniel.stoller-schai@collaboration-design.ch

© Springer Nature Switzerland AG 2021
S. Güldenberg et al. (eds.), *Managing Work in the Digital Economy*, Future of Business and Finance, https://doi.org/10.1007/978-3-030-65173-2_11

designed and negotiated, computer-mediated context (common space of meaning, cooperative setting) and using common resources (see Stoller-Schai 2003, 2019, S. 45).

The topic "Making Collaboration Work" is developed in four parts: In Part I, we look into the year 2030. For this purpose, we look at the everyday life of the young data specialist, Nadire, who works virtually as well as face-to-face in different contexts and with people from various countries. In Part II, we look back: Where did this all come from, and what were points of departure to established norms? The future Collaboration Landscape will be introduced in Part III. Here, we will explored the question, what have we undertaken in schools, companies, and governmental organizations and globally in the last 10 years to develop collaborative competence on individual and organizational levels that have become a decisive competitive factor in 2030. The final part addresses the question, which steps do we have to undertake in the coming years to achieve the realization of the "Collaboration Landscape 2030" (see Sect. 3.1)?

Let us first read about a typical working day of Nadire in 2030.

1   A Day in the Life of Nadire in 2030

Nadire is a young data specialist whose grandparents immigrated from Turkey to Switzerland. She studied in London and now works in Zurich, where she lives in an international community, who, by nature, is globally networked through cultural ties and today's work culture. Collaborative work in different virtual contexts is quite routine for her and so is working in different physical locations face-to-face.

07.00 a.m.
It's 27 March 2030; Nadire wakes up and spins around on her futon once more before preparing a fresh green tea in the kitchen. Zurich has grown in the last 10 years. At its core, the city has been compacted, and the agglomeration has also been expanded. Surprisingly, however, there has not been a total collapse due to the rise in traffic. Since the Corona crisis in 2020, home office, remote work, and digital collaboration have become widespread. In addition, many people have sold their cars and switched to car sharing, e-bikes, and e-scooters, or self-flying vehicles. All this has helped to resolve the potential major traffic problem. Nadire briefly checks her body readings on a large windowpane, which gives a view of a green inner courtyard. With just an oral command, the large windowpane becomes a screen on which all her bodily readings are made visible. Nadire moves the individual blocks of information around using eye contact, thanks to a body chip, which she had inserted under the skin of her forearm. The chip gives her continuous feedback on her most critical bodily functions and displays them on the windowpane or on the device which is closest to Nadire at the moment.

08.00 a.m.
Time to meet others for the daily meeting. Every day, the team meets at a different team member's place. Today, it's Nadire's turn. The other team members are represented by holograms and take a seat at Nadire's dining room table. A short check-in gives the opportunity to make small talk. "The weather is a perennial topic," Nadire thinks, "the subject will probably always be topical." After the check-in, all team members give a short update on where they stand with their work. Again, the large window front in Nadire's apartment serves as a screen for everyone. The 7 m × 2.5 m area offers enough space to place all the essential facts, pictures, graphics, and films so that everyone has a clear overview of things. The team consists of three groups, divided into three large time zones. The morning meeting always brings together the EMEA and APAC parts of the team. Although English is still the standard language of communication, each team member is always able to express themselves in their national language, even in their dialect, so that everyone can get the feeling of having expressed themselves clearly on the matter. The collaboration infrastructure translates any language directly and into the desired target language. In this way, misunderstandings have been significantly reduced, and the understanding of intercultural nuances has grown.

09.00 a.m.
After the daily meeting, Buana from Indonesia and Nadire stay on. Just a few years ago, they had each met through data glasses in a virtual 3D room. Since this function has been integrated into a lens, this possibility is available at any time and can be activated by calling up the feature. Buana and Nadire connect their infrastructures in this 3D space so that they can continue working together on their project. They are in the process of designing molecules for new drugs and are moving around molecule chains for this purpose. By moving their hands, they can change the scale and thus either immerse themselves in a molecule or view the entire context from a distance. This form of collaboration is very intensive, and after an hour, they say goodbye. They are satisfied with what they have achieved and have managed to initiate the production of a molecular chain. They now leave their work to an idea development algorithm, which will move their idea further along independently and which they will be able to review during their next meeting.

10.30 a.m.
Nadire leaves her apartment for a short walk in the park nearby. She goes into off-line mode and closes all communication connections. It is important to her that she can log off once or twice a day and be on her own. At the end of her walk, she always goes to a teahouse. Sometimes, she meets an older lady there, with whom she likes to talk. Mrs. Walter is 70 years old and tells her about her childhood in the 1960s when there were no computers, no smartphones, and no Internet. For Nadire, these are stories from another world, and she can hardly imagine that one could have ever lived like that.

12.00 p.m.

Back at home, Nadire prepares lunch for herself. She is a member of a neighborhood garden project that uses empty spaces on flat roofs to grow vegetables, berries, and fruits. From this, Nadire receives a box of fresh vegetables every now and again. Today, it is eggplants that she processes into a gratin. Sometimes, the two IT students from the flat next door come to visit for lunch. They are also studying data science and can benefit from Nadire's experience and her networks. Today, they are talking about the services they want to use to set up their own business in a year's time. The innovative power of the start-up scene in the early 2000s has meant that many people are now self-employed and can quickly form flash organizations for projects, where they complete a job together and then separate again just as quickly. The social security and tax systems have had to be adapted for this. Social security benefits and taxes are calculated according to a simple pay-per-use principle. For the billing of the project work to the individual project members, the services are mutual and mutually evaluated. A distribution algorithm automatically distributes the fee to the accounts of the members according to a consensus decision.

01.00 p.m.

In the afternoon, Nadire starts her quiet working phase, at least for about 2 h. She dictates new ideas to her digital assistant, which are automatically transcribed, summarized, and indexed. She draws other ideas with a virtual pen on her universal windowpane and turns them into a 3D object as required. She reads her curated news from various data sources or switches on a live stream for more details.

03.30 p.m.

Today was a good day: 2.5 h of work in peace—that doesn't always happen. Now, Nadire is ready for real contacts. She leaves her apartment again and rides her e-bike on well-built cycle paths directly to her favorite coworking space. These were created from 2020 onward and have developed into local work centers, bazaars for exchange, workshops spaces, makerspace sessions, and much more. Nadire meets a new client and two colleagues (Sue and Jana), with whom she has already worked on numerous projects. The four of them retire to a "huddle room" and discuss the assignment. Via an app, Jana orders a round of coffee for everyone, and after 10 min, it is brought by Bobby, the barista robot. The project idea takes shape, the tasks are distributed, and the budget is discussed. After the client left, the three women stay together and discuss the next operative steps and set up a virtual project space.

06.00 p.m.

Nadire is going back home. Markus, her boyfriend, is waiting for her there. He works for a large machine manufacturer and is responsible for sales in the USA. He has already prepared a light dinner. Nadire meets briefly for her "Lately," as she calls her daily meeting with her American colleagues. Markus stops by and says, "Hello"; in the meantime, they have got to know each other well, and Markus has already been able to use Nadire's contacts for his American sales tasks. At 6.45 p.m., the meeting is over, and Nadire and Markus treat themselves to a cozy dinner and a glass of red wine. They talk about their next holidays. They want to go to Indonesia. Nadire finally wants to get to know her team colleagues, with whom she has been working with for the last 2 years. Markus is interested in the country, the culture, and the language. In the last few weeks, he has even started learning the Indonesian language with his AI tutor. Automated translations are quite practical—but learning a language by yourself and being able to speak it have another quality.

08.00 p.m.
That's it for today. Nadire does not want to talk anymore and watches a series in 2D. Markus reads a book. He loves the haptic experience, the weight, and the smell of a book, even if it seems very anachronistic in 2030. It is important to him to do things in a completely analog way, as a counterpoint to his mostly digital work. That is why he likes to work in a wood workshop on weekends and improve his skills in furniture making with solid wood together with others. Meanwhile, some objects have been created for their shared apartment. Nadire thinks it's great and likes to sit in a lounge chair made by Markus, especially in the morning during the "Daily."

10.30 p.m.
Nadire goes to bed; Markus joins a little while later. Nadire takes a quick look at the automatically curated daily summary on her tablet and checks her body values: she has taken 11,000 steps today—not bad. She is satisfied with the day and falls asleep.

2   A Look Back: Where Did We Start in 2020?

This chapter aims to describe the initial situation in 2020. Where did we stand in terms of collaboration? What had we already achieved? What were we proud of and didn't want to lose? What were our predictions for the skills we would probably need in the future to work collaboratively?

The year 2020 was marked by the Corona crisis. Thousands of people died worldwide. The only effective measure against the spread was social distancing. This led to people being sent home, entire cities being quarantined, schools being closed, and companies and shops being forced to close. Suddenly, the only way to communicate was via the Internet and mobile networks. Schools had to switch immediately to homeschooling and businesses to home office work. After a short period of shock, the message was finally accepted that people really did need to stay at home. This started a creative and solidary push started on four levels:

- *Mind*—In 2020, a new attitude and a new view of school, the world of work, and the home office developed.
- *People*—There was a new assessment of the value of analog and digital encounters.
- *Organizations*—There was more discussion about leadership and new organizational models.

- *Machines*—The Corona crisis led to new experiences with digital tools and intelligent systems.

Mind

A new attitude and a new approach to issues such as social vulnerability (fragility), questions of sense and purpose (purpose), and, in general, questions about the ethical foundations of a digital network society (ethics) developed.

- **Fragility:** Perhaps one of the most important things to come from the Corona crisis was a new global awareness of the vulnerability of economic and social systems. Not because this was not known beforehand, but because for the first time it become evident and tangible to the general population. At the same time, there was a great deal of solidarity, leading to numerous creative initiatives such as the Versus Virus Hackathon in Switzerland in April 2020. LinkedIn further established itself as an important platform to exchange experiences and to get to know new events, ideas, and people.
- **Purpose:** Many things were questioned. Why do we actually travel around so much when it is possible to do so much digitally? How do we have to prepare ourselves so that we are ready and able to continue working and generating revenue even during a pandemic? What will we use our face-to-face meetings time for in the future? What competencies and skills do we need in the future so that we can work together virtually?
- **Ethics:** A rethinking of digital ethics also took place. If we are increasingly working together—and perhaps in the future especially digitally—then we will have to establish rules and measures for data security, protection of personal data, and intellectual property. A study by Gartner stated, "Legislators and companies must clarify ethical issues surrounding the use of AI, in particular, 'emotional computing' (analyzing the feelings of a human counterpart) moves in a grey area in the EU" (see https://www.cio.de/a/gartner-nennt-5-megatrends-bis-2029,3606088)

People

With regard to the comparison between machine and human capabilities, the following topics came to the forefront: awareness of typical human strengths (value judgment, self-directed goals, creativity, handling dilemmas, intuition, dreaming, imagination, abstraction, empathy, etc.), the value of shared experiences, and the importance of exchanging it, both in analog and digital form.

- **Potential:** Another insight into the ingenuity of machines and the ingenuity of people had already been pointed out in 2015. Colvin (2016) stated that we often underestimate ourselves in the face of the possibilities of intelligent machines. Humans have the ability to adapt flexibly to all environmental changes, and they will further increase their options when working together with digital assistants and robots. Emotional intelligence, empathy, lateral thinking, and intercultural competence became important values.

- **Presence:** But the Corona crisis also showed that we want to see and experience how each other live: Before and after the crisis, a real boom for presence-oriented learning and working forms began. Working out Loud (Stepper 2018), Liberating Structures (Lipmanowicz and McCandless 2014; Steinhöfer and Weinert 2020), Design Thinking (Lewrick 2018; Lewrick et al. 2018), Lego® Serious Play®, and Eigenland® are just some of them (for a detailed overview: Stoller-Schai 2020a). Further, makerspaces were set up, and coworking spaces were opened to collaborate directly with each other.
- **Exchange:** With Meetup groups, LinkedIn networks, BarCamps (Muuß-Merholz 2019), and coworking spaces, the willingness to share and collaborate across company boundaries increased. Co-creation became a significant trend. With these forms of creative exchange, the boundaries between experts and nonexperts became blurred. Depending on the role and setting, everyone was once an expert and, then again, a nonexpert. In the spirit of the holacracy (Robertson 2016), the person who was currently best suited to take on a role or task was always the one to do it.

Organizations

2020 was also the starting point for a strategic rethink of the home office and in regard to remote work in general. Completely virtual companies such as "required" (https://required.com/de/) were suddenly no longer unusual but the yardstick for the new normality.

- **Virtual-Analog:** Virtual leadership became an important development topic in leadership training. Karin Christen, CEO of "required," said, "Virtual leadership is our default setting. However, for specific issues, we often rely on real-time communication with video calls or even meetings to minimize asynchronous communication and thus waiting times and misunderstandings. We use video calls, for example, for weekly team or planning meetings, job interviews, complicated tasks, briefings, or bugs. We do not hire an employee until we have met at least once. We also combine employee interviews with a physical meeting, and for team building, we also meet once or twice a year for several days" (Stoller-Schai 2020c).
- **Cell-Network:** The classic top-down organizations with a pyramid structure continued to crumble. New approaches like "BetaCodex" were intensively discussed. Organizations were switched to networks (Bensmann 2018; De Vet and Lowette 2018, Gray 2012) or cell structure design (Pflaeging and Hermann 2019). Organization are organized as cell networks. Decisions are made at the periphery of the network, where the contact to the market exists. The core of the network serves to support the periphery. This is a radical shift away from the classical pyramid organizations, where decisions are made at the top and then executed at the bottom. Large corporations like Novartis started an "Unboss Program." The role of top management and the CEO changed. Decisions were no longer made at the top but on the periphery. Where the company and associates

have direct market contact, decisions were also made on investments, products, and distribution.

- **Flash-Gig:** For the implementation of project orders, more emphasis was placed on flash organization. According to the principle "Build a Team, Do the Job, Say Goodbye" (Scheiber 2017), temporary teams are formed that are made up of experts from all over the world. Matching platforms (e.g., https://www.comatch. com/de/) specialize in bringing companies and consultants together and supporting the creation of flash organizations.

  The gig economy also continued to develop. To meet the requirements of social security and tax authorities, new possibilities for accounting, invoicing, and social security had to be designed for the numerous freelancers and service providers who did not want to start their own company (GmbH or AG). Companies such as PayrollPlus (see https://payrollplus.ch) specialize in providing social security and payroll solutions for freelancers and self-employed service providers.

Machines

The Corona crisis led to new experiences with digital tools and intelligent systems. The web conferencing provider "Zoom" extended its user base from 10 to 200 million. Virtual reality and the collaboration in 3D spaces became commonly known. Artificial intelligence and deep learning became two of the most discussed terms.

- **Zoom and Co:** The year 2020 was the year of "Zoom" (www.zoom.us). Hardly any other provider of web conferencing systems was in such a good starting position as Zoom. They could offer a stable and user-friendly service. Zoom was used for meetings, distributed workshops, broadcasting, coaching sessions, and much more. The Corona crisis led to the realization that digital collaboration is the backbone for collaboration in networked organizations. Teams from Microsoft was offered license-free. Many providers also offered their systems at very low prices. Projects were increasingly managed with Trello, Jira, Monday, Asana or Planner, etc. Surveys were conducted with Mentimeter, SurveyMonkey, or Slido. Communities were started via Slack, Yammer, Facebook, Meetup, Beekeeper or Glowing Blue, etc. Information was shared via LinkedIn, WhatsApp, Instagram, Telegram, TikTok, or Twitter.
- **Spaced Collaboration:** But there was also a lot happening in the 3D area: BarCamps (e.g., the corporate learning community BarCamp Hamburg 2020; see https://colearn.de), which should have been a physical meeting, were held in 3D worlds (see https://tricat-spaces.net and Herkersdorf 2018). Entire trade fairs (such as Interpack 2020 or TalentPro) were virtualized and took place entirely online. These experiences led trade fair organizers and stand builders to consider the question of which trade fairs and conferences should be physically held in the future. Some booth builders went bankrupt in 2020; others understood early on that trade fairs and conferences can also take place digitally and developed appropriate platforms and services.

  Collaborative products such as the "SmartBoard," which often stood around unused in companies, were revived by new concepts such as the "CollaBoard."

With the CollaBoard (see https://ibvsolutions.com/de/collaboard/), it was possible to work on a physical board that was digitally networked with the boards of others, thus creating a networked collaborative workspace.

• **Deep Learning:** It became obvious that the gap between the elite of artificial intelligence researchers and users in companies was vast. New training programs were offered for managers in the fields of data science (e.g., www.dsfm.ch/dsfm) or artificial intelligence. Max Tegmark expressed his hope for this as early as 2016: "Everything we love about civilization is the product of human intelligence, so if we can amplify it with AI, we obviously have the potential to make life even better" (Tegmark 2017).

To summarize, the year 2020 was a real turning point in terms of collaboration and laid the foundations for the social, economic, and technological developments of the next 10 years.

3 "What Have We Done to Reach Where We Are Today?"

3.1 The Collaboration Landscape 2030

This chapter explains the Collaboration Landscape 2030. It looks at what we have undertaken in schools, companies, and governmental organizations and across regions, in general, to encourage collaboration, make it work, and thus contribute to competitiveness.

The Collaboration Landscape 2030 (Fig. 1) consists of four areas. At the center is the collaborative mindset, which drives the Collaboration Landscape from within. The three most notable examples are listed for each area.

Collaboration Mindset
A collaborative mindset is at the heart of the Collaboration Landscape. Leaders must have an understanding of the importance of digital and analog collaboration and must have concrete experience of it themselves. This implies an understanding of networks (Bensmann 2018) in general and an understanding of networked companies (Gray 2012) or organizations according to the cell structure design (e.g., Pflaeging and Hermann 2019) in particular. Leading in the virtual company becomes a central challenge for managers (Stoller-Schai 2020c).

Example

The company FrontRunners (fictitious example) specializes in the creation of digital signatures, which can be applied to all kinds of digital and analog objects. The company is organized sociocratically. Decisions concerning product development are made on the periphery of the company, as it is closest to the market. The founders and employees are aware that the company can only flourish if there

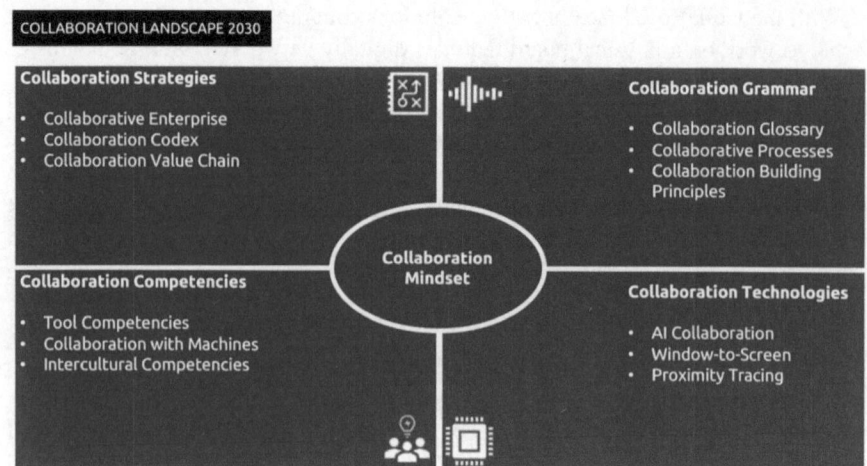

Fig. 1 Collaboration Landscape 2030 (Source: Stoller-Schai)

is open, transparent, and creative cooperation. For this reason, all documents are available to all employees. This requires a well-established culture of trust. Whenever that trust comes under pressure because decisions are not comprehensible or because one does not know exactly what the others are actually doing, this is immediately addressed to prevent an erosion of culture that is difficult to restore. The principles of cooperation have been summarized in a Collaboration Codex. All employees have signed it. Collaboration culture is also regularly discussed in town halls, in brown-bag sessions, and other events. In this way, an understanding and an in-depth knowledge of collaboration have developed. This also has an impact on the leadership culture. Leadership is always given to the person who is best suited for the current task. Leadership takes place almost exclusively in virtual or hybrid contexts. This means that the people who lead must know how to communicate with their teams and address difficulties. This happens—if necessary—mainly in one-to-one conversations. All these experiences and the development of a Collaboration Codex have led to the development of an actual "Collaboration Mindset" in the company. ◀

Collaboration Strategies

The collaborative mindset is the basis for the development of collaboration strategies. A collaboration strategy defines how to collaborate with all stakeholders of a company:

- Collaborative enterprise: In 2030, the collaborative enterprise is the standard. Product development with customers, collaboration with competitors, and fluid company boundaries are the basis for business success.

- Collaboration Codex: The Collaboration Codex defines which channels are used to communicate and collaborate and how.
- Collaboration value chain: Collaborative processes are developed along the value chain: From social hiring, to crowdfunding and community marketing, to crowd support.

Example

The company "VisitYourDreams" (fictional example) has established itself in the field of eTourism. On a platform, it offers various holiday destinations that have been compiled using contributions from its platform users. The cooperation between the users of the platform is an essential success factor in its success. To do justice to this important factor itself, the company "VisitYourDreams" has converted its entire value chain to collaborative processes.

Market research is solved via a crowd research approach. Instead of commissioning market research institutes, data and user impressions are systematically collected. Holiday reports and photos are evaluated using AI-based algorithms. Holiday films are analyzed for positive and negative impressions using sentiment analysis and rated accordingly.

Innovation and design are redeemed via an open innovation approach. There is also an open exchange with competitors and numerous universities that have specialized in the field of tourism. The financing of new functions is started via crowdfunding. In this way, the users of the platform also become co-owners and identify with the latest developments. On this basis, it is only logical that HR management also finds new employees via social hiring. It is sufficient to advertise a position in their own network. The people who apply are therefore already well known to the company. Prototyping and testing of new products are also solved via crowd testing. The users of the platform test new functions and thus receive bonus points for their next series. The production and manufacturing of new products are then realized via crowd-based manufacturing. Small orders are assigned to the entire network via micro-tasking. This enables fast and parallel development. Marketing and sales take place in the form of community marketing, and after-sales is also handled by crowd support. In this way, "VisitYourDreams" is a living network organism that can quickly adapt to new needs and situations. ◄

Collaboration Grammar

It needs a "collaboration language" to make collaboration work better:

- Collaboration glossary: The basis for a collaboration language is the glossary. Basic terms like "grounding," "concluding," or "performing" are defined here.
- Collaborative processes: The profession of collaboration designer has become established. They design collaborative processes, discover chessboards, advise,

and support in complex projects. By analyzing and graphically representing collaboration data, it becomes easier to develop better collaborative processes.

- Collaboration building principles: The analysis of data from numerous collaborative processes is used to derive collaborative principles. These collaboration building principles are, in turn, used to continuously improve the collaboration enterprise.

Example

The company SmartAdminstration (fictitious example) specializes in improving work processes and cooperation in administrations. For this reason, they have developed a collaboration grammar, which uses AI-based analysis of workflows to show where collaboration can be improved. For this purpose, not only are all activities of the social enterprise network are analyzed but also the external communication with the different stakeholders. Initially, the employees in the administrations were reluctant to take part. But they quickly realized that the data had been anonymized and that they were receiving confidential and personalized tips that only they could see. Collaboration grammar describes how the various phases of collaboration can be designed. This includes the following five phases (Stoller-Schai 2003, 2019):

1. Team building (forming)
2. Determining common language (grounding)
3. Designing the procedure
4. Simultaneous cooperation (performing)
5. Reaching conclusions (concluding):
   - Recording results (results)
   - Summative reflection

With this approach, Smart Administration has succeeded in increasing the understanding of collaboration. The different phases can be described, and the data from the daily collaboration show how well this works. Each employee is individually supported through personal tips. This increases the efficiency of work and makes for better and more economical use of tax money. ◀

Collaboration Competencies

- Tool competencies: The use of collaborative tools is already practiced in primary school. Collaboration literacy becomes a basic competence.
- Collaboration with machines: Collaboration with intelligent systems, robots, chat systems, and language assistants has become the norm and enhances the abilities

of an individual. With a set of intelligent systems, freelancers and self-employed people can solve tasks that would have required entire teams just a few years ago

- Intercultural competencies: The use of automated language translation makes it easier to work with people from other language regions and cultures. Since cultural nuances are also taken into account, it becomes easier to work with people from entirely different cultural backgrounds.

Example

The company LiquidMotors (fictitious example) is a company that specializes in the development of hydrogen-powered vehicles. Various virtual and artificial reality environments are used for the development of the engines. The mechanics and technicians work with VR and AR lenses that they can put on and are, therefore, always part of a global network. If necessary, colleagues from other regions can quickly be called in to solve a very specific problem on an engine. To make this possible, the company had to invest heavily in the collaborative skills of its employees. The tool competence and the cooperation with machines but also the intercultural competencies had to be developed substantially. The intercultural competences could be improved in two ways. The real-time translation of languages and dialects into a target language has led to a significant increase in intercultural understanding. At last, it was possible to understand even subtle cultural nuances. The cooperation with the machines was also improved via language assistants. The intelligent machine was no longer seen as a competitor but as a partner. The handling of the VR and AR lenses took a little longer. In the beginning, there were still deficiencies in usability. The lenses hurt after a 6-hour working day, and the eye also had to get used to handling information on different levels. In the meantime, however, this has become well established, and many employees also use the lenses privately, for example, when it comes to operating kitchen machines intelligently at home. ◀

Collaboration Technologies
- AI collaboration: Collaboration is organized through intelligent platforms that bring together people with similar issues. The collaboration is analyzed and evaluated, and the results are continuously used to improve the algorithms.
- Window-to-screen: Every window becomes a screen. This makes it possible to make better use of the window surfaces of buildings. Large screens and projectors become superfluous.
- Proximity tracing: The technology used to combat the pandemic has been further developed. It is now used to record patterns of behavior, interests, skills, projects, and much more. This makes it even easier to bring the right people together to solve current problems.

The company NextScreen (fictitious example) develops technologies that enable smooth surfaces such as windows, mirrors, or building facades to be used as a medium for screen content. In this way, it is possible to display content from small devices on large surfaces. As a result, traditional screens were no longer needed. On the road, small screens are used and, if necessary, applied to large surfaces when several people need to work together. The technology is called "window-to-screen" and has revolutionized collaboration. But NextScreen has other fields of activity. The collaboration, which now takes place over large surfaces, is continuously analyzed by AI algorithms. AI collaboration makes it possible to support teams that are stuck and no longer able to continue with their collaboration. Situational help, recommendations, or proposals for solutions can now be played onto the large surfaces, which help a team to discover the right solutions and next steps itself. Proximity tracing can also be used to bring together people with similar ideas or problems. Each person working on a large surface is linked to the topics and solutions worked on there and can thus appear on the screen of other teams when specialized expertise is required. ◀

3.2   On the Way Toward 2030

The world was a different place after the Corona crisis. Nadire was in her early twenties and can well remember how numerous initiatives, business continuity planning (BCP), concepts, and many new projects emerged from the Corona crisis. The Swiss government formed its own department for digitization. Organizations such as "digitalswitzerland" (www.digitalswitzerland.com), Mindfire (www.mindfire.global), SwissCognitive (www.swisscognitive.ch), and numerous start-up incubators (e.g., EdTech Collider (www.edtech-collider.ch) and Venture Kick (www.venturekick.ch)) became members. The State Secretariat for Economic Affairs (SECO) formed a task force to finally regulate the topic of home offices in terms of labor law. Together with the employers' associations and the trade unions, models were drawn up to regulate commuting, home office, weekend work, and work at off-peak hours when employees themselves regulated their work in terms of time and place.

2021 After Corona
What was started in 2020 was implemented in 2021; there was a real boost in initiatives such as hackathons to draw conclusions from the Corona crisis. Gartner had to readjust its hype cycle and was able to shift some trends and technologies toward the "Slope of Enlightenment." Many companies have questioned their entire work organization. Home office became standard. Bring your own device became part of the typical IT infrastructure.

But there were also critical voices. It was apparent that there were still significant shortcomings concerning "digital literacy." New competency models were developed based on studies by Ashoka (2018), Institute for the Future (IFTF) (2011), and the Stifterverband (2018). The Swiss Informatics Society founded a new specialist group, "digital literacy." The meetup scene picked up momentum again and discussed the experience of the Corona crisis in numerous presence meetings. Ideas for new collaboration technologies and digital business models of start-ups were taken up in the coworking spaces. Technology providers such as Zoom and Microsoft Teams were able to establish themselves in the working world across the board.

2022 Achievements

One year after the Corona crisis, the initiatives entered the production phase. "Teams" had become the standard for collaboration. But there were also new niche players who were able to benefit from the Corona crisis. CollaBoard was able to place its creative board, which connects the digital with the analog world, in many companies. Adobe Connect returned with a completely new version and once again took the lead in web conferencing solutions. At universities and technical colleges, there were new training courses on the subject of "collaboration." These covered not only technological topics but also social, psychological, and cultural ones. It was understood that digital collaboration is a new cultural technique that is already part of the curriculum in primary schools. In teacher training colleges, prospective teachers were trained to create didactically meaningful digital lessons.

2023 Backslash

The valley of disillusion had to be crossed in 2023. There was criticism of home office models, students wanted to participate more in in-classroom courses again, and self-organized organizational models were partly replaced by top-down structures. After the visionaries and masterminds, the skeptics and traditionalists led the discourse. And they were partially right. There were still gaps in the social security models for freelancers and micro-companies. Employees working from home worked 7 days a week, although sometimes only 3–5 h a day, which led to difficulties with the accounting of working hours. Productivity in online meetings had partly decreased again, as no time was invested in proper planning and moderation. It became apparent that thousands of years of working and learning in copresence could not be replaced within a few years by an online presence. This insight led to a more detailed analysis of methods, processes, and, above all, technologies for digital collaboration. Numerous new collaborative UX companies dealt with the details of the user experience (Steimle and Wallach 2018). The moderation of online meetings was supported by intelligent assistants, which warned the moderator when a break was appropriate or made suggestions for interaction and group exercises. Chatbots reported independently in online meetings and thus stimulated the discussions.

2024 Paris Olympics

The 2024 Olympic year gave a new impetus, and after the 2020 Olympic Games had to be canceled, everyone looked forward to a fresh start. There were some technical innovations. For example, the drones of Volocopter (www.volocopter.com) and Airbus circled over Paris, and the spectators could participate live and directly in the games via VR glasses and in VR arenas. Microsoft distributed millions of HoloLenses for this purpose; Logitech came out with a new camera for holograms and thus made it possible to bring the athletes directly into their own homes. Those athletes who wanted to were able to use chip implants that continuously monitored their body values and share them with fans around the world. Numerous implant start-ups worked to turn the vision of "Johnny Mnemonic" from the 1980s (https://en.wikipedia.org/wiki/Johnny_Mnemonic, Gibson 1981) into a reality and make it available to companies. Many employees experimented with the new technology and used it to improve their teamwork. In every meeting and workshop, the selected body values of all participants were displayed on large screens for all to see. Together, they analyzed, discussed, and reflected on the changes in body values in different phases of the collaboration (an extension of Gasparyan 2020).

2025 World of 5G

By the end of 2025, nationwide coverage with the 5G mobile communications standard could be completed. This made it possible to address practically every object via a unique IP address and to advance networking between objects. Cooperation with IP-integrated objects in combination with speech recognition and digital assistants increased the opportunities for freelancers and small companies in particular. Collaboration and learning with machines (Stoller-Schai 2020b; Wilson and Daugherty 2018) took on a new significance. It led to the implementation of a "Knowledge Navigator" as Apple had already presented it in a short film in 1987 (see https://www.youtube.com/watch?v=9bjve67p33E).

2026 Literacy

This year, the UNO held another world congress on the topic of "digital literacy." It was found that digital literacy in countries with good education systems has been significantly improved on average. However, there were significant differences within and between countries. A new digital divide manifested itself between those with access to technology, education, and the Internet and those who were unable to get similar access. Large corporations such as Microsoft, Alphabet, Tencent, Apple, and Alibaba formed a consortium that took on the task of closing this digital divide and providing Internet access, hardware, software, and, above all, education.

2027 Displays

The introduction of wall-sized displays led to a new intuitive form of collaboration. Window surfaces could be transformed into large-format screens with the latest technology, so that all objects of a collaborative process could be viewed. These visualization options greatly simplified digital collaboration. "Collaboration on any

Window" became a buzzword and turned even the smallest apartment into a collaborative space. Pinboards, flipcharts, and even tablets became increasingly less relevant.

2028 Holograms

A further step followed a year later. Hologram technology finally made it possible not only to make people visible on a screen or a window but also to place them in a three-dimensional space where they could interact with one another. This significant improvement in the immersive experience made working with people in other places even more accessible and more intuitive. This also had an effect on mobility behavior. It became less necessary to travel to another place to meet with others. Thanks to hologram technology, all participants are able to gather in one place and do so in a very real way. This gradually had an effect on traffic, as commuting to work slowly became less important.

2029 Language

Natural language processing and automatic speech recognition have been so successful in recent years that it has become possible to translate not only the main languages but also any dialect from an input language to a target language. In the process, intercultural background information was always included, which led to a drastic improvement in cooperation in internationally distributed projects. Finally, one understood one's counterpart and was able to deal with subtle cultural aspects and develop more empathy and understanding for each other, thus improving productivity and the success rate in projects.

2030 Nadire's Work

The ten years between 2020 and 2030 brought about similar changes as the first 10 years after Steve Jobs' keynote speech on the launch of the first iPhone on 9 January 2007 (see Steve Jobs' keynote: https://www.youtube.com/watch?v=x7qPAY9JqE4). Nadire's way of working has become the norm. Nadire works alone but always together with others and in constantly changing constellations. Digital collaboration and the connection of companies with a temporary team of freelancers and specialists have proven its worth after the employment law foundations were created. Nadire looks confidently into the future. The technological development of the last 10 years has not aggravated global problems but has partially reduced them through new forms of local and digital collaboration. The physical need for mobility has been replaced by a digital one. But Nadire is also aware that there is still a lot to do. Even in Zurich, opportunities and resources are not fairly distributed, and Nadire has decided to pass on her knowledge of digital collaboration to others in the form of free courses and coaching. She will participate in a global hackathon next year, which will be about "Future Collaboration."

4 Recommendations to Implement Collaboration Landscapes

To implement the above-described Collaboration Landscape 2030, the following recommendations should be taken into account:

1. We must develop our own collaboration strategies in companies, schools, universities, and institutions. A collaboration strategy defines which
   - stakeholders collaborate with each other through which channels,
   - competitive advantage is to be achieved through better collaboration,
   - collaborative forms are implemented,
   - competencies are required for which roles,
   - technologies and systems are required and made available.
2. We need to build, promote, and maintain collaborative cultures:
   - Collaboration within a company aims to dismantle silo structures and promotes work together across departmental boundaries.
   - Collaboration requires intercultural skills in dealing with stakeholders from other cultures.
   - Collaboration builds on a culture of trust. All stakeholders have to take a leap of faith—those who abuse it lose trust and thus the basis for collaboration.
   - A culture of collaboration requires a collaborative attitude and attitude of leaders.
   - A collaborative culture requires leaders who can lead virtually.
   - A collaborative culture is based on everyone taking on leadership tasks when necessary. There are no more rigid pyramid hierarchies.
3. We need to better understand collaboration processes in the digital and analog domain and develop a real collaboration grammar (Terkessidis 2018) so that we can speak a common language of collaboration:
   - A collaboration grammar defines all elements needed to describe collaborative processes: people, places, actions, outcomes, and processes.
   - A typical collaborative process goes through five stages (Stoller-Schai 2003, 2019):
     - Team building (forming)
     - Determining common language (grounding)
     - Designing the procedure
     - Simultaneous cooperation (performing)
     - Reaching conclusions (concluding), recording results (results), and summative reflection
   - How we talk about collaboration needs to be more differentiated: The phrase "I'm working with you" can have many different meanings and describe a wide variety of activities. For a collaborative grammar, such a sentence must be better describable so that one can build on it and build the right collaborative structures and processes.
4. We must keep an eye on equal opportunities and ensure access to technology,

networks, and training for all:

- Access to collaborative technologies and the right networks determines how successful someone is. Collaborative technologies and access to networks must be guaranteed for all in order to create equal opportunities.
- Successful collaboration is based on the heterogeneity of the people involved. The more heterogeneous the group of people involved, the more creative the result can be, provided the five process steps are successfully completed.
- Collaborative competence is a crucial qualification for the competitiveness of individuals and companies. Collaborative competence must be trained and educated, both in a digital and in an analog context.

5. We must experiment with new forms of collaboration, both digital and analog. Only if we gain experience ourselves can we develop new forms of collaboration:

- Collaboration lives from self-application and self-reflection. The more you collaborate with others in different forms and channels, the more you see possibilities for new forms and the need for new technologies and new solutions.
- Only those who collaborate with others can speak confidently about collaboration. Managers must be collaboration professionals and support and accompany others in this process.
- How we will collaborate effectively in 10 years, we do not know yet, but we do know that the new forms of the future will grow out of the lived forms of the present.

References[1]

Ashoka Germany, McKinsey. (2018). *The skilling challenge. How to equip employees for the era of automation and digitization – and how models and mindsets of social entrepreneurs can guide us* (This work is licensed under a Creative Commons Attribution 4.0 International License (CC BY 4.0, details: http://creativecommons.org/licenses/by/4.0/).

Bensmann, D. (2018). *Netzwerke - Eine innovative Organisationsform nutzen und managen. Haufe Fachbuch.*

Bornemann, S. (2012). *Kooperation und Kollaboration. Das kreative Feld als Weg zu innovativer Teamarbeit.* New York: Springer.

Burow, O.-A. (2015). *Team-flow. Gemeinsam wachsen im Kreativen Feld.* Weinheim: Beltz.

Colvin, G. (2016). *Humans are underrated. What high achievers know that brilliant machines never will.* London: Hodder & Stoughton.

De Vet, A., & Lowette, F. (2018). *The fluid organisation. An ideal mix of self-management and hierarchy.* Own Publishing House.

Ebert, H., & Pastoors, S. (2019). *Psychologische Grundlagen zwischenmenschlicher Kooperation. Bedeutung von Vertrauen für langfristig erfolgreiche Zusammenarbeit.* New York: Springer.

Gasparyan, A. (2020). *How graph visualization helps us understand collaboration.* Blogpost. Accessed from https://miro.com/blog/features/graph-visualization-understanding-collaboration/

---

[1]The basics of collaboration can be found in Bornemann (2012), Burow (2015), Ebert | Pastoors (2019), Ghanbari et al. (2018), Groth | Ritter (2019), Leimeister (2014), Parnow | Schmidt (2019), and Stoller-Schai (2019). All the mentioned websites and URLs were accessible on 30 April 2020.

Ghanbari, N., Otto, I., Schramm, S., & Thielmann, T. (Eds.). (2018). *Kollaboration. Beiträge zur Medientheorie und Kulturgeschichte der Zusammenarbeit*. Paderborn: Wilhelm Fink Verlag.

Gibson, W. (1981). Johnny Mnemonic. *Omni Magazine*.

Gray, D. (2012). *The connected company*. Sebastopol: O'Reilly.

Groth, S., & Ritter, C. (Eds.). (2019). *Zusammen arbeiten. Praktiken der Koordination und Kooperation in kollaborativen Prozessen*. Köln: Transcript Verlag.

Herkersdorf, M. (2018). *Kollaborative virtuelle 3D-Welten (Whitepaper)*. TriCAT GmbH.

Institute for the Future for the University of Phoenix Research Institute. (2011). *Future Work Skills 2020*.

Leimeister, J. M. (2014). *Collaboration Engineering. IT-gestützte Zusammenarbeitsprozesse systematisch entwickeln und durchführen*. Berlin: Springer.

Lewrick, M. (2018). *Design thinking. Radikale Innovationen in einer digitalisierten Welt*. Munich: C. H. Beck.

Lewrick, M., Link, P., & Leifer, L. (Eds.). (2018). *Das design thinking playbook* (2nd ed.). Munich: Vahlen.

Lipmanowicz, H., & McCandless, K. (2014). *The surprising power of liberating structures: Simple rules to unleash a culture of innovation*. Seattle, WA: Liberating Structures Press.

Muuß-Merholz, J. (2019). *Barcamps & Co.: Peer to Peer-Methoden für Fortbildungen*. Weinheim: Beltz.

Parnow, H., & Schmidt, P. (Eds.). (2019). *Zusammen arbeiten, zusammen wachsen, zusammen leben. Wie wir unsere Zukunft gemeinsam gestalten*. Berlin: Springer-Gabler.

Pflaeging, N., & Hermann S. (2019). *Zellstrukturdesign. Eine Sozialtechnologie von Red42. Broschüre Nr. 3*. Betacodex Publishing.

Robertson, B. J. (2016). *Holacracy: The revolutionary management system that abolishes hierarchy*. London: Penguin.

Scheiber, N. (2017, July 12). The pop-up employer: Build a team, do the job, say goodbye. *New York Times*. Accessed from https://www.nytimes.com/2017/07/12/business/economy/flash-organizations-labor.html

Steimle, T., & Wallach, D. (2018). *Collaborative UX design. Lean UX und design thinking: Teambasierte Entwicklung menschenzentrierter Projekte*. DPunkt Verlag.

Steinhöfer, D., & Weinert, C. (2020). *Liberating structures: Entscheidungsfindung revolutionieren*. Munich: Vahlen. in print.

Stepper, J. (2018). *Working out loud: For a better career and life*. New York: Ikigai Press.

Stifterverband der deutschen Wissenschaften, Mc Kinsey (2018). *Das future skills-framework. 18 Skills in drei Kategorien*. Accessed from https://www.future-skills.net/future-skills-framework

Stoller-Schai, D. (2003). *E-Collaboration. Die Gestaltung internetgestützter kollaborativer Handlungsfelder*. Universität St. Gallen 2003 (English Version 2019).

Stoller-Schai, D. (2019). Collaboration matters! Adventsserie 2019. *HR Today*. ALMA Medien AG Zürich. Accessed from https://www.hrtoday.ch/de/article/adventsserie-2019-collaboration-matters

Stoller-Schai, D. (2020a). Digitales Lernen führt zu einer Renaissance des analogen Präsenzlernens. In *Jahrbuch 2020 eLearning & Wissensmanagement* (pp. 10–15). Hagen im Bremischen: Siepmann Media.

Stoller-Schai, D. (2020b). Praxiseinsatz Künstliche Intelligenz - Wie lernen wir mit Maschinen? *eLearning Journal | Trend Report 2020/2021: Corporate Learning Trends und Innovationen für, 6–9*.

Stoller-Schai, D. (2020c). Micromanager sind fehl am Platz. In HR Today Nr. 4/2020: Thema "New Work".

Tegmark, M. (2017). *Leben 3.0. Mensch sein im Zeitalter Künstlicher Intelligenz*. Berlin: Ullstein.

Terkessidis, M. (2018). *Kollaboration* (2nd ed.). Berlin: Suhrkamp.

Wilson, H. J., & Daugherty, P. R. (2018, July–August). Collaborative intelligence: Humans and AI are joining forces. *Harvard Business Review*. Accessed from https://hbr.org/2018/07/collaborative-intelligence-humans-and-ai-are-joining-forces

Daniel Stoller-Schai is an experienced digital collaboration and learning expert and the managing director of Collaboration Design GmbH (www.collaboration-desgin.ch). At the University of St. Gallen, he was involved in setting up the learning center and completed his doctorate on "E-Collaboration." As a manager for digital learning and work technologies, he has implemented customer projects at numerous companies and start-ups and gained experience with the global use of Internet-based learning and work projects.

Vignette: Ella's Day—Work Anywhere Anytime

Barbara Josef

A glance at the personal assistant, which is displayed on the kitchen window right behind the coffee machine, indicates that another "colorful" day lies ahead of Ella; colorful means many different time pods. White stands for allotment, blue for deep work, red for project work, green for personal growth, orange for socializing, amber for personal priorities, and yellow for pooling time.

While enjoying the first coffee of the day, Ella quickly skims through the special attention list. 18 out of 20 events have automatically been resolved based on the programmed values and recent decisions. Only two need Ella's attention. The meeting with her practice circle lead takes place at the same time as the theater play of her godchild. She sends a quick voice message to the practice circle lead, asking whether it would be possible to have a brief exchange at 930 pm. Knowing that they are both "integrators," who aim at mingling work and private life, she is convinced that this is the best of all the available options displayed. The second alert reminds her that her last sporting activity was more than 3 days ago. Based on the local weather forecast, the smart assistant suggests a light run through the park nearby together with Amy, one of her learning partners, who lives in the neighbourhood. Amy seems to be available at the same time and due for training too. The newly popped-up green amber field indicates that Amy's personal assistant has accepted the suggestion.

After a quick shower and breakfast, Ella takes her bicycle and heads for the local coworking space "Wunderraum." During her 20-minute ride, she does the allotment (correspondence, documentation, etc.) via voice control. When she approaches the building, she is automatically checked in in the virtual community platform "G-Hub." The software does not only show who is in the building today but also displays the current projects, interests, skills, and free timeslots of the community members.

B. Josef (✉)
5to9, Zürich, Switzerland
e-mail: barbara.josef@5to9.ch

© Springer Nature Switzerland AG 2021
S. Güldenberg et al. (eds.), *Managing Work in the Digital Economy*, Future of Business and Finance, https://doi.org/10.1007/978-3-030-65173-2_12

Ella has 30 minutes before the project work begins. She grabs a coffee and starts working at the workbench in the community zone. "You should meet Steven. He has just entered the space and has a similar profile to you," suggests her smart assistant. Ella declines and continues doing her preparation for the day. Meeting new people is usually a nice distraction, but today she is very focused. Or let's say she was focused until she sees a stranger entering the community zone, dressed in shimmering green colors, which is a nice contrast to her short red hair. "Forget it. You're out of this project. Our values simply don't match," she yells in her phone before she slams it back in her bag without any further comments. "Oh hi," she says, totally absorbed in thoughts toward Ella, "I didn't mean to disturb you. Are you new?". After a few words of introduction, Ella starts immediately talking about her projects and areas of interest, although she has never met Rose, the lady in green, before. Without the discreet reminder of her smart assistant, that her project work is due in 3 minutes, she would have forgotten the reason why she came to the Wunderraum this morning. "Why don't you join us—we need exactly someone like to cope with the current challenges."

Three hours later, the group leaves the project room called "Wunderlabor" and heads for a joint lunch in the city farm garden, for which they had recently worked for on its new distribution strategy, on a volunteer basis. The writing on the wall and smart table is automatically converted to a protocol that is added to the shared notebook of the team members. The tasks are in parallel integrated into the personal diary of each project member—not as a to do, but as an appointment in the agenda in consultation with the personal biorhythm and place preferences. A quick video done at the end of the workshop summarizes the main output—not only to record the key findings but also to update those members who could not participate in the session. Rose spontaneously decides to join the community on their journey. Of course, it was an intuitive decision, but her learning score—a quick individual reflection guided by the smart assistant—went through the roof. Not only because the topic was new for her, but mainly based on the diverse composition and open discussion culture of the project team.

The afternoon is blocked for deep work. It's around 3 p.m. when Ella heads back to the Wunderraum. A few years ago, she would have felt bad about spending more than 2 hours for a community lunch, but this was mainly due to the outdated time tracking system that still existed in the old days. Since her main employer introduced a system called "Spark" that tracks energy, output, and learning, things changed drastically for the good of everyone—profits skyrocketed, the burnout rate went down, and the employee engagement score continually rose. She spends 2 h focused in the library of the Wunderraum—a place where all incoming messages and reminders are automatically muted. When she is through with her topics, she browses through "the pool" and checks the projects, where support is needed. She assigns one task to her that fits well with her skill set and interests. The introduction of the concept "pooling time" a few years ago helped her company enormously to gain velocity—it was a reaction to all the failed agility initiatives they tried before. Before she heads back home, she has a "Feedforward Session" with a new team member in a live meeting box. After the corona pandemic back in 2020, her company stopped doing performance reviews and feedback sessions—realizing that digging in the past does not help to foster strengths and acquire new skills. And of course, this proceeding helps her employer to match future challenges with individual growth paths.

It's already past seven when Ella finally arrives home. During summertime, she works 120%—being a passionate ice hockey player, she prefers to have more time for sports in the winter season, where she usually works around 60%, also depending a bit on the nature of projects that are available in the marketplace. While relaxing with a lovely tea that she got as a present from the city farm, she captures her main learnings of the day in the personal growth journal.

Her employer introduced the "Job Crafting Model" back in 2021 as a consequence of the movement that started from the Feedforward Sessions. They agreed that they would keep a minimal form of the line organization and also main functions, based on the skill set and individual growth paths, but that everyone could choose projects in the company as well as voluntary assignments with externals in addition to their core responsibility. That was also why Ella, being a communication specialist, accepted the project at the city farm. She wants to build up sales and distribution skills in a real-life environment, accompanied by a team coach, who not only joins their project sessions but whom she can consult whenever she wants to review complex topics.

Before going to bed, Ella spends an hour writing on her second novel—a habit that she truly loves, as it helps her to not only relax but also deal with the rich experiences made with different people during the day. She started writing 3 years ago, when she realized that due to the introduction of "Spark," she had suddenly much more energy in the evening to pursue her own personal projects. Maybe it was also because she started working at the Wunderraum during her autonomous time—back in the 20s called "home office days"—so suddenly her home was not associated with writing attritional emails and doing presentations any longer. Before she falls asleep, she glances at her smart assistant. How great, the next day is totally free of appointments as it is an "office" day. Of course, her company's community hub has nothing in common with the headquarters of the past, where people sat at individual desks and in windowless meeting rooms. However, unofficially they still affectionately refer to it as "the office." Consequently, the smart assistant has already programmed the "in the community hub message" to notify people that she is not available for externals that day—"Wouldn't it be a pity not to spend the day with her team and have time for serendipitous moments?"

Barbara Josef initially trained as a primary school teacher before later studying business administration at the University of St. Gallen followed by a PhD in business innovation with a focus on "coworking from a corporate perspective." Before founding her company 5-9 AG in 2016, she worked in various functions and industries, most recently as head of Communication and Corporate Social Responsibility and as a member of the Executive Board of Microsoft Switzerland.

Part IV

Careers in 2030

Smart HRM in 2030: Conversational HR, Connected Robotics, and Controlled Analytics

Christian Gärtner and Dieter Kern

Shenzhen, February 29, 2030

Startup SpinerHR announces the next release of SPOON, the virtual HR management suite.

Based on the latest analytics and automatization technology, SPOON shifts the way of using HR services to the next level: it offers end-to-end HR process support, customized for line managers, employees, and the few people left in the HR department. SPOON offers all functionalities needed to provide administrative, first- and second-level support for internal and external customers of the HR function. For workforce planning, the system automatically calculates the quantitative and qualitative skill gaps in the workforce based on internal employee and freelancer data as well as external information about demand and supply on various labor markets, education systems, and competitors' recruitment initiatives. It manages the recruiting process for commodity hires from job posting, CV screening and matching, interviewing, and contracting, including the whole real-time conversation with candidates. A "pay for skills" functionally crawls the talent market for hot skills and adjusts salary offerings accordingly. Employees get personal career coaching from the Avatar GO-WORN, a third-generation chatbot that generates original answers and learns from previous discussions. The new SPOON release comes with a FutureMe-well-being module: GEKKO, a friendly robot advisor that provides employees recommendations on how to optimize their investment portfolio—financials as well as investments in skills—throughout their lifetime. GEKKO uses data and statistical analysis to isolate demographic and behavioral characteristics to find the most successful options and tactics for employees.

C. Gärtner (✉)
Department of Business Administration, Hochschule München University of Applied Sciences, Munich, Germany
e-mail: christian.gaertner@hm.edu

D. Kern
Mercer, Munich, Germany

© Springer Nature Switzerland AG 2021
S. Güldenberg et al. (eds.), *Managing Work in the Digital Economy*, Future of Business and Finance, https://doi.org/10.1007/978-3-030-65173-2_13

1   The Times They Are A-Changin'. . .?!

Of course, Bob Dylan was right: times are changing. But what direction will change take? And how will change practically materialize? To answer, one can try to picture the (HR) world in 2030—which immediately means to run the risk of making a fool out of yourself, as "nothing is more amusing than the prognosis of the past" (Peterson cited in Radkau 2017, p. 222). The anxiety that SPOON, GO-WORN, and GEKKO or the like will be deployed in every company by 2030 is rather unsubstantiated. Nevertheless, there are already prototypes that are, in principle, able to perform these tasks. In addition, technological changes are only a part of all the changes that we have seen in recent years: globalization, protectionism, re-localization, global warming, epidemics, terrorism, etc.

If we position ourselves in the year 2030 and look back, we see that while change is manifold, some fundamental topics remain, particularly if the focus is solely on human resource management (HRM). Since the mid-1990s, experts have been arguing that (HR) work is changing, primarily as a result of new information and communication technologies and secondly due to sociodemographic changes, above all the ageing population in western countries, and economic policy factors such as the internationalization of value creation chains, including outsourcing (Scholz 1995; Hoss 1996). Very little has changed since then. This is why we are focusing on the effects of information processing technologies, which lead to more strongly data-based and automated HRM (see Gärtner 2020).

Regardless of the drivers of change just mentioned, there has been one other constant in the discussion about HRM for decades: the issue of whether a person is just a means of economic action and performance or an end itself that should be at the focus of all actions. In other words, do companies primarily conceive of and manage their employees as a resource or as a value driver? The relevance of HR's function depends on how this question is answered. While proponents of the second perspective view HR as (almost) the most critical function in the company, it merely plays a supportive role for all the others (they even think it may be done away with entirely). This dissent is in no way one which has only occurred in the past few decades with the increase in knowledge-intensive work. It can be seen in one of the first overview articles on the state of human resource departments in the USA (Donald and Donald 1929). It is most likely that the strategic and operational relevance of HRM have remained the same in 2030: organizations and divisions whose value creation is based on innovation, human interaction, and empathy or which provide knowledge-intensive services will put people (and therefore HR departments) at the center of their strategy. Others merely view them as a means among others.

In the next section, we describe three episodes that illustrate specific employee experiences of selected personas (Chap. 2). Before we outline HR practices that will be common along the HR value chain by 2030 in Chap. 4, we will explain four fundamental principles that underpin these HR practices in Chap. 3. The final chapter summarizes how the described changes in HR practices also lead to a change in the roles and responsibilities of the HR department.

2 "I Program my Home Computer, Beam Myself into the Future": Employee Experiences in 2030

Kraftwerk, the pioneers of electronic music, anticipated a computer world in songs like "Home Computer" and others already in the 1970s and 1980s. We use parts of their songs as an intro for the three episodes on employee experiences and HR practices. We also adopt the persona approach which has become quite popular for analyzing and designing customer or employee experiences.

2.1 Sophia: "I Call This Number, for a Data Date"—*Kraftwerk, Computer Love*

Sophia is part of what happens to be known as Generation Z+, so she was born in the early 2000s (see Fig. 1). She studied computer and data science at one of the top universities in Europe (she was lucky enough to start her bachelor right after the coronavirus which boosted digital learning at universities throughout the world). After finishing her bachelor's, she earned a master's degree and achieved one of her most desired goals: to finish her PhD before she turned 30. While working on her thesis, she gained some experience as a freelancer and completed a couple of smaller data science projects for medium-sized companies. In the future, she aims to maintain a good work-life balance, so while she is familiar with working extra hours, she is not willing to do this every week. She is an open and agreeable person, but not too extroverted. There are a couple of things that she does not like—although not all of them keep her up at night ("pains")—and some others that make her glad ("gains"). Some of the software packages she works with every day were introduced 15 years ago (around 2015, e.g., Keras, TensorFlow); others such as Python are even older but are still in use. When she interacts with machines, she either uses her hands (if there is a touchscreen) or a keyboard or just talks to them. The latter has been quite common for communication between machines and (end)users, but recently, it seems to work for developers as well. Apart from work, she has also tried some wearables, but most of the time she uses her smartphone to scan shopping items, view them in 3D, connect with beacons to see discounts, etc. Her motto shows that she is a firm believer in doing something right. Her motto helps explain why she contributes to various "maker communities" (just as her parents did), for example, Raspberry Pi and GitHub. Of course, she also uses and benefits from the version control and source code management functionalities that GitHub provides.

Since Sophia aims at achieving a good work-life balance, she is looking for a permanent job, at least for the next 2 years or so. Therefore, she attends a job fair that takes place at her university. There she meets a humanoid robot called "Pepper Jr." She asks the robot some general questions about the company, compensation and benefits, usual career paths for data scientists, and the opportunity to take a sabbatical. Although the robot answers these questions satisfyingly, she is about to end the conversation and move on to the next booth. Unexpectedly, the guys from the booth next to them start playing the new Ped Sheran single. Sophia turns her head toward

Pains

- If cybersecurity is not taken seriously (e.g. if there are only little investments in IT-security)
- "management clowns" who only talk about costs and sales, but not about the quality of the apps and products
- If software code is written cumbersomely (by a few specific colleagues who grew up with C and Cobol)
- Too few sockets and USB ports in meeting rooms (mobile phone & laptop cannot be charged)

Gains

- Getting to work at 9:30 am without stress and with no delayed trains and buses
- Taking time to work on a software problem, discuss it with colleagues and experts via Github until the problem is solved
- Having access to the latest hard- and software (in particular in-memory-computing, machine learning libraries)
- Watch the crime scene on Sundays and chat with others via a second screen

Personality

Neuroticism
Extraversion
Openness
Agreeableness
Conscientiousness

Goals
(business, private)

- Work in and publish papers on Data Science
- Maintain a good work-life-balance

Technology-/media usage

GitHub
K Keras
python

Scenes from an ordinary (business) day

Picture

Motto

Actions speak louder than words.

Peers

Tom (friend)

Lilian (colleague)

Fig. 1 Description of persona "Sophia" (own illustration)

the music and so does Pepper Jr.—and the robot asks her whether she likes Ped Sheran. Since he has been one of her favorite singers since her youth (in the late 2010s), she confirms—and they linger on the past for a minute or so. Sophia is impressed that the dialogue module of the robot seems to be trained on a broad variety of topics and really can engage in a short chitchat.

Back at home, she sees a job advertisement from the company when she clicked on Ped Sheran's new video on YouTube. It seems that Pepper Jr. and the job advertising system of the company are aligned and that the company is running a job advertising campaign on YouTube. Moreover, she sees not only the job ad but also the news about the company's new investments in IT security—did she tell the robot about her interest in cybersecurity? Or did the company run a background check on her on social media and found some of the posts she left on one of the makers' communities? The latter would have neither surprised nor shocked Sophia because she knew for a long time that almost nothing stays private in online communities. In fact, for Sophia, this is an indicator that the data science team seems to have done a good job: they seem to have the skills but also the hardware and software to achieve high accuracy on Natural Language Processing tasks and to make inferences across channels. The latter also means that processes and not only technologies are well prepared. These positive aspects outweigh the slightly scary feeling that she now has when she listens to Ped Sheran songs. So, she pushes the "apply now" button that automatically pulls the necessary information out of her LinkedIn account.

2.2 Ashley: "Interpol and Deutsche Bank, FBI and Scotland Yard—Business, Numbers, Money, People" – *Kraftwerk, Computer World*

Ashley is a woman in the prime of life. She was raised using progressive methods, and she sends her children to a Montessori school. Despite her post-heroic fundamental understanding of management, she has read her Machiavelli and knows about the role of power games. Something can still be achieved with "sufficient communication" in a few projects, but not without power—particularly in times in which changes need to be implemented against resistance. She has seen a lot of this in her many years in middle management at an automobile supplier, particularly between 2020 and 2030, with almost a third of the workforce being replaced and a further third needing to learn new skills. She now has to manage an organization of 500+ heterogeneous employees—and she has to cope with all the new digital-enabled HR services.

Last week and after a lengthy and nerve-wracking process, her company won a large double-digit million-euro contract with a premium car producer against their key competitor in this field. They are going to develop, produce, and supply next-generation sensors for autonomous driving. Integrating and connecting these hardware components with the software of other vendors require know-how in system architecture, software programming, and testing. To deliver in time and on budget and meet the client's rigorous quality standards are supposed to be the greatest challenge—as it always has been. Given the importance of this project, Ashley will be personally responsible to ensure its success.

Before she assigns the operational project work to a project manager, Ashley wants to understand how feasible the promised delivery in time and budget is. Over the weekend, Ashley puts together an initial project plan for the next 24 months, including the qualitative and quantitative resource needs. Back in the office on Monday, she plugs this into HR software. The result shown on her dashboard is better than expected. Only two out of the 15 roles (system architect and test engineer) that are needed to deliver are marked "red" and show a significant shortage.

Moreover, only a couple of the 25 "main tribe members" in her tribe have a high flight score risk, which means that the machine learning algorithm predicts that the vast majority is not about to leave. For those two high performers that have a flight score risk above 80 percent, the system recommends some retention measures that fit their personality profile (money and promotion for one, sabbatical for the other). Nevertheless, Ashley needs to prepare for the worst. Together with her HR business partner and a seasoned HR analytics expert, Ashley is running "close the gap" simulations on Tuesday and develops measures to overcome the skill gaps. The machine learning module of the HR software immediately recommended some measures based on past projects. Those measures, however, appear to be slightly off as they do not match her specific requirements. Nevertheless, they help get the thinking and discussion going. By the end of the week, the plan is finished and goes to the board for sign off.

2.3   Jeff: "I'm the Operator with my Pocket Calculator" – *Kraftwerk, Pocket Calculator*

After completing a degree in business administration in 2010, Jeff worked in the accounting division of a large logistics group for many years. He was never that interested in leadership tasks but in numbers and accounting rules. Unfortunately, the expert careers offered by the group rapidly turned out to be pure lip service and HR marketing jargon.

Many efficiency and reorganization programs in finance at his former company led to Jeff being happy he could still do his job for a while. When he started working, many partial processes were carried out by a service provider in India (e.g., updating master data, managing open posts, checking and booking travel expense bills, creating reports). From early 2020 onward, however, the outsourcing activities were gradually taken back, because software robots and machine learning algorithms were now cheaper. This affected debtor and creditor accounting (e.g., creating, validating, and updating customer and supplier master data but also the entire invoice production, including travel expense bills). Since the bots and algorithms still needed to be supervised in the beginning, Jeff helped with their introduction and training. This was an exciting and new task, but it took over 6 months for the machines to be able to handle the numbers and rules better than humans.

Jeff, therefore, made an effort to work on new activities, such as the creation of consolidated financial statements and liquidity management, and wanted to learn how to use various corporate financing tools. A couple of things had changed since he had originally studied them (or he simply forgot a few things). When Jeff contacted the HR department about this, a chatbot forwarded him a few videos and online tutorials that were freely available on the internet. After several emails to the HR department, Jeff found the HR consultant responsible for him. She told him, however, that due to the corporate crisis, personal and specialized training would not be offered at all until 2021 and after that would no longer be offered centrally to a significant extent. She did, though, encourage him to work on it himself and to train himself using one of the many online learning platforms. Ultimately, he would have a better idea of which qualifications and competencies were in demand in his area of expertise. Jeff started several online courses but did not manage to complete them. Learning alongside his work without any real contact with the teachers (one course had a reasonably good chatbot as a learning coach which tailored the tasks to Jeff's needs but that was the only one) caused Jeff to lose his motivation quickly.

Jeff's attempts to engage in the union and as an employee representative were too half-hearted and somehow petered out. Since 2025, he has been increasingly annoyed with his employer and wonders about what it will mean for the logistics industry if self-driving trucks and cars are allowed to drive within cities, which is still prohibited but has been subject of an ongoing debate over the last 5 years. The major distribution centers near the motorways have become more autonomous, and the intralogistics are already fully automated. What was horrifying to see was that all the hardware and software were delivered by Amazon's logistics division.

Somehow Jeff does not think that his employer will survive on the market for very long, so he has also applied to the IT company which developed the software robots for his department. He actually thought he was already too old to start something new and focus more on the software side. The official reason he was rejected, though, was a mismatch in the cultural fit. Jeff had to do a half-hour online assessment with a personality test. The result was fast and sounded nice, but the content was devastating. The employees in the IT company, with whom he had worked on the introduction of the software robots, found him to be not particularly social or team oriented. And now his deficiencies were being flagged up. That, at least, was what it said in the report on the automatic assessment of the video taken during the online evaluation.

Exasperated, Jeff resigned from the logistics group 2 years ago. Initially, he was still used as a tester and quality assessor via an online platform when companies wanted to introduce software robots in the field of finance. But these were just occasional projects, and now there is not much of the work anymore—there are too many freelancers, clickworkers, etc. who undercut one another on these platforms. Since then, he has kept his head above water with fixed-term contracts and temporary employment. Both produce significantly lower earnings than he made years ago. He was recently even hired as a backup driver for his former employer. It transpired that the last mile in the cities was not so easy to supply autonomously. Too many real but mainly almost accidents with cars still being driven by humans led to robot cars being banned from the centers of towns. The delivery process became bogged down, so in the short term, more subcontractors were commissioned to deliver packages.

3   The Three Plus One C of Smart HRM

In 2030, there are still three main activity areas that a Chief Human Resource Officer (CHRO) must take care of: (1) People and Talent Management, (2) Organization Design and Change, and (3) Management and Leadership of the HR Department. The primary tasks in the activity area "Talent Management" were the same as in 2020: attract and select, plan and deploy, perform and compensate, and develop and retain. In 2030, however, the delivery pattern of these four essential tasks is significantly influenced by technology that automatically processes data and communicates with humans. While the tasks remain somewhat stable, there are significant changes in how they are done. We circumscribe the latter in terms of the three Cs of Smart HRM that characterize HRM in 2030: "Conversational HR," "Connected Robotics," and "Controlled Analytics."

Conversational HR denotes that the most used technology within HR and for interacting with HR is chatbots. The field of Natural Language Processing has improved due to new methods that combine the ever-increasing amount of data with domain-specific symbolic knowledge. This progress boosted not only the breadth and depth of topics that chatbots can cover but also the accuracy of their answers and tasks they can automatically process. Consequently, voice-based chatbots have achieved high levels of usability and performance for most tasks in the activity area "Talent Management," which means that using these chatbots is the most common way of interacting with HR.

Connected Robotics encompasses the relation and collaboration between human workers and both physical and digital technologies. Humans are connected with various devices which are themselves connected: manufacturing and software robots, wearables (glasses, watches, phones, etc.), sewn or implanted sensors, and actuators. The implications of collaborative robotics for the three activity areas are manifold. Technologies that produce virtual and augmented realities are mostly used in the areas "attract and select" and "develop and retain": For example, to provide candidates a "realistic" job preview and to have them perform tests virtually. In addition, the use of digital technologies to transfer information and virtual environments to acquire knowledge by conducting training has been pushed by the Corona pandemic. Wearables, on the other hand, are preferably used to "plan and deploy" employees as well as to measure their performance, because these technologies gather data about activities in a certain location at a certain time. The processing of these data is part of "Controlled Analytics."

Controlled Analytics denotes the prevalence of data- and evidence-based recommendations to design work environments and processes (highly relevant for "Organization Design and Change" but also the other activity areas). This is a double-edged sword. On the one hand, making decisions based on scientifically processing data is likely to replace prejudice and biases in decision-making. On the other hand, data protection and security issues become vital and give rise to different forms of worker resistance that range from individual action to platform organizing, discursive framing, and legal mobilization (Kellogg et al. 2020). The term "Controlled Analytics" reminds us that data and algorithms can be used to control workers (e.g., by recommending and restricting what they should do, evaluating their performance or replacing them) and thus should be controlled.

Together, the three Cs of Smart HRM drive HR practices in 2030, both in terms of efficiency and in terms of quality. The three Cs have produced, however, another "C" as an unintended consequence: they corroborate a *chasm between digital winners and digital losers*, and HR needs to address this divide. This divide is not only digital but has an effect on the analogue or physical world: it creates a divide between those who have lovely jobs and those who have lousy jobs and those who exploit and those who are exploited, and it separates those who are tech-savvy from the "people people" in the HR department. The three episodes illustrate several divides which form the great chasm.

First, there are "digital winners" such as Sophia and "digital losers" such as Jeff. Of course, the former encompasses not only data scientists and software and robot developers but also those who have accumulated a lot of monetary and social capital (e.g., owners of real estate in large cities, influencers, and others with a vast and robust social (media) network or the creative class). The digital losers are victims of what has been called digital capitalism and digital Taylorism, which denotes that software packages capture and codify an increasing body of professional knowledge that can then be automated and transferred to any location, where it is monitored ubiquitously (Brown et al. 2010, p. 71ff.). The profits that these efficiency enhancements generated have been distributed unequally, i.e. those who do the work still benefit less. In contrast, those who distribute work through technologies and data benefit more. In addition, working and employment conditions have deteriorated for clickworkers, self-employed or temporary workers, and others who work based on project-related contractual arrangements because traditional forms of employment and participation, which allow employees in companies to exercise influence and receive support for developing their employability, do not apply for them (see De Stefano 2016).

Second, the work itself and the jobs built on it are likely to be polarized. They might be characterized along dimensions such as "high tech" vs. high touch" or "lovely jobs" vs. "lousy jobs." For example, some high-tech and lousy jobs have emerged in the (social) media industries and include the assembly line like the publishing of cheap content or doing quality and compliance checks of posts in social media. Some critics referred to these as "digital sweatshops" (Cohen 2015, p. 104; Garson 1989). Of course, some lousy tasks have been automated. However, looking back, we see that for every lousy job that existed, new lousy jobs have been created.

Lastly, and as a consequence of what we have just described, there is a physical divide between those who exploit and those who are exploited in real, "analogue" sweatshops. In these factories with poor working conditions, humans perform highly manual work that cannot be digitalized or automated, at least not as cheaply as it can be done by exploiting human resources. In this regard, focusing on and providing the human touch are still an essential aspect of human resource management. In 2030, however, the "people people" no longer represent the majority in HR departments as their new colleagues are robots, gig workers or clickworkers, and the like.

4 Smart HR Practices Along the HR Value Chain

We describe some selected use cases along the HR value chain that put the three Cs of Smart HRM (Conversational HR, Connected Robotics, Controlled Analytics) into practice (see Fig. 2 for an overview and Gärtner 2020, S. 51ff., for further use cases).

4.1 Attract and Select

In terms of attract and select, the three Cs can primarily be seen in the fact that chatbots automatically answer candidate questions, collect and analyze data, and prepare it for further decisions. In 2030, language-based bots have mostly replaced their text-based predecessors. They are able to carry out dialogues on a broad range of topics (job vacancies, career topics, or general information about the company) and not just retrieve topic-specific responses. They interact with most candidates before a human HR specialist is involved, both in the virtual and in the physical environment (e.g., the company website but also in the form of humanoid robots at job fairs). In the case of high potentials in narrow employment markets and high-ranking jobs, the primary contact is person to person, but there still are bots running in the background to identify information about skills, integrity, and intentions from the language patterns—of both the candidate and the recruiter. Before, during, and after the job interview, bots collect data to help both parties to decide (e.g., background information that bots found in the company's databases or crawled on the internet such as qualifications confirmed by a candidate's contacts on business platforms). We see here that chatbots are not just prominent examples of Conversational HR, but can also connect people via different devices (Connected Robotics) and use the data obtained in a controlled manner to make decisions (Controlled Analytics). Since these chatbots interact with people, aspects such as user experience, trustworthiness, security, and social support become as crucial as carrying out the task they were designed for.

Candidates are assessed by digital selection systems to estimate their suitability for a job: from the automatic assessment of CVs and web-based personality or creativity tests, to online games, to selections based on language samples or video interviews. Games or playful elements have been used in both internal and third-party selection since around 2010, which is why we also talk about game-based assessments or "recruitainment." There have been various developments of language and video analyses: after the initial euphoria, there were then concerns about the relevance of their content and their ability to predict a candidate's suitability and subsequent success (Gärtner 2020, p. 87). Most concerns with multimodal analysis

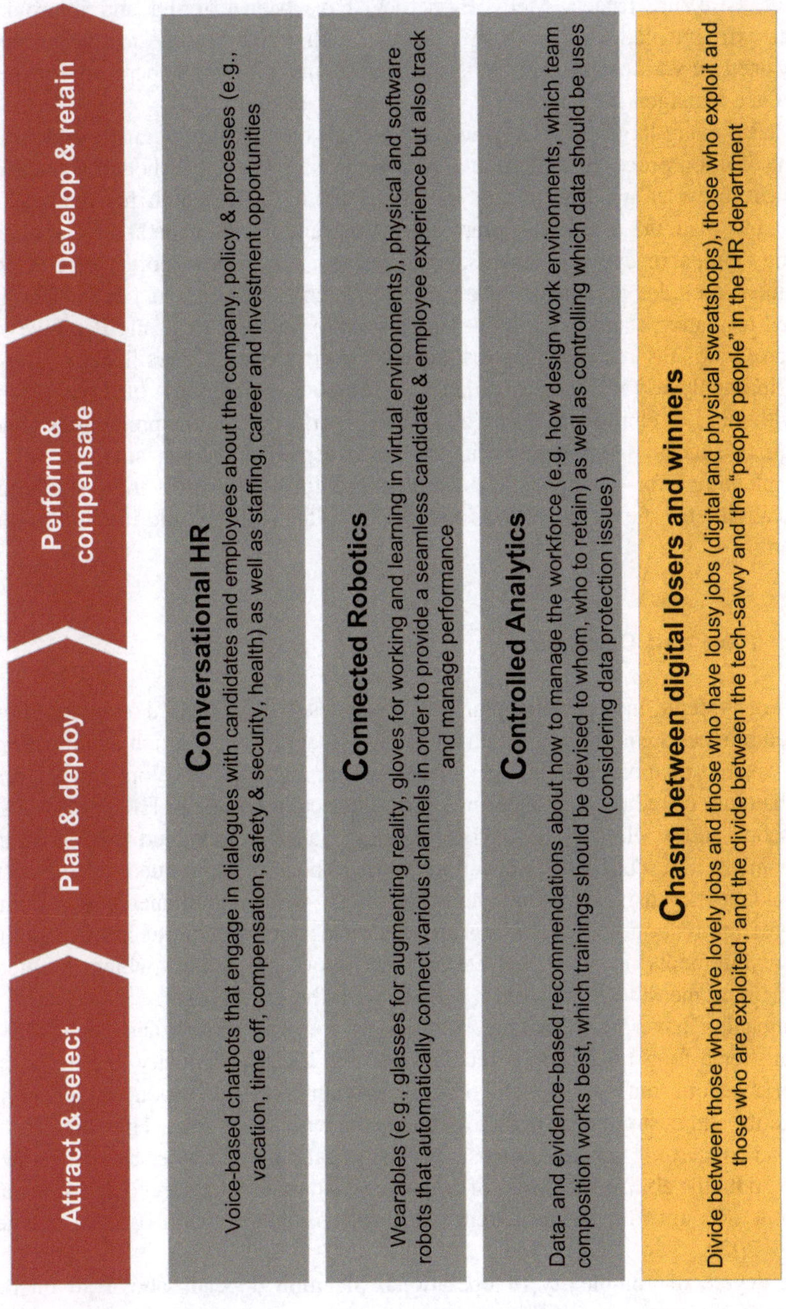

Attract & select	Plan & deploy	Perform & compensate	Develop & retain

Conversational HR

Voice-based chatbots that engage in dialogues with candidates and employees about the company, policy & processes (e.g., vacation, time off, compensation, safety & security, health) as well as staffing, career and investment opportunities

Connected Robotics

Wearables (e.g., glasses for augmenting reality, gloves for working and learning in virtual environments), physical and software robots that automatically connect various channels in order to provide a seamless candidate & employee experience but also track and manage performance

Controlled Analytics

Data- and evidence-based recommendations about how to manage the workforce (e.g. how design work environments, which team composition works best, which trainings should be devised to whom, who to retain) as well as controlling which data should be uses (considering data protection issues)

Chasm between digital losers and winners

Divide between those who have lovely jobs and those who have lousy jobs (digital and physical sweatshops), those who exploit and those who are exploited, and the divide between the tech-savvy and the "people people" in the HR department

Fig. 2 Overview of principles and Smart HR practices (own illustration)

systems have been alleviated by the constant improvement over the course of the 2020s. Our confidence is mainly rooted in the fact that several providers (e.g., Cyquest, HireVue, Knack, Mettl, Pymetrics) have been offering and improving their assessment platforms since the 2010s, which is why online testing became widely used for various groups of jobs and professions (e.g., developers, apprentices, and trainee managers).

In 2030, many large companies use technologies to analyze language and video data in selection processes. These analyses encompass not only whether somebody leaves the browser window during an online test (e.g., to search for the answer online) but also the tonality, pattern of words, and facial expressions, such as blinking, jumps in eye movements, and staring at a specific point. Part of the assessment includes personality analyses, in which language and image data are checked for patterns and links to known personality features (e.g., the Big Five) or other professionally relevant features (such as assertiveness and resilience). Simple regression analyses (and more sophisticated statistical techniques) of the applicant data with those of employees deemed to be high performers allow predictions about subsequent success. Applicants who are not accepted are given suggestions for career planning, for example, how they should further develop their skills and qualifications for future positions and which other roles could be interesting for them.

4.2   Plan and Deploy

As part of strategic and operative planning processes, HR is required to analyze how many employees are needed in which location at what time with which qualifications and at what costs in order to initiate suitable recruitment, staff development, succession planning, or redundancy measures. Metaphorically speaking, HR needs both a microscope and a telescope to analyze existing data precisely and predict future developments and scenarios for different futures. The aim is to reduce staffing costs by avoiding expensive overtime and idle times while simultaneously keeping employee motivation and increasing customer satisfaction, without infringing any legal requirements as well as ethical or moral principles—which includes implementing measures that avoid a deepening of the great chasm.

Companies have been making predictions for operational and quantitative planning for a long time: (food) retailers and the logistics industry use historical data on checkout transactions, new orders and quantities to be produced, incoming complaints, and customer inquiries to estimate the work to be done. They predict the workload concerning several dimensions time, location, and matter-based perspective. In 2030, the ability and desire of employees and their behavioral disposition are taken into account to a greater extent to put teams together in an optimal manner (Gärtner 2020, p. 94).

The degree of complexity of operational planning depends above all on the number of different groups of employees and how many features (e.g., skills, needs, company agreements, or rules) are considered. In what is known as contingent workforce management, nontypical employment contracts (part-time, consultants, freelancers, contract workers, etc.) are considered in addition to classical full-time workers. Depending on the employee group, staffing and personnel costs vary. Companies, therefore, use their talent ecosystem to plan and deploy the increasing numbers of nontypical employees (gig workers, freelancers, etc.) efficiently. Employee questions with regard to working hours, absences, holidays, benefits, etc. can mainly be answered by chatbots, which are also used in medium-sized companies. Unlike their predecessors from the 2020s (e.g., Vinni, the HR chatbot run by Invia), in 2030, these chatbots can understand open questions and generate responses.

Here, too, the double role of Controlled Analytics must be considered: the algorithms control the staff but also need to be checked themselves because discrimination could creep in. If, for example, the data fed into the training of a machine learning algorithm are already biased, the results will also be biased. Also, an algorithm that aims at cost optimization could learn that female employees are more cost-effective (because they work part-time to a disproportionate degree and earn less for comparable jobs) and, therefore, would recommend female employees more often. In addition to gender-based discrimination, there are also other unwanted biases. If, for example, unionized employees receive additional payments for working at nights or on Sundays (but those who are not in unions do not), an algorithm aiming to minimize costs would systematically allocate cheaper employees who are not part of a workers union to the unpopular night and Sunday shifts, thereby discriminating against this group (Gärtner 2020, p. 95).

The qualitative dimension of planning (i.e., considering competencies, needs, etc.) will become more important than it has been at the start of the century. Strategic workforce management considers these abilities and develops long-term measures which ensure that competencies are available in the company and can be used. Companies such as 8works or Burning Glass currently provide external and internal data on the demand and availability of specific skills in the employment market. Microsoft offers something similar through its subsidiaries LinkedIn and GitHub and the Microsoft Workplace Analytics division. With the help of employee-based data and skills inferencing (i.e., drawing conclusions about skills profiles based on gathered data plus previous knowledge about employees' skills), companies will find it relatively easy to create transparency about the current level of competence within the company, to identify skilled persons and to discover skill gaps (see the next section for more on this). In sum, there will be four Bs in workforce strategies: build, buy, borrow, and bot.

4.3 Perform and Compensate

Performance management covers several areas, ranging from the definition of the activities, processes, or structures to be measured (including suitable parameters), to deviation analyses, to the feedback and control process. Many companies used to measure and monitor individual aspects such as leadership styles (e.g., delegation, information), work results (e.g., sales, percentage of positive quality tests), and personality features (e.g., openness, diligence). These formed the basis of assessments and feedback. In 2030, these individual, intra-department aspects are (at least in part) supplemented and in some cases even replaced by team- and customer-based criteria (e.g., project completions, recommendation rate).

Data from outside of the company will also be included automatically to identify competencies or strengths and weaknesses that drive performance. In business networks such as LinkedIn, participants can confirm one another's skills and qualifications. Companies can either crawl this data or can retrieve it via performance management software solutions (e.g., BambooHR or WebHR) to validate their employees' actual competencies. It may be the case that these endorsements, mutual assessments, and references are not as valid as those from independent third parties because there might be courtesy votes and competencies that can only be confirmed and not denied or rated negatively (Kern and Haep 2016, p. 14). Nevertheless, these critics may also apply to current assessment systems, and the benefits are the timeliness and effortlessness of the peer assessments. In this context, it is interesting to note that Microsoft acquired LinkedIn, GitHub, Lynda, and Glint. This means that Microsoft has access to both data about qualifications, competencies, strengths, and weaknesses of employees from their online profiles (LinkedIn, GitHub), the feedback they received (Glint), and their daily work behavior (Office products)—and it can offer them training via the learning platform Lynda (Gärtner 2020, p. 108).

There are various options for analyzing what the most important drivers and influencing factors for work performance are. In the simplest cases, the data needed for this are specially collected via employee surveys, so it is possible to check whether drivers which are theoretically possible are actually in place. Simple multiple regression analysis or a Bayesian network may be used to predict which factors are the most important ones and which measures are likely to influence these factors and what the overall impact on work performance is. The collection of performance data using wearables is a bit more complicated (technically, legally, and ethically). However, manual activities, for example, can be measured using beacons or position and acceleration sensors (Pentland 2014).

In large companies, remuneration is often based on a grading system in which the requirements of a position are assessed using defined criteria, for example, the breadth and depth of specialist and management skills which are required to work successfully in the role or the significance of the impact on the operating result. In contrast to performance assessment, it has thus far been the anticipated input rather than the output, which is measured to rank roles internally and to set the remuneration in a manner that reflects the requirements and the market (Skenes and Kleiner 2003). There are several digital tools on the market from established providers such as *Mercer, Willis Towers Watson*, or the *Hay Group* but also startups such as *Gradar* and *Content. Content*, for example, has developed a model that represents all the tasks and associated capacities as well as costs in a relational database. One advantage in comparison to the standard assessment process is that changes to job intersections can be shown more easily because the smallest units of a role—the tasks and services carried out—are identified and recorded in the system. This flexibility is important in a dynamic work environment. The connection between input (grading) and output (performance assessment) goes one step further. In the simplest case, information about the requirements of a role is placed in what are known as calibration rounds, where they are used to determine target achievement and bonuses. An example for this is *Zalando*'s feedback and assessment system, called "Zonar," which stores role structures and career paths in order to document the expectations and requirements of a job, conditions for promotion, and levels of development (Staab and Geschke 2019, p. 17). Another idea is to link the tasks not only to costs and capacities but also to the service provided in an IT system. The latter is achieved to some extent by technically enabling peer-to-peer performance assessments, although this comes with all of the problems and criticisms linked to an approach of this kind (see Gärtner 2020, p. 107 et seqq.).

In order to motivate employees to achieve their goals, some providers integrate gamification elements (levels, point or star ratings, leader boards, badges), which should keep players' (intrinsic) motivation levels high. *Betterworks* and *Engagedly* offer these types of functions. For example, employees can collect points which can then be redeemed for vouchers or other rewards, or they can go up a level when they have achieved their goals. The visibility of what has been achieved within the organization is often used as a lever to offer immaterial stimuli such as recognition and an increase in status. Ultimately, the aim of gamification is for employees to be intrinsically motivated and encouraged to achieve self-optimization through play. The hype surrounding the use of gamification in the workplace has now, however, given way to more critical and realistic considerations (Vesa and Harviainen 2019).

While pay for skills has been challenging to master in 2020 due to lack of solid information on both pay and skills, in 2030, this approach has gained ground. For example, IBM asked managers to rigorously identify skills throughout the organization. The segmentation of skills today is strict: rewards are linked to those with in-demand skills, while those with skills that are not needed do not get any increase. Identifying and rewarding the right technical skills allow the company to innovate continuously. Employees whose skills appear to be obsolete are encouraged either to learn new skills—for which there are extensive training budgets—or to move on (Mercer 2020). Maintaining this link between planning, performing, developing, and outplacing (or retaining) is one of the robust principles within HRM that has not changed throughout the years—but in 2030, the technologies are ready to enable seamless integration.

4.4   Develop and Retain

In general, the digital tools for developing and retaining are primarily about analytics and chatbots that should enable adaptive, personalized learning as well as virtual and augmented reality as a replacement technology for face-to-face training sessions. In particular, the use of digital tools changes several aspects of training and competence development (see the chapter on "Learning in 2030" in this book or Gärtner (2020)):

- Learning content can more easily be tailored to individual needs and be adapted to the learning progress or learning objectives through "learning analytics" (a synonym for this is "Educational Data Mining").
- Development methods and learning locations become more diverse: they range from informal and tactile learning in the workplace with or from others; to virtual training on the computer or via smartphone with the help of video libraries, curated blog posts, e-coaching sessions, playful tests, simulations, or online communities; to the use of sensors and augmented or virtual reality. Through these media and technologies, the previously text-intensive content can be communicated through images, with sound, interactively, and in a tactile manner. Digital technologies thereby enable multimodal and interactive learning, which both increase the quality of the training provided (Niegemann and Heidig 2019, p. 3). When it comes to how digital tools can support the self-organized or (partially) automated creation of learning content, it is less about quality and more about cost reduction (Meier et al. 2018, p. 22, 25).
- More responsibility is transferred to employees in development planning, with the employer in turn permitting more transparency. Tools like Fuel50, a career pathing platform, provide means to personalize career paths and connect with mentors, coaches, and colleagues. They use gamification, AI, and 360° feedback to drive succession and talent development as well as performance management.
- When controlling HR development measures, (almost) real-time data from the training situation can be used. In addition to the data which is typically collected about participants, trainers, and training sessions (equipment) such as the number, costs, times, and competencies, data are now available on the actual training process and the progress participants are making with their learning.
- The changes mentioned above result in new requirements placed on the skills of HR developers. In particular, they need to be able to estimate the opportunities and limits of the tools of digitized learning. Regardless of whether they consider them positive or negative, it is evident that digital technologies are the media of knowledge and action: we know more when we have access to global databases, and we act differently because we have these opportunities.
- Along with the tasks, the roles and expectations of HR developers, managers, employees, and providers of educational services change too. Since digital tools enable new forms of needs-driven, self-controlled, and social learning, the learners become the focus to a greater extent but also take on a driver role, with HR becoming the curator of learning content (Jenewein 2018, p. 273; Liebert and Talg 2018, p. 203 et seqq.). Learners determine the form, content, time, and fellow learners themselves, and the corresponding demand is satisfied through internal or external cloud services (from push to pull learning). HR is then responsible for providing continuously relevant, high-quality, and current learning content and will become the Spotify of learning because the content will be offered as a personal playlist. At the same time, the learners will be made more responsible for their development and "employability" than they used to be. A nontechnical argument for this is that where candidates are more specialized and the economy is more dynamic, it is increasingly only the management and the

employees themselves who know what they need. Another argument is that the training budgets do not cover the investment that is needed, and "employee self-service" is cheaper for the company.

It is not, however, just technologies that are changing but also the working conditions and, therefore, the sought skill profiles, which in turn results in an adjustment to strategic and operative knowledge and competency management (North and Maier 2018). This includes strategic issues about the knowledge and competencies which will be needed in the future based on the corporate strategy and about which business models are possible on the basis of the changed competencies. These questions are not addressed below, nor are aspects of pre-company or inner-company socialization (e.g., onboarding, cultural development) and career management (e.g., career pathways such as management, specialist, and project careers).

5   Conclusion

The described changes in HR practices also lead to a change in the roles and responsibilities of the HR department:

- Established IT providers and HR startups, fuelled by readily available risk capital, play an even more significant role in terms of new service offerings but also data security. Since these third-party providers reliably and continuously supply the market with new products, HR employees must be able to assess the offerings, negotiate contracts, and manage the collaboration.
- HR professionals need to know how "Natural Language Processing," "machine learning," "Robotic Process Automation," and other techniques and technologies work in order to evaluate possibilities and risks. While these techniques and technologies translate into appealing labels such as "Conversational HR," "Connected Robotics," or "Controlled Analytics," many of these ideas are rather buzzwords or fads. They are driven by vested interests and portray simple organizational concepts or long-standing ideas in HR in bright new colors and with a digital flavor. When such buzzwords are presented at conferences or award ceremonies, some HR managers will find themselves fidgeting in their chairs, cringing with embarrassment for the speaker, or are simply irritated—and buy the products and services just because they heard people say that "Google is also doing it." Understanding the underpinning technologies, methodologies, and tools is a prerequisite to professionalize HR (for some of these underpinnings, see Gärtner 2020, p. 17ff).
- The Chief Human Resource Officer (CHRO) must manage and lead a more diverse HR team, composed of specialists who are data- and tech-savvy and often work as freelancers. In addition, there are a couple of "people people" and several of robots, gig workers, and clickworkers.

We suppose that digital tools will significantly influence the delivery of HR services. Of course, tools do not solve challenging organizational matters. The weather app and the iPhone won't help if you have to go out in miserable weather because the dog needs a walk or the daycare center is closed. What you really need are good shoes, an umbrella, and a good understanding of the terrain (where to find shelter, which roads to avoid and which to take, etc.). And since it is often the case that you are not alone out there, you should also have learned how to behave as a social being in specific environments appropriately.

We believe that in 2030, the HR function will have made further progress both in terms of an increasing understanding of tools and the terrain. If HR lacks the motivation to move in this direction, there are external drivers: one is that the business is merely requesting HR to use these tools because they can improve the efficiency and effectiveness of HR practices. And even in 2030, an inability to attract, retain, and motivate the right numbers and right kinds of people will mean that human and nonhuman resources are wasted. Another driver is that managers of other functions threaten to overtake HR or vote for getting rid of HR. In our opinion, this is not going to happen until 2030. Still, those HR departments that do not consider the use of digital tools will attract less investment, and their reputation is going to deteriorate just as Scholz (1995) and others have projected.

References

Brown, P., Lauder, H., & Ashton, D. (2010). *The global auction: The broken promises of education, jobs, and incomes*. Oxford: Oxford University Press.

Cohen, N. S. (2015). From pink slips to pink slime: Transforming media labor in a digital age. *The Communication Review, 18*(2), 98–122.

De Stefano, V. (2016). *The rise of the 'just-in-time workforce': On-demand work, crowd work and labour protection in the 'gig-economy'. Conditions of Work and Employment Series No. 17.* Geneva: International Labour Organisation.

Donald, W. J., & Donald, E. K. (1929). Trends in personnel administration. *Harvard Business Review, 7*(2), 143–155.

Garson, B. (1989). *The electronic sweatshop: How computers are transforming the office of the future into the factory of the past.* New York: Penguin Books.

Gärtner, C. (2020). *Smart HRM: Digitale Tools für die Personalarbeit* [Smart HRM: Digital tools for HR management]. Wiesbaden: Springer Gabler.

Hoss, D. (1996). Personalwirtschaft an der Schwelle zum 21. Jahrhundert [Human resources at the eve of the 21st century]. *Personal, 48*(12), 632–634.

Jenewein, T. (2018). Ansatze zum Lernen im Digitalen Zeitalter. Darstellung am Beispiel SAP. In T. Petry & W. Jager (eds.), *Digital HR. Smarte und agile Systeme, Prozesse und Strukturen im Personalmanagement* (pp. 259–274). Freiburg: Haufe Lexware

Kellogg, K. C., Valentine, M. A., & Christin, A. (2020). Algorithms at work: The new contested terrain of control. *Academy of Management Annals, 14*(1), 366–410.

Kern, D., & Haep, M. (2016). Wie Konzerne ihr Performance Management modernisieren können (Interview by G. Birkner). *Comp & Ben Magazin, 2*, 12–14.

Liebert, K., & Talg, A. (2018). Kunstliche Intelligenz und das Lernen der Zukunft. In K. Schwuchow & J. Gutmann (eds.), *HR-Trends 2019: Strategie, Digitalisierung, Diversitat, Demografie* (S. 197–208). Freiburg: Haufe Lexware.

Meier, C., Bäcker, D., & Seibold, D. (2018). Digitale Transformation und L&D: Ergebnisse einer Standortbestimmung und Handlungserfordernisse. scil Arbeitsbericht Nr. 29.

Mercer. (2020). *2020 global talent trends study.*

Niegemann, H. M., & Heidig, S. (2019). Interaktivitat und Adaptivitat in multimedialen Lernumgebungen. In H. Niegemann & A. Weinberger (eds.), *Lernen mit Bildungstechnologien* (pp. 1–25). Berlin/Heidelberg: Springer.

North, K., & Maier, R. (2018). Wissen 4.0 – Wissensmanagement im digitalen Wandel. *HMD Praxis der Wirtschaftsinformatik, 55*(4), 665–681.

Pentland, A. (2014). *Social physics: How good ideas spread - The lessons from a new science.* London: Penguin.

Radkau, J. (2017). *Geschichte der Zukunft – Prognosen, Visionen, Irrungen in Deutschland von 1945 bis heute [History of the future – Forecasts, visions, mistakes in Germany from 1945 until today].* München: Hanser.

Scholz, C. (1995). Ein Denkmodell für das Jahr 2000? Die Virtuelle Personalabteilung [A conceptual lens for the year 2020? The virtual HR department]. *Personalführung, 28,* 398–403.

Skenes, C., & Kleiner, B. H. (2003). The HAY System of compensation. *Management Research News, 26*(2/3/4), 109–115.

Staab, P., & Geschke, S. C. (2019). *Ratings als arbeitspolitisches Konfliktfeld: Das Beispiel Zalando* (Study der Hans-Böckler-Stiftung, No. 429). Dusseldorf: Hans-Böckler-Stiftung.

Vesa, M., & Harviainen, J. T. (2019). Gamification: Concepts, consequences, and critiques. *Journal of Management Inquiry, 28*(2), 128–130.

Christian Gärtner is a professor of human resource management at Hochschule München University of Applied Sciences (Germany). His main research interest is in the (digital) transformation of work. He has authored or co-authored five books and published widely on the subject. He has worked as a management consultant at Capgemini Consulting and still supports companies as a freelance consultant, speaker, and workshop facilitator.

Dieter Kern leads Mercer's Leadership & Organizational Excellence Practice. Before joining Mercer, Dieter worked for Capgemini Consulting as head of HR & Change Management Consulting and co-headed the Business Transformation Practice in Central Europe. His clients are mainly large, international companies, many of them listed in the DAX 30 and the tech industry.

Learning in the Year 2030

Klaus North

Los Angeles, June 15, 2030
  Upload Knowledge to Your Brain
  Researchers from the California-based HRL Laboratories developed an innovative way to make learning quicker and more effective by neuro-stimulation. They use a headset to feed electric signals from the brain of an experienced airplane pilot to the brain of trainees. HRL Laboratories claim that by this new technology, trainees learned how to pilot airplanes in a flight simulator 33 percent better than non-stimulated candidates did. Transcranial direct current stimulation (tDCS) has become the latest fad in learning settings this year. Researchers argue that tDCS strengthens synaptic connections and thus enabling faster learning. Sales of DCS starter kits (called Halos), which contain cables, electrodes, straps, batteries, sponges, and a current stimulator, are booming. Biomedical engineering expert Monica Werner, however, warns that it is not enough to just to put on a neuro-stimulation headset and hope to master a musical instrument or improve your golf handicap. You still need to practice, but researchers argue that the device will assist your brain to memorize and supports a quicker creation of synapses.

1   Introduction

Hoping that we can upload knowledge while sleeping and wake up enlightened is still a dream in 2030. What, how, when, and where we learn, however, is changing rapidly. While there is a widespread discussion about which skills and competencies will be needed in the 2030s, there is an overall education and learning challenge: To develop "agency." As EAEA (2019) states, *agency*—the ability to make informed choices about one's life and a sense of responsibility to participate in the world and

K. North (✉)
Wiesbaden Business School, RheinMain University of Applied Sciences, Wiesbaden, Germany

© Springer Nature Switzerland AG 2021   223
S. Güldenberg et al. (eds.), *Managing Work in the Digital Economy*, Future of
Business and Finance, https://doi.org/10.1007/978-3-030-65173-2_14

to influence people, events, and circumstances—is at the center of learning and, consequently, of any change in society. In their Education 2030 report, OECD (2018) argues that two factors, in particular, help learners enable agency: "The first is a personalized learning environment that supports and motivates each student to nurture his or her passions, make connections between different learning experiences and opportunities, and design their own learning projects and processes in collaboration with others. The second is building a solid foundation: literacy and numeracy remain crucial. In the era of digital transformation and with the advent of big data, digital literacy and data literacy are becoming increasingly essential, as are physical health and mental well-being."

As boundaries between remunerated work, voluntary activity, and leisure blurred, the same thing happened to the learning spans across these activities. Do you remember that 10 years ago, learners sat in rows in classrooms? Today, people learn in a museum setting, out in nature, and together with robots in a factory or other places. Students know to break up the rows of chairs to create pods and place themselves around the room or join in a multidisciplinary superlab. "Learning everywhere" by choosing the time, place, media, and content that best meet the learners' goals, intentions, and wishes has become a reality.

In work contexts, learning and performance management are increasingly linked. This is supported by on-demand (micro)learning, often supported by virtual reality applications. "Mass-personalization" of content and delivery modes address and engage learners individually. Data-driven identification of learning gaps is the basis for creating personalized learning experiences based on open education resources available on mobile devices. The learning experience platform (LXP) market is growing up fast, which makes the content easy to find and consume. Face readers, eye trackers, and wearables help learners to show and develop appropriate learning strategies and behavior. Gamification links emotions to learning. In 2030, self-directed and social learning has gained in importance over standardized institutional learning programs. Synchronizing human and machine learning is still a problem to be solved.

In the following chapter, we will discuss the state of the art of adult learning in the fourth decade of the twenty-first century. While this contribution mainly focuses on work-related learning, many of the developments discussed are pervasive in all spheres of education and learning.

2   Learn-Work-Live: Lifelong Learning Has Become a Reality

The shift toward knowledge work, artificial intelligence, digitalization, and robotics will definitely disrupt our classical stages of life and our workplace in profound ways. It will make it much more fluid and thereby interesting. In 2030 education and training, work-life and career followed by (partial or temporary) retirement will no longer be separated stages but much more intertwined. Therefore, we will have to organize these three stages in a fundamentally new and more synchronized way.

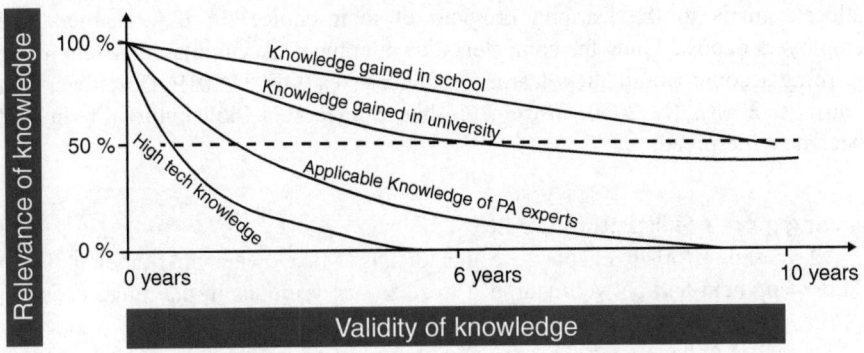

Fig. 1 Half-life of knowledge (own illustration based on Machlup 1962)

Lifelong career guidance centers on-site, for example, in shopping malls or as online platforms will assist citizens in shaping their career life.

In the past, it was common to have one job and one professional career. The US Bureau of Labor Statistics (2019) found out that "individuals born in the latter years of the baby boom (1957–1964) held an average of 12.3 jobs from ages 18 to 52." These numbers are expected to increase for millennials (born between 1995 and 2010) and require them to renew their professional expertise during that time. These phases are interrupted by further education, not just reading a book or attending a two-day seminar, but rather a fundamental overhaul and renewal of knowledge and skills. Figure 1 illustrates this need for lifelong learning as relevance and validity of knowledge decrease rapidly. Learning becomes "fluid" throughout our lives.

Under the concept of "Fluid learning," Falconer et al. (2013) describe the radical change in cultural perceptions of learner agency and learner-teacher roles, associated with changes in technology: "After completing compulsory education, the focus of each learner moves from learning pre-defined knowledge to filling gaps between areas of knowledge, integrating different areas of expertise, as well as learning new knowledge. People do not turn automatically to formal institutions for large blocks of learning. Instead, they consider it natural to make use of open learning resources and open courses, making their own decisions about what to learn, when and how. Learners naturally employ open learning practices, creating new knowledge for future learners to benefit from. They expect to contribute to the learning of others as well as learning themselves, viewing themselves as the experts in their own situation."

Bélanger (2016) widens the term of "lifelong" to "lifewide" learning which comprises learning in institutions, families, communities, and workplaces.

Fluid and lifewide learning imply that people take responsibility for self-organized learning and manage their competence portfolio by blending formal and informal learning. This also raises the question of how to finance lifelong learning (ILO 2018). In 2030, many increasingly flexible financing instruments such as vouchers and individual learning accounts (ILA) will give learners the freedom to make training rights "portable" from one job or employment status to another or allocate funds to the learning provider of their choice. In ILA, learners and employers deposit funds for competence development. Accumulating assets in the learning account would allow learners to defer taxes (OECD 2019; Oosterbeek and Patrinos, 2008). By 2030, instruments like Singapore's SkillsFuture Credit will become widespread.

> **Singapore's SkillsFuture Credit**
>
> "As part of efforts to encourage Singaporeans to take ownership of their skills development and be well-equipped to seize opportunities in the future economy, a one-off SkillsFuture Credit top-up of $500 will be provided to every Singapore Citizen aged 25 years and above. Eligible Singaporeans can start using their one-off SkillsFuture Credit top-up on more than 8000 courses offered by the Institutes of Higher Learning (IHLs) and NTUC LearningHub and also on other SkillsFuture Credit-eligible courses. Take timely action to upskill and reskill, to seize new career opportunities! This top-up will expire on 31 Dec 2025."
>
> Source: https://www.skillsfuture.sg/Credit

3   People Take Responsibility for Self-Regulated Learning and Manage Their Competence Portfolio

What has been your learning journey so far? Was it characterized mainly by being a consumer of formal education? Or have you gained experience with self-organized learning and managing your competence portfolio?

In switching to self-organized learning, you might need to overcome two challenges: "the extent to which learners need guidance and, depending on the learning goals, the extent to which learners need recognition and certification" (Castaño Muñoz et al. 2013, p. 171).

Depending on the needs and personality of the learner, Castaño Muñoz et al. (2013) suggest four complimentary scenarios of open adult learning. The *learning for life scenario* is based on the learner's interests and curiosity without a need for formal recognition. Learners select learning resources according to their needs with no or a minimum of guidance. In case learners seek more guidance, orientation, and structure, in often confusing and in transparent training market, learners would rely more on assistance by communities and groups or on trusted gateways to knowledge (*learning café scenario*). *My learning certified* scenario responds to the need for recognition or certification to fulfill an externally set curriculum or standard. In this scenario, learners might still have a high degree of freedom regarding learning resources and approaches. The *open training* scenario lies between the learning café and my learning certified approach: "Here the learner chooses to study a particular subject that is linked to an externally set standard (even if this is loosely defined) in a more structured, supportive, collaborative learning environment. This scenario may lead to a certification, but the latter is not necessarily its principal aim" (Castaño Muñoz et al. 2013, p. 176).

To support these scenarios, self-regulated learning is increasingly assisted by adaptive learning systems with AI-based tutors that are powered by algorithms to customize individual learning journeys. In *personalized scaffolding*, artificial tutors "provide successive levels of temporary support that help learners reach higher levels of comprehension and skill acquisition that they would not be able to achieve without assistance. Like physical scaffolding, supportive strategies are incrementally removed when they are no longer needed" (so-called fading scaffolds) (www.edglossary.org/scaffolding/). In such a system, there might be four tutors or "agents": "Gavin the Guide" supports students' navigation in the learning environment and provides questionnaires for self-assessment. "Pam the Planner" monitors the planning process during self-regulated learning and helps users to set sub-goals or to activate their preknowledge. "Mary the Monitor" presents the meta-cognitive monitoring of self-regulation during learning by stimulating self-assessments on text comprehension or estimated sub-goal achievement. "Sam the Strategizer" encourages cognitive learning strategies (Azevedo et al. 2016).

As learning broadens, so too must *assessment and accreditation*. Assessment is performed by a range of different types of people, including peers and experts, not just by teachers. Open technologies offer new means of accreditation through expert consensus and/or online activity tracing on mobile devices (Falconer et al. 2013).

In 2030, a variety of formal or informal certifications are available. This is especially useful as regards competencies that are not recognized in frameworks or official curricula. Micro-credentials, badges, and social certification are widely spread, making it difficult to understand how valid these certifications are. There is an increasing number of organizations and firms offering the management of e-portfolios. As an example, the box below explains the Open Badge concept of the Mozilla Foundation. To verify resumes and competence profiles, blockchain protocols allow for the creation of personal profiles that certify academic credentials, participation in nonacademic training courses, skills, previous work experience, and recommendations received. This is what the start-up *Skillchain* proposes.

In 2030, personal trusted portfolios, where individuals can store and manage their own "demonstrators" of competences, are common. Professional platforms such as LinkedIn are trying to develop their business as "human capital banks." Competence portfolios are increasingly generated automatically by analyzing the "digital footprint" of users across digital media and applications. Even though these applications claim that users have full command of their competence portfolio, there is some doubt if these systems can be trusted and privacy is respected. Courses on "What skills, competencies, and experiences do you share online?" and how "Do you 'showcase' your talents?" have become popular in 2030. Consequently, the monopoly held by the public sector in certification is fading or has become more flexible and open.

Open Badges

Open Badges promoted by the Mozilla Foundation are verifiable, portable digital badges with embedded metadata about skills and achievements which can be shared via the web. They represent a continuously updated picture of a person's lifelong learning. Each Open Badge is associated with an image and information about the badge, its recipient, the issuer, and any supporting evidence. All this information may be packaged within a badge image file that can be displayed via online CVs and social networks. Badges may represent many different types of achievements and claims: Hard skills such as proficiency in a programming language, soft skills like collaboration, official certification, community involvement, and new skills and literacies not recognized by traditional education providers.

Because the system is based on an open standard, recipients can combine multiple badges from different issuers to tell the complete story of their verifiable achievements—both online and off-line. Open Badges can be displayed wherever recipients want them on the web, including on social media profiles and through services that store and display badges. Badges can be shared for employment, education, or lifelong learning.

Anyone can issue a badge, receive one, verify that a badge is real, or inspect the metadata and any associated evidence. Badge issuers can certify that their badges are technically compliant with the specification and, therefore, can be readily moved among backpacks and display sites. Badges can be used to set goals, motivate behaviors, connect learning environments, and communicate achievements across many contexts.

Source: https://openbadges.org

4   How We Learn in 2030

In 2030, people do not only take responsibility for self-regulated learning, but also how and where we learn has changed significantly. That is why on-demand learning and microlearning, combined with action, have become the primary learning approach, often linked to performance analytics. People bring their own devices (BYOD) and increasingly rely on virtual or augmented reality applications. On-demand learning suits in particular freelancers who change jobs frequently and combine different projects at different organizations.

Let us have a look at how learning has become more attractive, relevant, and up-to-date.

Learning on Demand Combined with Action

In the past, people often had the feeling that they were forced to learn things that they will never need. The current generation of learners wants to be able to solve problems now and demand personalized content in real time, anywhere and anytime. This immediacy has changed people's expectations of learning and is challenging traditional learning and development structures in organizations that take too long to respond. Haenisch (2017) describes modern learning on demand (LoD) systems as follows: LoD enables continuous learning in small nuggets to enable immediate action or to stay current with the ever-changing knowledge required. From your app where you perform a certain task, you may directly jump into learning about this task if needed. You can ask a "learning bot" what you want to know "and the bot puts together a great explanation out of the myriads of content available, tailored to your pre-knowledge and preferred learning style. Moreover, it won't be only about you asking questions. The bot might reach out to you and pro-actively inform you about new things you should learn" (Haenisch 2017). As a learner, you might have access to a learning experience platform (LXP) that looks more like YouTube or Netflix to search and select relevant content. In addition, interactive labs and clinics create environments for teams to learn together close to work situations.

When learning comes closer to action, it is only one step further to link it to performance management. Analytics about learners, programs, and experiences link learning with individual, team, and organizational performance. In 2030, comprehensive learning analytics allow us to optimize learning based on data about learners, learning experiences, and learning programs. Learning and development (L&D), HR professionals, and operational management have overcome their relative isolation from each other, which was still the case in the 2020s.

Linking Learning and Performance

"A manufacturing company seeks to increase efficiency across their supply chain, as measured by the number of rush orders. Through the performance management process, managers set relevant goals for supply chain team members, assign training to streamline their processes, and track performance after training. If rush orders drop, the learning was a success. By setting a clear metric (number of rush orders) that speaks to a business goal (supply chain efficiency), the L&D team can work with managers (who lead the performance process) to deliver the right training to the right individuals."

https://www.peoplefluent.com/blog/learning/linking-learning-performance-management-drive-business-outcomes/

Microlearning[1]

With shorter attention spans and the pressure for quick and ubiquitous learning, short digital lessons that workers can access at their convenience have become popular. Microlearning consists of short, focused learning nuggets designed to meet a specific learning outcome, typically designed and delivered in rich media formats. Often,

---

[1]This paragraph widely follows https://www.itcilo.org/stories/microlearning.

augmented or virtual reality solutions allow to closely link training and real situations. In healthcare, for example, a display of organs via holograms can support surgeons to prepare for complicated operations.

These flexible, portable, and personalized microlessons give learners the freedom to choose to learn wherever is convenient. "Breaking up content into microlessons increases learning outcomes, makes it easier to author and also easier to engage with. The method is most effective on specific tasks or to rapidly fill performance gaps."

Microlearning with Virtual and Augmented Reality

Vanessa is a junior labor inspector and wants to get fit for inspecting a specific kind of ship. On her tablet, she opens the "The Maritime virtual tour," which is a virtualization of a ship to guide labor inspectors on a maritime deck. She puts on her virtual reality glasses for an immersive learning experience with simulated real-life situations on a ship. She virtually goes through all kind of default situations an inspector could encounter (FOL 2018).

Marc operates *a machine in an Industry 4.0 setting*. In the morning, when he signs in at the control panel of the machine, he is regularly offered short learning nuggets to deepen or update his knowledge on specific operations. He can only start operations after having gone through the learning nugget. When the machine asks for a maintenance operation, he scans a QR code on the machine with his tablet, directs the camera to spot where maintenance is needed, and is guided by an augmented reality solution, where the real-world image is overlaid by virtual information with example maintenance instructions.

"No Thrill-No Skill": Games to Learn

Daniel starts his first day in a customer care team by a gamified onboarding training to help him acclimatize with the culture of the organization. The game uses virtual reality (VR) features, personalization through avatars, and leaderboards and analytics to understand the efficacy of user interactions.

Gamification builds on people's natural desires for socializing, fun, mastery, competition, achievement, and status. The main strategy to keep players engaged is to reward them by points, badges, or levels and compare players in a competitive environment.

Kapp (2012, p. 10) defines gamification as "using game-based mechanics, aesthetics and game thinking to engage people, motivate action, promote learning, and solve problems." In social networks, where reward and status elements are embedded in implicit and explicit forms in people's interactions, game elements and competition are interspersed throughout the platforms. In the 2030s, gamification has shifted toward the construction of open gameworlds, which are 3D immersive locations that players can explore. In 2030, gamification software can understand each user and provide him or her with a tailored experience (Growth Engineering 2018). Pervasive games that extend the gaming experiences out into the physical world by weaving the games into the fabric of players' real environments are increasingly applied as serious games in work contexts. Readers looking back from 2030 might remember the game Pokémon Go which was popular 15 years ago.

Pulse!!: Serious Gaming in Healthcare

"Pulse!! reproduces the conditions of an emergency ward in a hospital. Thanks to this video game, future nurses can practice all they have learned in their theoretical classes and gain experience handling real situations. The goal of the players is to identify each patient's problem, giving priority to the most severe cases, and applying the appropriate measures depending on each person's condition."

Source: https://www.game-learn.com/all-you-need-to-know-serious-games-game-based-learning-examples/

Learning Is Social and Open

Learning has always been a social phenomenon in the family and at school, work, and society at large. Professional networks of colleagues and contacts have been an essential source for workplace learning. The last 10 years, however, have leveraged learning via social media applications, where learners network, share, collaborate, and exchange ideas to solve problems. Simulations take learning closer to real-world events. Tools such as (micro)blogs, wikis, Twitter, interactive instant messaging, YouTube or "Edutube" channels, podcasts, and social bookmarks or social tagging have become important sources so that everybody can become a content provider and a consumer of learning resources. Since the 2020 Covid-19 crisis, platforms for webinars and live presentations are blossoming. Increasingly popular are formats like "radio talk show," a free web-based service in which anyone can create, join, or listen to live interactive content. Talk shows can be recorded, making them available as podcasts later. Social networks like LinkedIn or Facebook have developed new business as learning providers.

The open education movement offering OpenCourseWare, MOOCs, and Open Educational Resources (OER), in general, has become a central player in the education market. There are a plethora of learning and research materials available in any medium, digital or otherwise. These mostly "reside in the public domain or have been released under an open license that permits no-cost access, use, adaptation, and redistribution by others with no or limited restrictions" (UNESCO no year).

Agile Learning via Communities

As many subject areas develop rapidly, quick learning loops are imperative. Sara is a part-time manager of a specialist community in healthcare. The community provides constantly updated training modules and certifies their users for skill blocks. The community started with the exchange and informal

(continued)

learning on a new topic in an informal setting of an online group space on a social media platform. Resources and materials on the subject area were collated (e.g., individual problem solutions, brief experience reports, visualizations on relationships). In the next step, resources and materials were systematized by the community manager or learning coach and made available to other users (e.g., intranet pages on the topic, webinars, podcasts, interactive tutorials). Sara also ensures the quality of the materials (inconsistencies, gaps). These quality-assured materials are an important basis for the development of training units and, if necessary, certifications (peer-to-peer assessments) on the new topic for larger target groups. Thus, learning from colleagues becomes more agile, relevant, and up-to-date than the traditional development of training programs.

5 Human and Machine Learning Are Increasingly Integrated

In 2030, the applications of "augmented intelligence" have changed a broad spectrum of domains, such as medicine, science, finance, and security intelligence. People train machines, learn from and with machines, explain their outputs, and ensure their responsible use. Wilson and Daugherty (2018b) call this *reciprocal apprenticing:* "In the past, technological education has gone in one direction: People have learned how to use machines. But with AI, machines are learning from humans, and humans, in turn, learn again from machines. In the future, humans will perform tasks alongside AI agents to learn new skills, and will receive on-the-job training to work well within AI-enhanced processes." For these tasks, new jobs as "machine trainers" emerge.

Machine-learning algorithms must be taught how to perform the work they are designed to do and how to best interact with humans. This requires understanding the two fundamentally different ways in which machines learn. In the *symbolic reasoning* approach, being supervised or unsupervised learning, developers encode and store knowledge in a knowledge base to solve tasks, drawing rule-based inferences from that knowledge. This form of machine learning is close to experience-based human learning and applied to, e.g., robots learning to interact with humans. The key advantage of symbolic learning is that the reasoning process can easily explain why a particular conclusion is reached and what the reasoning behind each of the steps had been. Codifying knowledge, however, requires substantial effort, and inference rules become increasingly complex with the breadth of the knowledge domain, which restricts these systems' capabilities. For these tasks, new jobs as "machine trainers" emerge, which often include interdisciplinary teams.

Training of Chatbots

"Microsoft's AI assistant, Cortana, required extensive training to develop just the right personality: confident, caring, and helpful but not bossy. Instilling those qualities took countless hours of attention by a team that included a poet, a novelist, and a playwright. Similarly, human trainers were needed to develop the personalities of Apple's Siri and Amazon's Alexa to ensure that they accurately reflected their companies' brands. Siri, for example, has just a touch of sassiness, as consumers might expect from Apple."

Source: Wilson and Daugherty 2018a, p. 5

In *deep learning*, on the other hand, systems perform tasks using statistical models "filtering" data in neural networks with several layers. This happens, for example, in face recognition and is applied, for example, to cancer screening. Developers optimize/train these models by extracting patterns from data of solutions to similar past problems or by letting the system gain experience from the feedback over time. The high performance of deep learning methods comes at the cost of high model complexity and low interpretability. Artificial neural networks' complexity usually prohibits determining why a system based on such models has reached a specific solution (Berger and Hess 2019).

Based on this understanding of how machines learn, the following *six challenges for effective learning of humans together with machines* will be discussed:

Narrow application challenge: "Most current AI systems are 'narrow' applications—specifically designed to tackle a well-specified problem in one domain, such as a particular game. Such approaches cannot adapt to new or broader challenges without significant redesign. While it may be far superior to human performance in one domain, it is not superior in other domains" (CSER 2020). Users of such systems have to be trained within which limits specific systems will deliver good results and what happens if these limits are surpassed.

Dependency challenge: While many people are no longer able to find their way without their car navigation system, professionals in 2030 are increasingly dependent on AI applications. Will a surgeon be able to operate without the help of AI systems? Will a pilot be able to land an airplane when algorithms fail? This increasing dependence on such systems requires developing strategies to learn, simulate, and regularly practice interaction with these systems to understand how they "tick" and how to act when systems fail.

Value alignment challenge: Norbert Wiener, the founder of cybernetics, had already stated in 1960 that "We had better be quite sure that the purpose put into the machine is the purpose which we really desire." To avoid misalignments between human and machine goals, algorithms have to be trained, and their behavior has to be closely monitored. This is an arduous task as human behavior is rooted in values and norms, which are mostly implicit knowledge. There is also a need for awareness training on the ethics of algorithms.

Bias challenge: This is a specific problem related to value alignment as algorithms may be trained on data containing human bias. Unfair machine-learning algorithms may reinforce social biases of race, gender, sexuality, and ethnicity. Examples are face recognition systems reflecting societal prejudices or biases in personnel selection or credit allocation algorithms. By 2030, developers and users have become aware of these possible biases and learned to mitigate them.

Black box challenge: The high performance of deep learning methods comes at the cost of high model complexity and low interpretability. Artificial neural networks' complexity usually prohibits determining why a system based on such models has reached a specific solution. Building and training accountable and interpretable AI-based systems are therefore a crucial task in fusing human and machine learning. This should be governed by the principle of algorithmic transparency. This principle refers to the transparence of factors that influence the decisions made by algorithms to the people who use, regulate, and are affected by systems that employ those algorithms. The Boeing 737 Max crashes around 2020 demonstrated the vital need that users are trained to understand how an algorithm reasons.

Competitive pressure challenge: The "launch and iterate" mindset in software development might lead to deficient testing and training due to time constraints and cost reduction pressure. Boeing, for example, wanted to avoid costly simulator training of pilots for the 737 Max resulting in reduced capabilities in using the Maneuvering Characteristics Augmentation System. It is evident that an efficient learning journey of developers and users is compulsory in particular for such critical systems.

Microsoft's 18 design guidelines for human-AI interaction (see Fig. 2) not only are valid for developers but also provide useful guidance for integrating human and machine learning, and this may provide answers to some of the challenges mentioned above.

6   Implications for the Stakeholders of Learning in the Year 2030

The developments discussed above lead to far-reaching changes not only for learners but also for the involved stakeholders, which will be described in the following.

1. *As a learner*, you take responsibility for self-organized learning and manage your competence and skill portfolio by blending formal and informal learning. You proactively set your learning goals and create your learning journey making the best use of digital tools and devices. If necessary, seek support by a learning coach or your personal AI-powered chatbot. Integrate yourself into communities and networks to benefit from sharing knowledge and experiences with peers. Collect your "badges" and certificates to prove and communicate your competencies and skills.

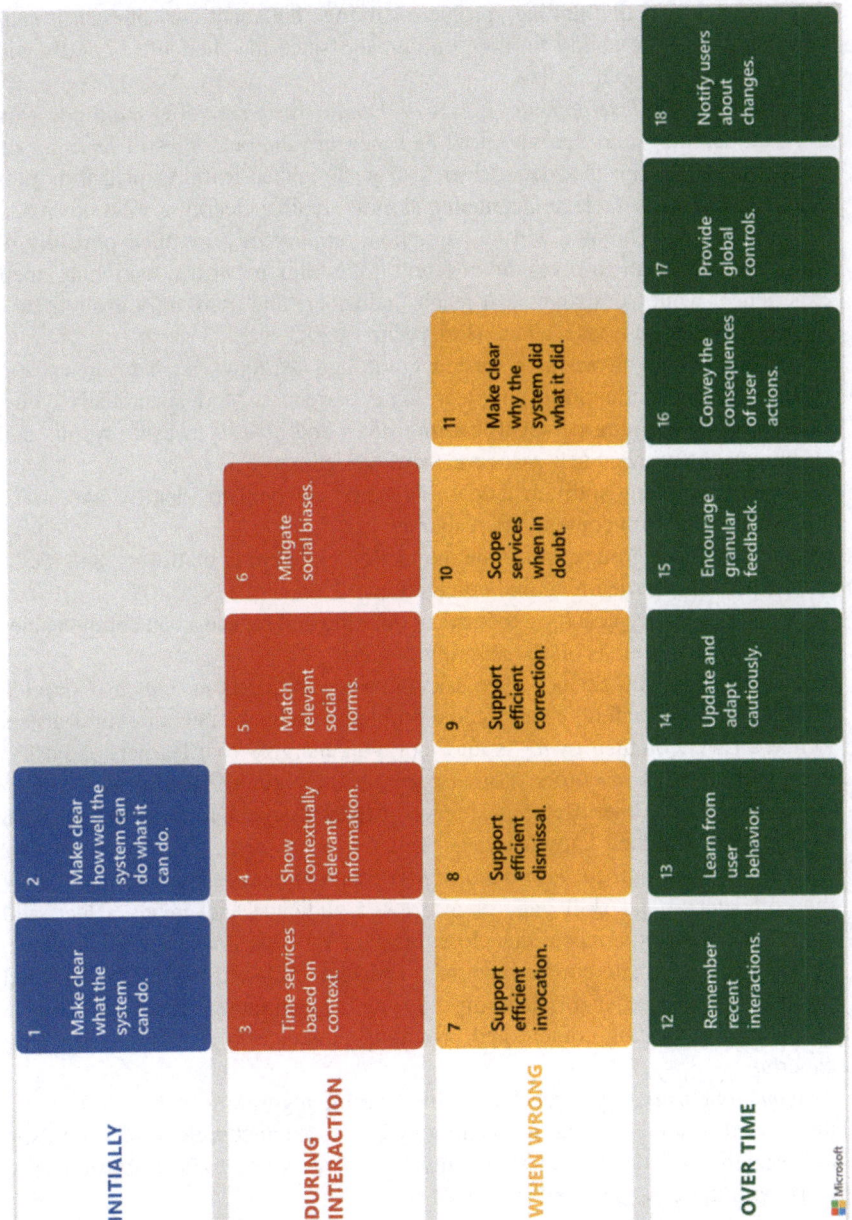

Fig. 2 Microsoft's 18 design guidelines for human-AI interaction. Source: https://docs.microsoft.com/en-us/ai/guidelines-human-ai-interaction; see also Amershi et al. (2019)

2. *As a manager*, you pay less attention to degrees while hiring new employees/ knowledge workers. Instead, focus more on competencies and values/attitudes to cope with complexity, uncertainty, and ambiguity. Such competencies include creative and critical thinking, problem-solving, collaboration, empathy, self-leadership, and the ability to learn on-demand since the shelf life of skills will be even shorter (OECD 2016).

3. *As learning and development (L&D) or human resource (HR) manager*, you integrate learning into the workflow and measure the outcomes of learning on performance. Ensure that data-driven and personalized learning platforms provide employees with relevant content and individualized learning solutions ready for application. "This is a win-win situation: employees grow their portfolio of skills and apply themselves in different roles and networks, enriching their experience, while companies can reach their goals and constantly grow thanks to highly skilled in-house talent" (Rallyware 2020).

4. *As an educator*, you act as a trusted guide and learning coach to create and accompany relevant and fulfilling learning experiences. More specifically, you
   • assist in developing personal learning goals and how to measure results and support the relevant self-assessments of the learner;
   • assist in defining individual learning path and help to identify and make available relevant content and resources;
   • coach learning groups, moderate interaction on learning platforms, and facilitate peer-to-peer learning and co-creation;
   • provide guidance/coaching for critical thinking and reflection on competencies developed as well as on the learning process.

5. *As a tutor bot*, you do not only ask and answer questions but also provide personalized scaffolding. You promote problem-solving by encouraging learners to find answers on their own. As tutor bot, you energize your learners and assist them with learning resources. You also give learners regular feedback. You also act as a sparring partner: Before learners take an assessment, they can engage with a tutor bot to test their knowledge.

6. *As a learning curator or learning designer* (instructional designer), you identify the competence and skill gaps of a targeted audience and create, select, and suggest learning experiences that close this gap. You research applicable content, suggest and formulate course materials, and then collate these newly designed resources. You also enable learning via online communities and social media technologies, curating content and providing guidance to faculty and teaching experts.

7. *As a machine trainer*, you teach machine-learning algorithms on how to perform the work they are designed to do and how best to interact with humans (Wilson and Daugherty 2018a). You also simulate use cases and train professionals to work with these AI-powered systems.

References

Amershi, S., Weld, D., Vorvoreanu, M., Fourney, A., Nushi, B., et al. (2019, May 4–9). Guidelines for human-AI interaction. In *CHI conference on human factors in computing systems proceedings (CHI 2019), Glasgow, Scotland, UK*. ACM, New York, p. 13. https://doi.org/10.1145/3290605.3300233

Azevedo, R., Martin, S. A., Taub, M., Mudrick, N. V., Millar, G. C., & Grafsgaard, J. F. (2016). Are pedagogical agents' external regulation effective in fostering learning with intelligent tutoring systems? In *International conference on intelligent tutoring systems* (pp. 197–207). Amsterdam: Springer.

Bélanger, P. (2016). *Self-construction and social transformation: Lifelong, lifewide and life-deep learning*. Montreal: UIL, Les Presses de l 'Université de Montréal.

Berger, B., & Hess, T. (2019). *AI-based systems' explanations: Still a topic for IS research*. Accessed April 22, 2020, from https://www.fim-rc.de/Paperbibliothek/Veroeffentlicht/1000/wi-1000.pdf

Bureau of Labor Statistics. (2019). *Number of jobs, labour market experience, and earnings growth: Results from a national longitudinal survey*. Accessed from https://www.bls.gov/news.release/pdf/nlsoy.pdf

Castaño Muñoz, J., Redecker, C., Vuorikari, R., & Punie, Y. (2013). Open education 2030: Planning the future of adult learning in Europe. *Open Learning: The Journal of Open, Distance and e-Learning, 28*(3), 171–186. https://doi.org/10.1080/02680513.2013.871199.

CSER. (2020). *Risks from artificial intelligence*. Accessed October 15, 2020, from https://www.cser.ac.uk/research/risks-from-artificial-intelligence/

EAEA. (2019). *The future of adult learning in Europe. Background paper - European Association for the Education of Adults*. Accessed April 21, 2020, from https://eaea.org/wp-content/uploads/2019/12/The-future-of-adult-learning-in-Europe.pdf

Falconer, I., Littlejohn, A., & McGill, L. (2013). *Fluid learning: vision for lifelong learning in 2030*. OpenEducationEuropa. Accessed April 18, 2020, from http://oro.open.ac.uk/id/eprint/52380

FOL. (2018). *The future of learning*. Accessed June 9, 2020, from https://issuu.com/delta51/docs/future_of_learning_04

Growth Engineering. (2018). *What is the future of gamification?* Accessed April 22, 2020, from https://www.growthengineering.co.uk/what-is-the-future-gamification/

Haenisch, S. (2017). *The future of learning – Top 7 predictions for 2030*. Accessed April 15, 2020, from https://blogs.sap.com/2017/11/22/the-future-of-learning-top-7-predictions-for-2030/

ILO. (2018). *Financing life-long learning for the future of work*. Accessed June 9, 2020, from https://www.ilo.org/wcmsp5/groups/public/%2D%2D-dgreports/%2D%2D-inst/documents/publication/wcms_646046.pdf

Kapp, K. M. (2012). *The gamification of learning and instruction: Case-based methods and strategies for training and education*. New York: Pfeiffer.

Machlup, F. (1962). *Knowledge production and distribution in the United States*. Princeton, NJ: Princeton University Press.

OECD. (2016). *E2030 conceptual framework: Key competencies for 2030 (DeSeCo 2.0)*. Accessed April 21, 2020, from http://www.oecd.org/education/2030/E2030-CONCEPTUAL-FRAMEWORK-KEY-COMPETENCIES-FOR-2030.pdf

OECD. (2018). *The future of education and skills*. Education 2030. p. 4. Accessed April 20, 2020, from https://www.oecd.org/education/2030/E2030%20Position%20Paper%20(05.04.2018).pdf

OECD. (2019). *Individual learning accounts - Panacea or Pandora's box?* Accessed June 9, 2020, from https://www.oecd.org/publications/individual-learning-schemes-203b21a8-en.htm

Oosterbeek, H., & Patrinos, H. A. (2008). *Financing lifelong learning*. Policy Research Working Paper 4569, The World Bank Human Development Network. Accessed June 9, 2020, from https://openknowledge.worldbank.org/handle/10986/6495

Rallyware. (2020). Rallyware blog. Accessed April 21, 2020, from https://www.rallyware.com/blog/human_machine_partnership

UNESCO. (no year). *Open education resources*. Accessed October 15, 2020, from https://en.unesco.org/themes/building-knowledge-societies/oer

Wilson, H. J., & Daugherty, P. R. (2018a). Collaborative intelligence: Humans and AI are joining forces. *Harvard Business Review, 2018*, 2–11.

Wilson, H. J., & Daugherty, P. R. (2018b). *Human + machine: Reimagining work in the age of AI*. Boston, MA: Harvard Business Review Press.

Klaus North is a professor of international management at Wiesbaden Business School, Germany, and was previously a senior researcher at the International Labour Office (ILO). He has widely published on knowledge and innovation management as well as digital transformation. His textbook "Knowledge Management: Value Creation Through Organizational Learning" (Springer Texts in Business and Economics) has been translated into multiple languages and has become a reference work on the subject. He frequently consults with major companies and public institutions worldwide and teaches in business programs internationally.

Vignette: Communities, Challenges, Curiosity, and Coaches—A Corporate Learner in 2030

Jochen Robes

Peter is just on his way to the Community Center. For the past 3 weeks, he has been meeting with several partners to further develop the concept of mobility in his city. The partners working with him on the project come from very different areas, administration, schools, and banks, some are from small local businesses, some are self-employed, and some are even retired but are still interested in the future of their neighborhood. Today they have made an appointment with a Swedish expert from Uppsala to hear more about the experiences the Swedish have already gained in this area. Peter is thrilled about the meeting. And he is pleased to be allowed to work on this project during his working hours.

Peter is 35 years old and married. He serves as a data analyst in a large management consultancy with clients and projects worldwide. The opportunity to get involved in projects that are not part of his actual field of work was an important reason for him to join the consulting firm 3 years ago.

What used to be called learning and development was dissolved at Peter's consultancy several years ago. The colleague with whom he conducted the interview when he was hired instead spoke a lot about the four Cs: communities, challenges, curiosity, and coaches.

Communities, he said, were cross-project networks in which sometimes external parties such as business partners, freelancers, or experts participate. They took care autonomously of everything related to learning, knowledge-sharing, and innovations in their respective fields.

Challenges would be internal or external assignments for which employees can apply. However, his colleague immediately let it be known that it was highly expected that he would be part of these challenges. The commitment to local projects, he emphasized, was one of the company's top priorities, a focus to which his company has remained faithful to this day.

J. Robes (✉)
Robes Consulting, Frankfurt, Germany

© Springer Nature Switzerland AG 2021
S. Güldenberg et al. (eds.), *Managing Work in the Digital Economy*, Future of
Business and Finance, https://doi.org/10.1007/978-3-030-65173-2_15

Curiosity is a response to the progression of AI and aims to allow employees to question routines and to never stop looking for new and better solutions. To measure the curiosity of its teams and employees, the company has developed a number of smart, internationally acknowledged parameters. They build on the curiosity scale developed by the German pharmaceutical firm Merck.[1]

Coaches, finally, would help with any questions that might arise, for example, regarding the choice of communities, the extent of involvement, or the dissemination of experiences, in other words, issues where managers and teams quickly reach their limits as advisors. Peter was immediately hooked by this concept. Nobody here talks about learning or training anymore.

Peter was asked for an interview at the time because he had been active in various networks and projects since midway through his studies. LinkedIn was then already the platform on which many activities converged. Nowadays, in April 2030, it does so more than it used to do. Thanks to its sophisticated algorithms, the platform not only provides its users with information about open positions and projects but also automatically updates the profiles of its users, makes recommendations for new projects, connects with other members, offers courses on current topics, and curates information to pass on to its users. Depending on their needs and license, LinkedIn also integrates companies' internal networks into their recommendations.

Peter values these services highly. With the help of his speech assistant, he usually accesses the platform several times a day, asks questions, and conducts short dialogues to check his calendars, appointments, and contacts. He only continues to struggle with some features, which are too playful and competitive from his point of view, e.g., to translate activities into points, badges, lists, and rankings.

At the end of his studies 10 years ago, AI, algorithms, and bots were the big issues. But it was the pandemic in 2020 that triggered another major leap in development—not so much in terms of technology, but mainly in terms of working culture and attitudes. After the crisis, the principle of "digital first" had become established in many companies. In other words, since then, it has been taken for granted that exchange with others and cooperation in projects should take place online. Personal meetings on-site must be justified and approved.

Today, employees have a wide range of technical options available—from simple videoconferencing systems to meetings in sophisticated 3D environments, something that was still in its infancy 10 years ago as the so-called virtual reality. The carbon footprint is shown for all communication and collaboration channels and activities and is tracked for the company, teams, projects, and each employee. Yet, for the Community Center project, it was advisable to meet on-site, as some of the partners there are not as technically well-equipped as would be desirable.

At the Community Center, Peter arrives a little before schedule. He takes the opportunity to quickly adjust some keywords for a current project on his mobile. The new project with a Spanish and a German retail chain includes a few topics that he

---

[1]https://www.merckgroup.com/company/curiosity/Curiosity_Full-Report_English.pdf.

has heard about but has not yet dealt with directly. The new keywords ensure that the daily curated compilations he receives from LinkedIn and some other networks contain the "right" information: information that is directly tailored to him and his projects as well as references to people in his networks he can approach. The service adapts automatically to how Peter uses and evaluates these information bites.

Peter does not intend to rely entirely on one system. His employer, however, does not consider this a drawback. They appreciate the principle of "everything from one source." Also, many features of the platform depend on having access to relevant user data. The promise of "personal" information tailored to the user is as relevant today as it was 10 years ago. Despite this, Peter immediately signed up with his old university once they offered him membership and access to scientific information, further qualifications, and some special networks.

The moment Peter enters the conference room of the Community Center, the expert from Uppsala just happens to appear on the large wall screen.

Jochen Robes has been advising companies and organizations on the optimization of their HR and corporate learning services for over 25 years. He focuses on the challenges of education and learning in the digital world—from knowledge management, eLearning, social media, and corporate MOOCs to the development of digital skills. He is an active blogger, lecturer, and speaker. He is a founding member of the Corporate Learning Community (CLC).

Epilogue: What Have We Learned?

Stefan Güldenberg, Ekkehard Ernst, and Klaus North

In spring 2021, when we finalized this book, the world was in a big mess: The COVID-19 pandemic was still not contained and had resurged in several countries. Large economies were either governed by populist demagogues or by autocratic dictators. Democracy versus command control was no longer only a philosophical question but shaped geopolitics and our multilateral system. Racism and xenophobia increased. We witnessed a deglobalization under the motto "my country first." The divide between winners and losers continued to deepen under the impact of the digital transformation of business and society. The forecasting firm Stratfor (2020) argues that "over the next ten years, the world will revert to a multipolar power structure that will encourage constantly shifting alliances and create a more contentious global system. In the midst of this dynamic change, pockets of economic opportunity will emerge."

Will this become a lost decade where artificial intelligence increases and collective human intelligence decreases? What will be the generic strategies used in this decade be, allowing us not only to survive but also progress towards justice, peace, and prosperity? Or, to formulate it in terms of the United Nations' Sustainable Development Goals, which aim, in particular, at "[p]romot[ing] sustained, inclusive and sustainable economic growth, full and productive employment and decent work for all" (UN SDG8). How close will we get to this goal in 2030?

To ease the digestion of this book and provide guidance to our readers, we have condensed the contributions in this book as *seven generic strategies towards* "sustained, inclusive and sustainable economic growth, full and productive employment and decent work for all."

Built on the Power of Meaning and Shared Value

In Chapter "The World in 2030: Looking Back Ten Years from Now," *Dewan and Ernst* argue for a new type of capitalism, stakeholder capitalism. This attempts to bring a company's various stakeholders—customers, workers, suppliers, the local community, and shareholders, closer together. In such an approach, the private

© Springer Nature Switzerland AG 2021
S. Güldenberg et al. (eds.), *Managing Work in the Digital Economy*, Future of
Business and Finance, https://doi.org/10.1007/978-3-030-65173-2

sector would align its interests automatically with broader social goals and no direct state intervention through regulation or taxation would be needed. However, a significant obstacle to achieving this transition is that the existing ownership and property rights structure of a company do not incentivize managers to move beyond the shareholder value principle.

Güldenberg shows in Chapter "The New Role of Leaders and Leadership in 2030" that purpose gives our lives meaning, it unlocks energies for change and engages employees to their work. This is also reflected in the five key pillars of the new work movement[1]:

- Empower employees to do tasks they really want to do.
- Work should be inspiring.
- Technology should work for people. The key is to use technology for human gain and not let it use us.
- Prioritize community: A sense of working for a community and goal gives people a purpose and helps them build a better world while they are at it.
- Make work about freedom: Freedom to choose your tasks, your projects, your location, your hours, and what you want to learn.

Develop Agency and Inner Balance

Agency—the ability to make informed choices about one's life and a sense of responsibility to participate in the world and influence people, events, and circumstances—is at the center of any change in society. This requires "Lifewide Learning," as discussed by *North* in Chapter "Learning in the Year 2030" and *Robes* in Chapter "Vignette: Communities, Challenges, Curiosity and Coaches—A Corporate Learner in 2030," covering learning in institutions, families, communities, and workplaces. Everybody has to take responsibility for self-regulated learning and the management of one's competence portfolio. People will have to take stock of their strengths, weaknesses, life goals, priorities, development potential, and limits, and assess how all of these fit within the competitive environment. Self-management will not function sustainably without an inner balance, as shown by *Heinke* in Chapter "How Humans and Machines Interact" and *Richert and Neef* in Chapter "Vignette: Cobot on a Couch—Living with Robotic Companions in 2030."

Consume Less: Work Less—Enjoy More

Triggered by COVID-19 and Fridays for Future, people in the highly developed economies are increasingly reflecting on their patterns of life: Does fast fashion and fast food, frequent flying and working long hours increase our quality of life and

---

[1]https://engage.kununu.com/en/blog/new-work-essential-guide-future-of-work/

happiness? Is there an alternative to the current capitalistic system? Would such an alternative be compatible with a new business model that is oriented towards stakeholder capitalism? More importantly, who would be in a position to afford to work less. The introduction of a universal basic income scheme, together with a drastic reduction in the number of regular working hours, could be a way to enable new patterns of work and life for future generations, as outlined by *Hamann* in Chapter "Values vs. Technology? Why We Need to Consider a New Foundation for Work" and *Josef* in Chapter "Vignette: Ella's Day—Work Anywhere Anytime."

Prefer Social Resilience Over Economic Efficiency

Resilience is the ability of a system to overcome disturbances and its capacity for continuous reconstruction (Hamel and Välikangas 2003). Resilience is related to agility, which is the ability of a system to respond to change rapidly. Efficiency is the quest for optimization between output and input of resources. In the long run, the need to balance efficiency with resilience is essential for a system to survive. It is a strategy that ecosystems have perfected throughout their evolution by adapting to diverse and changing environments (see Ulanowicz et al. 2009). In unstructured working environments, agile organizations and well-educated, resilient individuals have the greatest chances for survival. *Samaan* hints in Chapter "Job Scenarios 2030: How the World of Work Has Changed Around the Globe" that hierarchical and bureaucratic organizations which function best in a well-structured environment with centralized knowledge and top-down approaches in decision-making will have difficulties to maintain their performance levels in turbulent and competitive landscapes. Well-balanced investments in digital technologies and AI will enable us to manage and efficiently organize these more complex work environments.

Resilience versus efficiency has remained a challenge that needs constant re-adjustment. Slack resources, that is, "inefficiency," can also provide room for experimentation, creativity, and possibly result in innovations. In Chapter "The World in 2030: Looking Back Ten Years from Now," *Dewan and Ernst* recommend strategies of social resilience to complement economic efficiency for countries to enter a sustainable and inclusive path. Societies, institutions, and firms need to be able to cope quickly and effectively with emerging threats and to reap unexpected opportunities. As some observers have aptly put it: One needs to leave money on the table to survive.

Lead Together, Not Others

New leaders in 2030 have to change their self-perception from the leadership generations of the past. The leader of the future does not know everything better than their followers but is the one creating a movement towards change and is asking powerful questions. This requires the leader to be curious and develop lifelong learning skills. In Chapter "The New Role of Leaders and Leadership in 2030,"

Güldenberg has proposed a new 5S model of leadership (self, situational, stakeholder, servant, shared). This will fit much better to the requirements of a new leader in 2030. It will make leaders more effective and knowledge workers more productive. It all starts with self-leadership, which will become even more critical than in the past. In a world where attention is a scarce resource, managing focus and attention of oneself and employees is the decisive factor in getting things done. Traditional leadership functions, such as performance measurement, incentivizing, or management control, will be increasingly replaced by AI solutions. Future leaders need to be masters of these technological solutions and possibilities, not their servants, as shown by *Güldenberg and Langhof* in Chapter "Digital Leadership and Technology". Leaders in 2030 have to concentrate on the innovative and creative tasks of leadership that cannot be replaced by machines. The main task of modern leadership is to cocreate the future of the organization in an unpredictable and turbulent world.

Develop Decent Digitalized Work

Digital transformation challenges traditional forms of employment and labor relations. *Hamann and Güldenberg* argue in Chapter "New Forms of Creating Value: Platform-Enabled Gig Economy Today and in 2030" that temporary, solo entrepreneurship, and self-employment are on the rise, not least thanks to opportunities provided by gig platforms to connect freelancers and businesses across countries and continents. According to *Gruber-Risak,* this brings new fragilities and undermines the capacity of social protection systems to provide support (see Chapter "Working in 2030: Heaven or Hell? Why Regulation, Standards and Workers' Representation Will Still Matter"). Social protection systems for the next decade will, therefore, need to find answers to this proliferation of new forms of employment while at the same time ensuring a stable funding base, for instance, through raising taxes on digital services.

At the same time, the structural change brought by the rise of the digital economy and other long-running trends requires constant adaptation of the workforce, as discussed by *Samaan* in Chapter "Job Scenarios 2030: How the World of Work Has Changed Around the Globe" and *Schnurr* in Chapter "Vignette: A Day in the Life of a Medical Doctor in 2030." As life expectancy increases and working lives lengthen, current and future workers are likely to experience more occupational transitions than their parents and grandparents. *Gärtner and Kern,* in Chapter "Smart HRM in 2030: Conversational HR, Connected Robotics and Controlled Analytics," outline that an economic environment conducive to strong job growth, together with establishing a universal labor guarantee and strengthening institutions that provide the right skills and competences, can ensure successful transitions and prevent occupational dead ends that leave people with little perspectives and deteriorating livelihoods.

But a human-centered approach to the Future of Work, as put forward by the ILO's Centenary Declaration, also requires strengthening collective representation and social dialogue (ILO 2019). New forms of collective action are necessary if stakeholder capitalism is to become the new business model over the next decade. Only by bringing in the voices of all people affected by current transformative forces can we expect to promote decent work for all.

Build Capabilities for Transformation

The profound changes we are currently witnessing and those lying ahead require people, institutions, businesses, civil society organizations, policymakers, and systems at large to challenge basic assumptions, identify possibilities of renewal, and in many cases, reinvent themselves or vanish.

To induce the necessary transformation, however, possible future needs to be imagined and assessed against current trends (Beckert 2016). This book is an attempt to contribute to such an exercise. Building scenarios and imagining different paths that various socioeconomic (sub-)systems are likely to take over the next decade constitute essential building blocks that help us to provide answers both individually and collectively to the challenges we all face. *Stoller-Schai* describes one of these decisive building blocks for transformation, which he calls collaboration competencies, in Chapter "Making Collaboration Work."

Turning collectively current challenges into future opportunities while minimizing risks requires a transformative policy agenda. No action is not an option but the choices that we make depend on the possibilities that we perceive. Transformative policies are only as good as they are formulated against real constraints. Policy objectives such as those developed by the United Nations Sustainable Development Goals need to be framed within the transformational forces that shape our societies in various ways. This book has been a contribution to this endeavor by illustrating the implications of the coming changes related to the digital transformation at both the societal and individual levels. By bringing in expertise from various fields and perspectives, we hope to have provided a framework to formulate policies for shared prosperity and decent work for all.

References

Beckert, J. (2016). *Imagined futures. Fictional expectations and capitalist dynamics*. Cambridge, MA: Harvard University Press.

Hamel, G., & Välikangas, L. (2003). The quest for resilience. *Harvard Business Review, 9*(1), 52–62.

ILO. (2019). *The Centenary declaration for the future of work*. Accessed from https://www.ilo.org/wcmsp5/groups/public/@ed_norm/@relconf/documents/meetingdocument/wcms_711674.pdf

Stratfor. (2020). *Decade forecast: 2020-2030*. Accessed August 27, 2020, from https://worldview.stratfor.com/article/stratfor-decade-forecast-2020-2030-risk-opportunity

Ulanowicz, R. E., Goerner, S. J., Lieater, B., & Gomez, R. (2009). Quantifying sustainability: Resilience, efficiency and the return of information theory. *Ecological Complexity, 6*, 27–36.